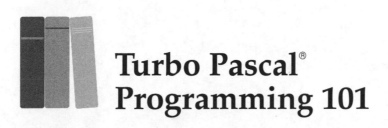

# Turbo Pascal® Programming 101

# Turbo Pascal® PROGRAMMING 101

Charles Calvert

SAMS
PUBLISHING

A Division of Prentice Hall Computer Publishing
11711 North College, Carmel, Indiana 46032 USA

*This book is dedicated to Margie.*

*Composed in Palatino and MCPdigital*
*by Prentice Hall Computer Publishing*

*Printed in the United States of America*

**Publisher**
Richard K. Swadley

**Acquisitions Manager**
Jordan Gold

**Acquisitions Editor**
Stacy Hiquet

**Development Editors**
Phil Paxton
Dean Miller

**Senior Editor**
Tad Ringo

**Production Editor**
Keith Davenport

**Copy Editors**
Gayle L. Johnson
Greg Horman

**Editorial Coordinators**
Rebecca S. Freeman
Bill Whitmer

**Editorial Assistants**
Rosemarie Graham
Lori Kelley

**Technical Editor**
Andrew Reiger

**Cover Designer**
Tim Amrhein

**Director of Production
and Manufacturing**
Jeff Valler

**Production Manager**
Corinne Walls

**Imprint Manager**
Matthew Morrill

**Book Designer**
Michele Laseau

**Production Analyst**
Mary Beth Wakefield

**Proofreading/Indexing
Coordinator**
Joelynn Gifford

**Graphics Image Specialists**
Dennis Sheehan
Sue VandeWalle

**Production**
Debra Adams
Katy Bodenmiller
Christine Cook
Lisa Daugherty
Brook Farling
Dennis Clay Hager
Carla Hall-Batton
Howard Jones
John Kane
Tom Loveman
Sean Medlock
Juli Pavey
Angela M. Pozdol
Michelle Self
Susan Shepard
Greg Simsic
Angie Trzepacz
Alyssa Yesh

**Indexers**
John Sleeva
Suzanne G. Snyder
Loren Malloy

# Overview

## Appendixes

# Contents

## Classroom 3          Structured Programming

### Lessons

**Classroom 4**      **Arrays and Text Files**

*Lessons*

## Classroom 9     Introduction to Pointers

*Lessons*

*Appendixes*

# Acknowledgments

I want to thank my father, who bought me my first computer, and my brother Jim, who taught me how to set it up (his voice on the other end of the phone saying, "Now write *copy con config.sys...*").

I also want to thank Wayne Simila-Dickinson, who taught me how to program in Turbo Pascal.

I owe a great debt to my colleagues at the Technical Support Department at Borland. These fine gentlemen are Lester Jackson, Rich Jones, Xavier Pacheco, Jason Sprenger, Peter Rolney, Robert Warren, and the redoubtable Lar Mader. There is no way I can express my gratitude for getting the chance to work with such a fine group of colleagues.

At Sams Publishing, I want to thank Stacy Hiquet, whose cheerful and understanding voice on the other end of the phone line helped get me through the long and arduous task of writing this book. I also wish to thank Keith Davenport, whose fine ear for language helped make this a better book.

Special thanks to Dan and Jen Richart.

# About the Author

Charles Calvert has a B.S. degree in Computer Science and a B.A. degree in Journalism from Evergreen State College in Olympia, Washington. He has worked as a journalist for *The Morton Journal* in Morton, Washington, and as an English teacher at an extension of Centralia College near Centralia, Washington. He has also worked as a programmer, doing contract work using Turbo Pascal. He is now employed as a Technical Support Engineer for Turbo Pascal at Borland International. He lives with his wife, Marjorie, in Felton, California.

# Introduction

Welcome to the world of Borland Pascal for Objects 7.0 and to the lands inhabited by its close cousins, Turbo Pascal 7.0 and Turbo Pascal for Windows. This is a great place to be whether you are a new programmer or an experienced pro who wants to learn a second language.

The purpose of this book is to present an easy-to-use, friendly introduction to the world's premier programming language, Borland Pascal 7.0. The approach used throughout this book will be conversational and friendly.

The basic premise of this endeavor is that Pascal is essentially a straightforward, elegant language that is not difficult to learn. Therefore, my job as a writer is to explain programming in Pascal in the plainest possible language. There is no need for me to bombard you, the reader, with lists of obscure facts, nor with examples of especially clever or convoluted programming. Instead, I wish to speak plainly about a straightforward and very elegant programming language.

Many introductory programming books aim to be both systematic and thorough. These are important concepts, and they will never be far from my mind. But my primary goal in this book is to be lucid. I want to be easy to understand at all times.

In short, I feel that the most important trait of an introductory programming book is that it be well written.

This book explores the basics of the language in considerable depth. The first step is to gain elementary fluency in Pascal and then to begin exploring how to structure programs so that they are robust and easy to maintain. Along the way, I want you to learn as much as you can about Pascal while having as much fun as possible.

I don't want you to misconceive my aims as frivolous just because I approach this project with enthusiasm. Having high spirits does not imply that someone is not serious about achieving a particular goal. This misunderstanding comes about because some people confuse drudgery with expertise. In my experience, almost all the real experts I have known exhibit enormous enthusiasm for their subject. They are experts in their field because they enjoy their field. It is fun for them.

So don't let my cheerfulness fool you into thinking that I regard this book as a trivial undertaking. In fact, by the time you are through exploring the language with this book, you will have covered, in considerable depth, all of the basic tools needed to write robust, powerful programs.

As I write this book, I am working for Borland in their Turbo Pascal Tech Support Department. Every day I talk to Pascal programmers who cover a wide range of experience levels. This has given me the best possible opportunity to learn what beginning Pascal programmers need to know.

So relax; take it easy. Those portions of the language which need to be studied in depth are going to be examined in ways that are both illuminating and exciting. In other words, if I find a nice juicy topic that needs to have some light shed on it, I'll do my best not to retreat behind the illusory safety of a stuffy and pedantic aura, but will instead find interesting ways to explore the topic.

Writing this book, I concentrated first on teaching you the basics, and second on preparing you for the moment when you will move from the beginning to the intermediate level.

I've read too many introductory programming books that let the reader down at this crucial point. These books get users started and then, all of a sudden, drop them into deep water. Readers of these books end up either: (a) sad and confused, or (b) sounding like marauders with chips on their shoulders and blood lust in their eyes.

Throughout this book, therefore, I work hard to keep part of my mind focused on this crucial transition. I want you to learn not only the basics, but also where the hot spots that well-prepared programmers look out for when they begin to explore how Turbo Pascal can be used to write professional-level programs.

# Why Turbo Pascal?

If you are new to programming, you may not be aware of just how fortunate you are to be learning Turbo Pascal. There is nothing second-rate about Pascal. It is one of the world's premier programming languages—one which I quite sincerely believe to be the best computer language in existence.

It is among the very fastest of all the high-level languages, and also one of the easiest to use. Turbo Pascal allows you to get in close to the machine without bogging you down in arcane syntax. It's like good prose that manages to be simultaneously concise and eloquent.

Leaning to master Turbo Pascal is the same thing as learning to master the IBM PC. With the help of this well-structured language, virtually all of the resources of a computer are at your disposal. Whether you want to write a simple program to help you balance your checkbook, or whether you want to write a complex communications program that will use serial I/O to communicate with a distant computer over a phone line, Turbo Pascal is the language best suited for the task.

So let's set your minds to rest about one thing: Turbo Pascal is a very fine, well-crafted language. Forget what you might have heard about Visual Basic or C++; forget the nit-picking intricacies of assembly language and the aesthetic crudity of C's tangled syntax. Pascal is a clean, elegant language that allows you to get the job done in short, concise statements that are both powerful and easy to read.

Turbo Pascal is nearly as easy to use as BASIC. But unlike BASIC, Turbo Pascal will allow you to work closer to the machine level. It will never leave you staring across a gulf at a goal you could reach if you had a tool nimble enough and strong enough to navigate the intervening currents.

Turbo Pascal is also every bit as fast as C. But unlike C, Pascal makes it easy for you to write concise code that comes together quickly, without ever resorting to the arcane syntax which appears all but incomprehensible to you only five minutes after you've written it. It also allows you to entirely avoid the unnecessary and gruesome task of wrestling with a linker.

If you ever become a true Turbo Pascal die-hard fan, you will one day have to face the ire of programmers who feel that their language is better than yours. This is particularly true of C programmers who will, despite considerable evidence to the contrary, claim that their language is somehow magically faster than yours.

Don't believe them for a moment!

In most cases well-written Turbo Pascal code is as fast or faster than well-written C code, which is nice. But perhaps even more importantly, Turbo Pascal code is easier to write. Projects that take two weeks to write in C can be written in a week in Pascal. Projects that take a year to write in C can be finished in six months using Turbo Pascal, without sacrificing any speed or power.

My purpose here is not to denigrate assembler, C, C++, or BASIC. I program in all of these fine languages and enjoy using them very much. But Turbo Pascal is my tool of choice. There are some types of programs that are easier to write in BASIC, and a few types of programs that can only be written in assembler, but 99 percent of the time, when choosing between BASIC, assembler, or Pascal, Turbo Pascal is the best possible tool.

I somewhat reluctantly have to admit that C, C++, and Pascal are so much alike that making a choice between them is often not so easy. C has the advantage of being very widely used, while Pascal has an edge because it is easier to use and because it has a very fast compiler. C and C++ are notoriously hard languages to learn because of their complex syntax and somewhat arcane structure. Pascal is a spare, elegant language which is easy to learn and easy to use. It is also a nice language to use when writing large projects, because the Turbo Pascal compiler is almost unbelievably fast. C programmers get to take frequent coffee breaks while their large programs are compiling. Pascal programmers get to go home early at the end of the day because they didn't have to sit around waiting for their compiler to finish doing its job.

So take heart. If you are beginning Turbo Pascal, you are at the beginning of a great adventure. The keys to the computer, that most exciting machine of our age, are at your fingertips. Computers, and especially IBM PCs, like Turbo Pascal. They come to life under its touch.

# How To Use This Book

While you are working your way through this book, take the time to enjoy yourself.

A good computer language like Turbo Pascal is simultaneously playful and austere. It forces you to be logical, to think things through to their conclusion. And at the same time, it allows you to exercise your imagination, to make new discoveries, and to have, above all, a good deal of fun.

I am very much aware of just how dreary most of the prose is that has been written about computer languages. I can well remember struggling over difficult texts that claimed to be "easy-to-understand introductions to computer programming." There is no doubt that some of them had the opacity of gnarled vinyl and the structural integrity of a shattered windshield.

But the ultimate offense of these wrecks masquerading as books is that they failed to reveal the beauty, excitement, and fun of the languages they attempted to describe. Many times when struggling over difficult material I mumbled to myself that there had to be a better way. I'm excited about the opportunity to show that there is, indeed, a better way. This book is not something I am churning out as a task that must be done. Instead, it is a project which engages my imagination; it is something that has been brewing in my mind for a long time.

There are, of course, a handful of well-written introductory books on Turbo Pascal. My goal is not to compete directly with those books on their own ground, but rather to take an entirely different approach—one that I feel has long been needed.

This approach means speaking in plain, simple language about the act of writing code with Turbo Pascal. If you want a systematic reference, you need look no further than the manuals that shipped with Turbo Pascal 7.0.

But few people can learn to program just by reading those dry and dusty tomes. What most people really need is a plain-talking friend who can sit down and explain the basics to them in simple English. That's what I'm here to do. I love the English language, and I love Turbo Pascal. My goal is to share this enthusiasm with you. In the process you will learn a marvelous thing: how to program a computer.

I should add, however, that there is nothing I can do here that will substitute for your willingness to write programs on your own. I can explain how things work, and I can prepare the ground for you, so to speak. But the real test of your ability comes when you sit down to write programs on your own. And it is never too soon to start those projects. So whenever you get the urge, set this book aside for the moment and try some experiments of your own.

It's a bit hard for me to admit that the preceding paragraph probably contains the single most important piece of advice I can give you in this book. The simple truth is that there is nothing I can do for you that will substitute for your willingness to write code on your own.

When I first started programming, I kept trying to write an editor. I failed once trying to write it in BASIC, then failed again in C, and finally managed to fail once again when I found Pascal. The problem, of course, was that I was a novice attempting a project that even an experienced programmer would find extremely challenging. Looking back on it now, I realize that my supposedly "failed" editor project was actually one of my great successes. I learned how to program while struggling with that challenge. When I returned to more reasonable tasks, I was able to surmount them all because of the tools I mastered while working on my infamous editor project.

Of course, I doubt that I could have learned anything at all if it weren't for the books which guided me through the process. Even my computer science teachers weren't as helpful as those awkwardly written books, which I struggled over night after night. But the key ingredient which turned the trick for me was my willingness to code on my own.

# Conventions Used in This Book

The following typographic conventions are used in this book:

- Code lines, variables, program names, and any text you see on-screen appear in `monospace`.

- Placeholders in statement syntax explanations appear in *`italic monospace`*.

- Information you enter at prompts appears in **`bold monospace`**.

- Filenames are in regular text, all uppercase (PDATA.TPP).

- New terms appear in *italic*.

# Index to the Icons

Unlike many other computer books, this book contains several items in the text that promote the workbook approach. You will run across many icons that bring specific items to your attention and that offer questions and exercises that you might want to answer. After many of the questions and exercises are blank lines where you can finish the problem. (In addition, each classroom has one page of blank lines that you can use to write entire programs or to make notes.)

The following icons appear throughout this book:

 The Lesson Objective icon appears at the beginning of each lesson. The goal of the lesson is stated so that you have a good idea of where the lesson is headed.

 This is the Think About... icon. When further thought is needed on a particular topic, the Think About... icon brings extra information to your attention.

When a topic becomes particularly difficult, the Still Confused? icon offers some help. The Still Confused? paragraphs are meant to further explain a concept that was taught earlier in the text.

The Try This icon marks a question or offers a small exercise for you to finish. After some of the Try This exercises, there is ample blank space so that you can answer the exercise before moving on to the next topic. The Try This icon gives you instant feedback that tests your understanding of what you just read.

Next to the Find the Bug icon you find a program listing that contains one or more errors. After some of these programs, room is provided for you to correct the error.

This is the Finish the Program icon. A section of a program is left unfinished, with ample space for you to fill in the missing code. The Finish the Program icon tests your ability to write programming statements that you just learned about.

In addition, tips and notes appear as screened text.

**TIP:** A tip shows you an extra shortcut or advantage possible with the command you just learned.

**NOTE:** A note brings a particular side effect or useful topic to your attention.

# Onward, into the Breach

So come along, and let's have some fun. Computers are not only very useful tools but also elegant toys. They are a canvas on which programmers can paint the pictures or ideas they conjure up in their imaginations. This book is about learning how to use that canvas. We'll start from the basics, have some fun on the way, and wind up knowing enough to begin work on a thousand exciting projects.

**NOTE:** If you own Turbo Pascal for Windows or if you own Borland Pascal 7 and want to use its Windows IDE, you should read Appendix B before beginning Lesson 1.

Let's not waste any more ink on this introduction. It's time to begin.

# Turbo Pascal
## CLASSROOM I

## Quick Start

**Notes**

# Output

***To explore basic output.***

I don't remember the first time someone asked me to draw the letter A on a piece of paper, but I do remember taking early penmanship courses. I remember little blue workbooks with letters and lines on them. We were supposed to trace over those letters so that we could learn to read and write the alphabet.

Now you are engaged in a similar task: learning the ABCs of programming in Pascal so that you can read and write one of the languages that computers speak.

This is a wonderful and exciting opportunity.

Okay, sit down at your computer and, as you did when first learning English, start at the beginning by creating the letter A. It's easy; just follow my outline.

# The Letter A in Pascal

This is how you write the letter A in Pascal:

```
begin
  Write('A');
end.
```

This is a complete program. It's not quite enough to guide a rocket all the way from the earth to the moon and back again, but it is a real program that will run correctly on a computer.

Now is the time to fire up your PC, bring up Turbo Pascal, and type this program. Type it exactly as you see it. Don't change any of it, and don't try to understand it yet. All that will come later.

Once you have typed the program *exactly* as it appears, press the F9 key. This tells the computer to compile your program, that is, to convert the code you have written in the edit window into code that the computer can understand. For now, all you need to do is compile. You still have to wait a few moments before you run your code.

If all has gone well, the message Compile successful should appear in the compiling dialog box, as in Figure 1.1. Immediately you will see the message Press any key in frantic, blinking letters.

*Figure 1.1.*
*The Integrated Development Environment (IDE) as it appears after a successful compilation.*

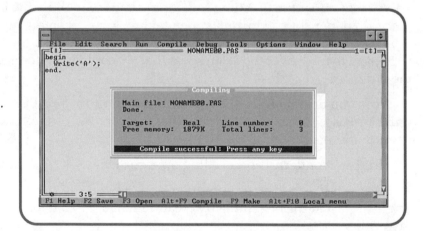

If you see this message on-screen, congratulations are in order. You have written and compiled your first Turbo Pascal program. Welcome to the cutting edge. Sit back and feel superior for a moment if you want to. After all, you are way ahead of most of the human race.

Don't worry about the begin...end pair surrounding the write statement. Its only purpose is to serve as bookends that delineate the beginning and end of a block of code.

If something went wrong when you tried to run the first program, you probably made a *syntax error*. Everybody makes syntax errors. If some programmer steps up to you and says: "I have never made a syntax error," then you can be assured of one thing: That individual is not being entirely truthful.

Syntax errors occur when you don't get the grammar of Pascal statements down correctly. For instance, if you had typed Write("A"); instead of Write('A');, you would have generated a compiler error. The computer would now tell you: Error 5: Syntax Error, and the cursor would blink beneath the first set of double quotation marks. To fix the problem, you would have to change the double quotation marks to single quotation marks and press F9 again.

Compilers are very patient. They let you try over and over again until you get it right. They may not offer you much sympathy, but on the other hand they will never let on if they're starting to get bored or impatient.

Those of you who got it right the first time might want to intentionally make the error just mentioned and then press F9. The more you can learn about error messages and how to correct your code, the better off you will be.

Try making or looking for the following errors in the preceding program:

1. See what happens when you leave the period off the word end.

2. See what happens when you type a colon instead of a semicolon at the end of the Write('A') statement.

Go ahead and make a few mistakes intentionally if you want. After all, you will make plenty of unintentional mistakes later on, so maybe we can get some sense of power by doing it once or twice on purpose.

> **TIP:** When an error message is up on the screen, you can get an explanation of that error message by pressing the F1 key. This starts up the help system, which supplies you with a little explanation of why the error message has appeared. You can use this explanation when you are trying to figure out how to correct the mistake that was made.

Okay, now that you have had a little experience with error messages, you are, I am sure, ready to run your program.

First, hold down the Alt key and then press the letter D. This brings down the Debug menu. Now press the letter O. An output window appears at the bottom of the screen. This is where the letter A will be printed when you run your program, as Figure 1.2 shows.

*Figure 1.2.*
*After you press Alt-D and then O, the output screen appears at the bottom of the IDE.*

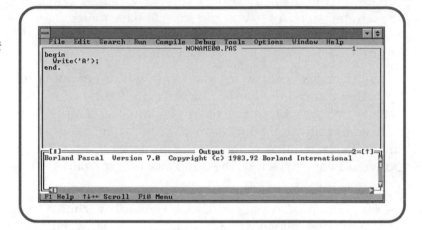

If the output screen does not appear, try pressing the Escape key a few times, then repeat the steps just outlined.

Now it's time to run the program. First hold down the Alt key and then press the letter R. This pulls down the Run menu. Now release the Alt key and press the letter R again.

What happened? Well, you just wrote the letter A with a Turbo Pascal program. Look down in the output window and you will see the result of your actions. If there are other letters or words on the screen besides the letter A, don't worry about them right now. You will learn how to erase them later on in this book. All that matters is that the letter A appears at the bottom of the output window.

Now press Alt-R and then R again. Do it as often as you like. The computer won't mind. It is just as indifferent to your success as it is to your failure.

That's a computer for you. They are very patient machines, and they don't tend to get caught up emotionally in what you are doing.

Try compiling these two programs and see whether you can find the errors in them:

```
begin
  Write;
end.
```

```
begin
  Write('A');
end;
```

# A Quantum Leap Forward

I've taken the time to give a detailed description of how to write the letter A on the screen. Now that you have taken this first step, you will find that it is easy to start doing much more complex things, such as writing an entire sentence to the screen.

To write a second program, you first need to get a clean window to work on. To do this, first hold down the Alt key and then press the letter F. This brings down the File menu. Now press the letter N. A new window appears on-screen with a title on the top if it that says NONAME01.PAS or something similar.

Now it is time to type in the second program. It looks like this:

```
begin
  WriteLn('You cannot step in the same river twice');
end.
```

This program is different from the first program in two ways. First, instead of placing the letter A in quotes, a phrase has been placed in quotes. Second, instead of using the Pascal command Write, WriteLn has been used. Don't worry about these differences. Believe me, there will be plenty of time for worry later on. For now, all you need do is type the program exactly as it appears.

You can run the new program by first holding down the Alt key, then pressing the letter R to bring down the Run menu. Now press the letter R again to run your program. Repeat this process.

If the output window is still open at the bottom of the screen, you see the most famous words of the ancient Greek philosopher Heraclitus written inside it. If the output window has been closed or obscured, or if you want to find out about a second way of viewing the output from your program, then hold down the Alt key and press the F5 key.

Now you can view your entire output screen as it would appear to a user who runs your program outside the Turbo Pascal environment. Again hold down the Alt key and press the F5 key. This toggles you back to the Turbo Pascal IDE.

Practice toggling back and forth between the *output screen* and the IDE until you feel comfortable with this method. You will do this often, so practice until you feel comfortable with the process.

When you are done, toggle to the output screen and pause for a moment to admire Heraclitus's words:

```
You cannot step in the same river twice
```

Heraclitus said these words because he wanted to comment on the fact that life is always changing. Each time you go to the river, new water from far away is rushing by you. It passes in just a few moments and then travels off, never to return in exactly the same form. *You can never step in the same river twice.*

Now look at your computer screen for a moment. It appears to be sitting very still. Like a river, it always appears to be the same, but it is not. Electricity is flowing through it, constantly renewing and changing it. Inside your computer, at this very moment, thousands of instructions are being executed at a fabulously fast rate. All this motion creates the illusion of stability. But that is all it is—an illusion, a sleight of hand, if you will.

Your computer is in constant motion. It's always changing.

Write and WriteLn are Pascal commands. They send output to the screen, or, in special cases, to a file or a printer. Notice that the commands have descriptive names: They write information to the screen, so they are named Write and WriteLn.

# Rolling on a River

Now that you have gotten started, it is nearly time for you to branch out on your own for a bit and experiment with your newfound ability to write text to the screen with Turbo Pascal. But before you do that, I want to pass on a few additional pieces of knowledge that might prove useful.

So it's time once again to press Alt-F for the File menu, then Alt-N for the New option, to bring up a fresh screen. If you find that doing this makes your desktop a bit cluttered, don't forget that you can press F5 to maximize the current window.

Earlier I mentioned the extra text that appears in the output window. You can clear this text from the screen with the ClrScr command. But in order to use this command, you must tell the compiler where to find the ClrScr command. You do this by including a *uses clause* in the program.

That last bit about the uses clause is bound to seem a bit confusing, but don't worry about that right now. At this time it's not important for you to understand *why* you are doing things, but only *how* to do things.

This is how to write a program that clears the screen before you write anything to it:

```
uses
  Crt;

begin
  ClrScr;
  WriteLn('The following sentence is false.');
  WriteLn('The preceding sentence is true.');
end.
```

After you have run this program, press Alt-F5 to view the output screen. Notice that it is blank except for the sentences you have written to the screen.

By modifying this program slightly, you can learn how to view the results of your work without having to open an output screen or *output window*.

Here is the modified program:

```
program StrangeLoop;

uses
  Crt;

begin
  ClrScr;
  WriteLn('The following sentence is false.');
  WriteLn('The preceding sentence is true.');
  WriteLn;
  WriteLn('Press the ENTER key to end this program.');
  ReadLn;
end.
```

After you type this program and run it, you see the following output on-screen:

```
The following sentence is false.
The preceding sentence is true.
Press the ENTER key to end this program.
```

If you press the Enter key as suggested, the program ends and you can view your code once again.

Notice that this program has a title—StrangeLoop. The title is preceded by the word program and ends with a semicolon. There is no real explanation of why programmers do things this way. It is simply a matter of tradition to place an optional title at the start of a program and to do it in this manner.

Because this program is a little more complicated than the ones written earlier, it might be worthwhile to examine it in detail.

The program begins by clearing the screen with the ClrScr command. Then it tells Pascal to print two sentences.

After writing these sentences, the program gives the command for writing a blank line to the screen. This is done by issuing the WriteLn command without passing it any *parameters*. (The words placed in parentheses after the WriteLn command are called parameters.) Parameters are discussed in more detail later.

Next the user is told how to end the program, and then the ReadLn command is issued. ReadLn can serve a number of purposes in a program. Right now it is used only to cause the program to pause until the user presses the Enter key. This is done primarily to save you the trouble of having to open the output screen or an output window in order to view the output from the program.

 When you run this program, the output from the two short Write statements appear on the same line, but the output from the two WriteLn statements appears on separate lines. As a result, the output appears cluttered. See if you can edit the program so that the output is easier to read.

```
program StrangeLoop;
uses
  Crt;

begin
  ClrScr;
  Write('The following sentence is false.');
  Write('The preceding sentence is true.');
```

```
   WriteLn;
   WriteLn('Press the ENTER key to end this program.');
   ReadLn;
end.
```

This find the bug exercise illustrates that the WriteLn command produces what is called a *carriage return*. A carriage return has the same effect on the screen that pressing the Enter key has when you are typing information on a word processor or a text editor.

> **TIP:** Turbo Pascal is not case-sensitive. This means that it does not care whether you write commands or syntax in small letters or capital letters. It treats the letters WriteLn exactly the same way it treats WRITELN or, for that matter, wRiTeLn.
>
> The style I use for capitalization, spacing, and line breaks is similar to the style followed by most of the developers of Turbo Pascal. You will not go wrong if you imitate the style of capitalization used in this book. If you want, you may develop a style of your own. Also, you might want to study any source code that comes with the product. It is as close to a standard language as you will find. As you will see, most of it is very similar to the coding style adopted in this book.

# Another Quantum Leap

Okay, now it's time to get really fancy. Since you learned how to clear the screen, you have found that a program's output appears in the upper-left corner of the screen.

Sometimes, however, you may want text to appear in the center or at the bottom of the screen. You can control these factors by using the GotoXY command. GotoXY is passed two parameters. The first parameter designates in which column on the screen the words are going to appear. The second tells which row. Most computer screens have 80 columns and 25 rows.

Here is an example of how to use GotoXY:

```
program GotoExample;

uses
  Crt;
```

11

```
begin
  ClrScr;
  GotoXY(1, 1);
  Write('Coordinates: 1, 1');
  GotoXY(10, 5);
  Write('Coordinates: 10, 5');
  GotoXY(40, 24);
  Write('Coordinates: 40, 24');
  ReadLn;
end.
```

 Type this program and run it. Try changing the coordinates you pass to GotoXY. Remember to always set the first parameter between 1 and 80 and the second between 1 and 25.

Congratulations. You've made it through the first lesson. Rather than rushing on to Lesson 2, "Talking to the User," now is a great time to practice what you have learned. In order to help you do this, I have provided a set of optional questions that will give you a chance to expand your skills.

If you would prefer to create your own experiments using what you have learned in this lesson, please go right ahead. The examples that follow are merely placed here for your convenience.

# Review Questions

1. What is the purpose of the Write command? _____
   _____

2. What is the difference between the Write command and the WriteLn command? _____
   _____

3. If ReadLn appears by itself on one line with no parameters, what effect will it have? _____

4. What piece of syntax is used to end a program? _____

5. What do we mean when we say that Turbo Pascal is not case-sensitive? _____
   _____

# Review Exercises

1. Write a program that prints your name on the top line of the screen.

2. Write a program that prints your name in the center of the screen.

3. Write a program that prints the following verses from Andrew Marvell's "To His Coy Mistress," written in 1681:

The grave's a fine and private place
But none, I think do there embrace.
Now therefore, while the youthful hue
Sits on the skin like morning dew,
And while thy willing soul transpires
At every pore with instant fires,
Now let us sport while we may;
And now, like amorous birds of prey,
Rather at once our time devour,
Than languish in his slow-chapped power.

# Lesson

# 2

# Talking to
# the User

*To learn how to get input from the user.*

In this lesson you are going to learn how to write programs that can have conversations with their users. Fortunately, one of Turbo Pascal's great strengths is its capability to set up a number of very comfortable interfaces between a computer program and a human being.

The command ReadLn, introduced in Lesson 1, "Output," is the primary focus of attention in this lesson. You will see how to use this command to conduct the rudiments of a conversation between a machine and a person.

Considerable effort is expended in this lesson introducing variables and explaining their purpose in a program. You will probably still feel a bit confused about variables after reading this lesson, but don't worry, variables are explored from many different angles in this book. By the time you're done, the subject will be old hat.

# An Introduction to Variables

When you are having a conversation with a friend, you don't usually have to think about finding a place to store the things he or she tells you. You just remember what your friend said. But when a computer program is talking to a user, the first challenge a programmer faces is finding a place to put the input.

Everybody knows that computers have a memory. As a programmer, you need to begin to learn how that memory works. Unfortunately, the first thing to learn is that computers don't remember what they are told unless they are told explicitly how to go about remembering a particular piece of information.

Here is an example of how to tell a computer to remember something:

```
program Bogart;

var
  S: String;

begin
  S := 'You must remember this: A kiss is just a kiss.';
  WriteLn(S);
end.
```

This program has a title, and then a peculiar piece of syntax that includes the words var and string. In Pascal, the word string refers to sentences, groups of words, and letters. Strings should be thought of in contrast with numbers. On one side of the fence are numeric symbols such as 1, 2, 3, 4, and so on. On the other side of the fence are strings, which are made up of words and letters.

The letters var are an abbreviation of the word *variable*. Variables are declared in a program in order to tell the computer to set aside places for it to store information. When you write var S: String, you are telling the computer to set aside a little place in its memory to store a few words, and to associate that location with the variable S.

You also are telling the computer that later on you will want to get those words back. Computers have a lot of information stored in their memory, so you need a method of telling the computer which bits of information you are interested in. You do this by creating a variable that represents and points at those words in the computer's memory. (Don't worry if some of this is not sinking in yet. Variables can be confusing at first, and so this subject is referred to over and over again in this book.)

16

In the preceding program I chose the letter S to be the variable that refers to those words to be stored in memory. I didn't have to use the letter S for the variable, I could just as easily have used a word such as Information or Info. Here is how the program looks when the abbreviation Info is used as the variable instead of the letter S:

```
program Bogart;

var
  Info: String;

begin
  Info := 'You must remember this: A kiss is just a kiss.';
  WriteLn(Info);
end.
```

The computer regards this program in exactly the same way it regards the previous program. In fact, the only thing the compiler cares about is that variable names begin with a letter. Specifically, the compiler doesn't like variable names that begin with numbers.

In this example, the computer is first told about the word Info and its significance in the program. Then the computer is told what words are going to be assigned to the variable that was created. This is done by typing the following line:

```
Info := 'You must remember this: A kiss is just a kiss.'
```

This line of code introduces the *assignment statement,* which is written by combining a colon and an equals sign. To say this line of code aloud, you would say:

> Info colon equals, quote, You must remember this: A kiss is just a kiss, unquote.

You might also note that in Pascal you use single quotes rather than double quotes to insert a string directly into a program. Perhaps this is because Pascal was originally created by Niklaus Wirth, who lives in Europe, where punctuation conventions are somewhat different from those in America.

Find the bug in the following program:

```
program VarBug;

begin
  S := 'Do I dare to eat a peach?'
  Write(S);
end.
```

# Listening to the User

Now that you know a little about variables, it is time to have your first conversation with a user. This conversation will be about the Frenchman for whom Turbo Pascal was named. This Frenchman's last name was Pascal.

His first name, however, was not Turbo. In fact, he had a romantic-sounding first name—Blaise, as in a fiery blaze.

Here is the program about Blaise Pascal:

```
program Blaise;
uses
  Crt;

var
  S: String;

begin
  ClrScr;
  WriteLn('Turbo Pascal was named after a Frenchman.');
  Write('Please type his first name: ');
  ReadLn(S);
  WriteLn('You entered: ', S);
  WriteLn;
  WriteLn('Press the ENTER key to end this program.');
  ReadLn;
end.
```

Type the preceding program and run it. Remember that if you press Alt-R, R, or Ctrl-F9, then your program will be compiled automatically, eliminating the need for you to perform that task separately. If everything goes smoothly, the on-screen output looks like this:

18

```
Turbo Pascal was named after a Frenchman.
Please type in his first name: Blaise
You entered: Blaise

Press the ENTER key to end this program.
```

If your program doesn't run smoothly, it is probably because you have made a syntax error. Please check your program over carefully. Pascal is very fussy about syntax. You have to get it right.

# Two Heads Are Better Than One

The preceding program uses one variable, but there is no reason to limit yourself in this respect. For instance, the next program uses two variables, FirstName and Town.

```
program TwoVars;
uses
  Crt;

var
  FirstName,
  Town: String;

begin
  ClrScr;

  { Get Input }
  Write('What is your first name: ');
  ReadLn(FirstName);
  Write('In what town were you born: ');
  ReadLn(Town);

  { Write reply }
  WriteLn;
  WriteLn('Hello ', FirstName, ' from ', Town);
  WriteLn('Good to meet you!');
```

```
  { Pause to view program }
  ReadLn;
end.
```

Type this program and run it. Be careful when typing this line:

```
WriteLn('Hello ', FirstName, ' from ', Town);
```

The syntax here is a bit subtle and, as always, it is important that you imitate it exactly. In a few moments I will discuss this line and explain what it means.

Here is the way the output from this program should look:

```
What is your first name: Elvis
In what town were you born: Tupelo

Hello Elvis from Tupelo
Good to meet you!
```

The first thing to note about this program is the choice of variable names. Two variables of type `string` are declared and set apart with a comma. In the first program the variables are named `S` and `Info`. Neither of these names tell much about what was intended to be done with the variable. In the preceding program, however, one variable is called `FirstName` and the other `Town`. These names tell you a good deal about what role these two variables play in the program: The variable `FirstName` will hold the user's first name, and the variable `Town` will hold the name of the user's town.

**NOTE:** Variables are a subset of a larger group called identifiers. There is a set of rules for making up the names of identifiers. If you don't obey these rules, the compiler will reject your input, usually by posting the message `Error 2: Identifier expected`. The most common mistake is to try to begin an identifier with a number. This is illegal. The other rule to remember is that identifiers may consist only of letters, numbers, and underscores. Thus, the identifier `One_CoolCookie` is legal, but the identifier `1_CoolCookie` will be rejected. `RadCat1` and `Rad_Cat2` are both legal.

When you have several identifiers of the same type separated by commas, you can either have them all on one line or place them on separate lines. There are no clear guidelines to help you decide which way to go in this case, but you should always strive to make your code as readable as possible.

Why should you care about the names of variables? Well, the goal programmers strive for is to make the *source code* of their programs as readable as possible. Source code is the text you type when you are writing a program. All programs have source code, and all the source code in this book is written in Pascal.

Strive to make your source code as easy to understand as possible, because one day you might want to revise or improve your program. When you do, you'll want to be able to understand how it works as quickly as possible. If you choose your variable names carefully, then it will be easier to understand how your code works.

While we're on this subject, it's important to note that the program TwoVars also introduces Pascal *comments*. Here are the program's three comments:

```
{ Get Input }
{ Write reply }
{ Pause to view program }
```

Comments in Pascal programs are written between *curly braces*. On most keyboards, the curly-brace keys are located to the right of the letter P. Programmers place comments in programs in order to write notes that explain the code to themselves or to other programmers.

Comments are created simply for the sake of clarity. The compiler does not care about them—in fact, it studiously ignores them. Writing comments does not change the way your program behaves.

Comments can appear anywhere in a program and can extend for more than one line. The Turbo Pascal 7.0 editor finds comments and prints them in plain gray type by default.

> **NOTE:** Some teachers and computer managers are utterly obsessed with the idea of comments. This is especially true of people who frequently work with relatively obscure languages such as C, C++, or assembler. Throughout this book, short comments are added when they are helpful, but well-written Pascal code is usually so easy to understand that it is virtually self-documenting. The main goal, therefore, is to learn how to write clean, readily comprehensible code.

Speaking of matters of clarity, there is one last thing to mention before we move on to another program. The following line may seem a bit confusing to you:

```
WriteLn('Hello ', FirstName, ' from ', Town);
```

Perhaps a simple way of showing you how this line works is to demonstrate an alternative way of writing it. Consider this chunk of code:

```
Write('Hello ');
Write(FirstName);
Write(' from ');
WriteLn(Town);
```

These four lines write the exact same thing as the single line. It is simply for convenience that the makers of Turbo Pascal arranged things so that you can condense these four lines of code into one line.

The trick, of course, is to separate the various portions of the line from each other with commas. Start by writing a string, then insert a comma, and then write a variable. Continue this pattern until you reach the end of the line.

If this makes sense to you now, then fine, if not, don't worry. I will come back to this again later in the book. And remember, don't worry: It's simple once you get the hang of it.

# Pascal Was a Mathematician

Blaise Pascal dedicated most of the first part of his life to mathematics and much of the second part of his life to philosophy and religion. Although the fundamentals of programming are explored in this book, time is also allocated for discussing the philosophy behind the art of creating successful programs. Occasionally, however, time is taken out to play some entertaining mathematical games.

To play mathematical games, you must learn how to use numbers while programming in Turbo Pascal. The best way to get started is by typing and running a simple program that adds two whole numbers. Whole numbers are numbers that do not include any decimals. For instance, the number 1024 is a whole number, and the number 1024.334 is a decimal number. You will learn how to work with decimals later, so for now you'll work only with whole numbers.

Here is the program to type and run:

```
program EasyMath;
uses
  Crt;

var
  Num1,
  Num2,
  Result: LongInt;

begin
  ClrScr;
  Write('Enter a whole number between 1 and 999: ');
  ReadLn(Num1);
  Write('Enter another number between 1 and 999: ');
  ReadLn(Num2);
  Result := Num1 + Num2;
  WriteLn('The sum of these two numbers is: ', Result);
  WriteLn;
  WriteLn('Press the ENTER key to end this program');
  ReadLn;
end.
```

The program's output should look something like this:

```
Enter a whole number between 1 and 999: 10
Enter another number between 1 and 999: 8
The sum of these two numbers is: 18


Press the ENTER key to end this program
```

This example introduces a new type of variable called a LongInt. Until now, all variables in this book have been strings. Variables of type string are meant for holding words or letters, while variables of type LongInt are meant for holding whole numbers.

The preceding program asks the user to limit his or her input to numbers between 1 and 999. Actually, variables of type LongInt can hold numbers as large as 2,147,483,647 or as small as –2,147,483,648. But before you start working with numbers that large or that small, you need to understand two important concepts:

- `LongInt` variables can never contain any commas. If you want to enter two million, type 2000000, not 2,000,000. If you add commas to numbers, your program will generate an error.

- If you are going to add two numbers and place the result in a variable of type `LongInt`, make sure that the sum of the two numbers is not larger than 2,147,483,647. That's the biggest number you can place in a `LongInt`. If you try to put a bigger number in a `LongInt`, you will produce totally unpredictable results.

Now that you know a little something about using numbers with Turbo Pascal, you can modify your program so that it works with numbers larger than 999 and less than 1. To do this, change your program so that it looks like this:

```
program EasyMath2;
uses
  Crt;

var
  Num1,
  Num2,
  Result: LongInt;

begin
  ClrScr;
  WriteLn('Remember: no commas');
  Write('Enter a number between -10000000 and 10000000: ');
  ReadLn(Num1);
  Write('Enter a number between -10000000 and 10000000: ');
  ReadLn(Num2);
  Result := Num1 + Num2;
  WriteLn(Num1, ' plus ', Num2, ' equals ', Result);
  WriteLn;
  WriteLn('Press the ENTER key to end this program');
  ReadLn;
end.
```

Go ahead and play with program for a bit if you want. If you get some unexpected results, it is probably because you are entering numbers outside the range requested by the program's prompts. If a user enters numbers that are too large or too small, the results can be very unpredictable.

That is why the range of numbers chosen for the program is such that a user cannot obey the rules and enter numbers whose sum is larger than

2,147,483,647 or smaller than –2,147,483,648. Notice also that when I wrote the example numbers, I omitted the commas. I did this to encourage the user to avoid using commas. As a result, the users have a template that they can follow. If the sample template includes commas, then the user is more likely to use commas.

These latter points may seem like minor details, but they are all part of making a program user-friendly—a subject discussed often in this book. In fact, Lessons 22 and 23 are devoted to this subject. But the preceding discussion can serve as an introduction to topics that are mentioned often throughout this text.

Before this lesson ends and temporarily curtails the discussion of LongInt, you might want to type and run the following program to see whether you can find what is wrong with it and correct the error:

```
program RangeError;

var
  B: Byte;

begin
  B := 5000 * 5000;
  WriteLn(B);
end;
```

_____

_____

_____

_____

_____

_____

_____

_____

# The Second Finale

Well, here you are at the end of Lesson 2, and you already know how to write to the screen and how to get input from a user. I hope you are finding that programming is not nearly as difficult as some people claim. Just remember

to mind your P's and Q's, dot your I's, and to always keep your sense of humor someplace handy.

If you feel a sense of claustrophobic frustration creeping up on you, get up and take a short breather. Remember the words of Cassius Clay: "Dance like a butterfly and sting like a bee." It's not that compulsive laboring over the old keyboard never pays off, but rather that the proper attitude for a programmer is obsession leavened with a touch of bright-eyed, good-humored irreverence.

# Review Exercise

1. Write a program that asks the user for his or her age and place of birth. Then write both pieces of information back to the screen in a single WriteLn statement.

# Using the Built-In Tools

*To learn about the debugger and online help.*

When you bought Turbo Pascal, you may have gotten more than you bargained for. You probably expected to get one of the world's great compilers, but chances are you didn't know about all the high-powered goodies that come along with the product. These extra tools make Turbo Pascal a boon for all programmers, whether they are just starting out or are world-famous pros.

This lesson explores some of the programming tools available inside the Turbo Pascal *Integrated Development Environment* (IDE). It concentrates on the built-in debugger and the online help services. While perusing these riches, you are also going to learn more about getting input and producing output.

Every programmer who uses Turbo Pascal has immediate access to a good debugger, editor, and compiler. Many programming packages isolate each of these functions in separate tools, or else expect you to turn to third-party vendors in order to purchase one or more of these essentials. One of the great strengths of Turbo Pascal is that the compiler, editor, and debugger are all brought together to form one tool called the IDE.

The icing on the cake is the online help system. With this tool at your fingertips, you can grab hold of almost any piece of programming information you desire in a matter of seconds.

# Free Code in the Online Help System

The best programmers don't write the entirety of their programs from scratch. Instead, they paste them together from snippets of premade code. Some of this prewritten code may have been created by the programmer, or it may have been written by others.

As you develop into an experienced programmer, you will begin to build your own libraries of code. You will find yourself mining these repositories whenever you sit down to do serious coding. In fact, this book contains several large veins of information that you will explore in later lessons. When you are done reading this book, you will want to keep these libraries of code for use on a rainy day.

Of course, right now you are just beginning to program in Pascal, and you don't have any libraries you've pasted together from years of hunting and searching. A good place to begin is with one of the most amazingly accessible mother lodes of code any programmer could imagine—the online help system which is built into the compiler.

Suppose you sit down one day to write a program that finds the square root of a number. You turn on the computer, fire up Turbo Pascal, press Alt-F to bring down the File menu, and then select New to create a blank editor screen. (Go ahead and do this now, so you can follow along as we proceed.)

Okay, so there you are with a nice fresh new screen and a good idea in your head. After contemplating the matter for a few moments, however, you might decide: "Well, actually I'm not really sure how to go about getting the square root of a number from a computer."

Don't despair. Help is only a few keystrokes away.

First, type the word Squareroot in the Pascal editor. Put the cursor under the word and press Ctrl-F1. (Or, if you prefer, you can point at the word with the mouse and press the right mouse button.)

When you do this, the help screen will pop up from out of nowhere, and you find yourself looking at a long list of words, all of which begin with S, as Figure 3.1 shows. This is the help index, and you've been placed in the middle of a section where the words that begin with the letters *Sq* are located.

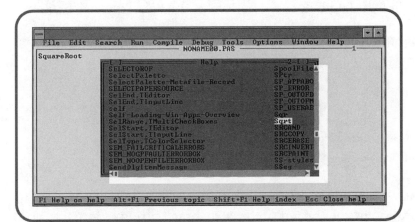

**Figure 3.1**
*The Turbo Pascal Help window.*

It just so happens that right under the cursor, or at least very near the cursor, is the word Sqrt. If it is necessary, highlight this word by using the arrow keys or the mouse, and press Enter. Or, if you have a mouse, point at the word Sqrt with the cursor and click the left mouse button. The help screen for the Sqrt function appears as shown in Figure 3.2.

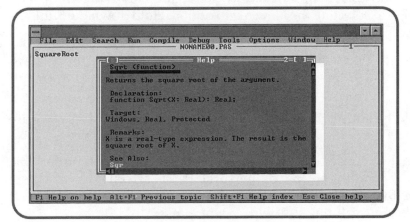

**Figure 3.2.**
*The Help screen for the Sqrt function.*

What have we here? The legend says that the Sqrt function returns the square root of the argument. Here is the very tool you need, and you found it just by opening the online help system.

Of course the online help system won't always solve your problems as easily as it did in the example, but it can come to your aid over and over again. The more you know about how it works, the more useful it will be to you.

Not only does the online help prove to be an easy way to find the function you need, but it also contains an actual example of how to use the function.

The example is hiding below the bottom of the help screen. To view it, click the scrollbar on the right or hold down the down-arrow key for a few seconds. The following example scrolls into view:

```
{ Example for Sqr and Sqrt }

begin
  WriteLn('5 squared is ', Sqr(5));
  WriteLn('The square root of 2 is ',
          Sqrt(2.0));
end.
```

To copy this example from the help screen to your program, first move the cursor to a location just to the left of the curly brace sitting before the word Example. Hold down the Shift key and press the down-arrow key six or seven times until the entire example is highlighted (or highlight the example using the mouse). Hold down the Shift and Control keys and press the Insert key once.

Even though you can't see it, the text of the example is now sitting in a Turbo Pascal-maintained buffer. In order to view the contents of this buffer, press Escape to close the help screen, and then create a new edit window by pressing Alt-F and selecting the New menu option. Hold down the Shift key and press Insert.

Voilà! There is the example program in the editor, ready to run. To see it in action, press Alt-R, R. Don't forget to press Alt-F5 to view the output screen.

What could be simpler? What could be more amazing? Computers are wonderful.

Work with the help system for a while until you begin to feel comfortable with it. The legend at the bottom of the Turbo Pascal screen is always there to remind you that if you need help on the current task, you can press F1. If you want to begin exploring the help system, press Alt-H.

Another fine option is to press Shift-F1. This brings up the index where you found the Sqrt command. If you want to move from the top of the index to the place where the words that begin with *V* are kept, for example, just press the letter *V*. Highlight the word Val and press Enter or click it with the left mouse button.

Notice that if you scroll the explanation of the Val procedure down a few lines, you will see the word Str highlighted in bright letters. Move the cursor onto the word and press Enter, or click it with the left mouse button. You are automatically moved to a description of the Str command.

Continue to explore the help system at your leisure. If at times it seems a bit confusing, don't allow yourself to give up too easily. The online help service is a valuable tool! Use it the way Robin Hood used his bow. Practice and practice with it till you can aim it just where you want, reaching your target every time!

Whatever happens, don't feel like a wimp just because you need to ask for help. Good programmers know how to use all the available tools they can get their hands on. The more experienced you are, the more useful the help system will be for you. Don't pass the opportunity by!

# The Heart and Soul of a Good Programmer

Now that you've had a look at the online help service, it's time to turn your attention to the debugger.

There are lots of myths about what makes up a good programmer. Some people feel it has to do with intelligence, and others put their faith in diligence. Some people feel you need a good background in math to be a top notch programmer, and others feel that writers are best at this particular job.

All of these ideas may or may not have some validity, but in my experience there is one thing that all good programmers have in common: They know their debugger inside out, and they use it all the time.

At this point, you might want to ask two questions:

- What is a debugger?

- Why does it have such a ridiculous name?

Well, a *debugger* is a tool for finding the mistakes programmers make. It gets its name from the fact that programming errors usually are called *bugs*.

Programming errors are called bugs because of a famous incident in programming history. In the 1950s, a computer pioneer, Admiral Grace Hopper, was working on a primitive computer when she noticed that it was producing erroneous results. After spending considerable time trying to track down the problem, someone discovered that the source of the error was a large moth. The moth had flitted into the computer, which was so big that it needed to be housed inside an entire room. The hapless bug had gotten caught in one of the computer's circuit breakers, and as a result the machine was producing erroneous output.

The key point of this story is that the problem was not a hardware error, or a programmer error, but the presence of an insect. The more you get involved with computer programming, the more you will understand a programmer's desire to blame computer programming errors on anything or anyone other than the programmer.

When programs run right, people say, "Wow, aren't computers amazing machines!" When programs fail, people say, "Who's the dumb programmer who put this hack job together?" Programmers get fed up with being on the hot seat. They want someone else to take the responsibility. Bugs definitely are the ideal culprit. Hence, the appeal of the word *debugger*.

At any rate, debuggers are a very important part of the art of programming. To understand better how to use them, analyze this sample program that features the Sqrt procedure introduced in the study of the online help system.

```
program SqrRoot;
{ Sqrt debugger program }

var
  Data, Result: Real;

begin
  Write('Enter a number and I will find its square root: ');
  ReadLn(Data);
  Result := Sqrt(Data);
  WriteLn('The sqrt of ', Data:0:2, ' is ', Result:0:4);
  WriteLn('Press <Enter> to exit');
  ReadLn;
end.
```

Before you start the debugger, type this program, and run it. The results should look something like this:

```
Enter a number and I will find its square root: 4
The sqrt of 4.00 is 2.0000
```

Notice that this program introduces a new type of number, called a real number. Real numbers are used when you want to work with decimals.

When printing real numbers to the screen with WriteLn, you need to add some special characters in order to format the output. Examine the following line of code from the program:

```
WriteLn('The sqrt of ', Data:0:2, ' is ', Result:0:4);
```

When the variable Data is written to the screen, it must be followed with a colon, the number 0, and the number 2. The number following the first colon is not important in this case, so just type a 0. But the second number designates how many decimal places the real number will have when it is printed to the screen. You write the number 2 in this place, so when you run the program, the first variable has two decimal places. The second variable, on the other hand, has the number 4 in this place. Therefore, the program prints this number with four decimal places after it.

It is possible for you to print numbers without formatting them in this way. But if you do so, they will appear in scientific notation, which may not be comprehensible to many of your users.

Now it is time to run the program in the debugger.

1. Make sure the SqrRoot program is in the editor, and then press the F5 key to bring it to full screen.

2. Press the F8 key. At this point, a highlighted line (blue on color monitors) should appear through the begin statement at the beginning of the program.

3. Press F8 twice so that the highlighted line is over the statement ReadLn(Data).

What has happened here? What are you looking at, exactly?

What you are doing is called stepping through a program. In other words, you are using the F8 key to tell the debugger to step through the program one line at a time. This is an amazing, very powerful, ability. Every time you press the F8 key, the debugger executes one more line of the program. So far you have written one line of text to the screen. (To view it, press Alt-F5 once to see the output screen, and then again to return to the editor.) With the help of the debugger, you can see exactly what output is produced by each line of the program. This is an inestimably powerful tool.

Debuggers can do much more. For instance, you can use them to examine variables.

1. Press F8 again to execute the ReadLn statement. You should now be looking at the output screen.

2. Type the number 346 and press Enter. Now you are once again looking at the Turbo Pascal editor screen.

3. Now you can take a look at the variable that contains the number 346. Hold down the Control key and press F7. The Add Watch dialog box appears on-screen. Enter the word Data and press Enter or click the Ok button. Now the current value of the variable Data appears in a *watch window* at the bottom of the screen. If you followed instructions and typed the number 346, you will be looking at that number.

4. Because you have added the watch window to the screen, it is probably a good idea to clean up the arrangement of the windows on-screen. Do this by pressing Alt-W to bring up the Window menu. Press the A key to select Cascade. Even if you didn't see exactly what happened, have faith in the fact that the windows have been rearranged in a way that will be helpful to you later.

5. Press F8 again. Examine the variable called Result. Press Ctrl-F7 to pop up the Add Watch dialog. Type the variable name Result and press Enter or click Ok. The variable name Result appears in the watch window, and the value following it is the square root of the number contained by variable Data.

6. Now step through three more instructions with the F8 key. When the output screen appears, you will see the results of the program.

By now you should be getting an idea of how the debugger works. Go ahead and press Enter once to return to the editor. Press F8 to end the program. If you want to step through the program again, you can start the process simply by pressing the F8 key once more. If you want to restart the program at any time while debugging, just press Ctrl-F2 to stop the program and then F8 to restart from the beginning.

Before finishing this lesson, it might be worthwhile to note a few things about the IDE and its interaction with the debugger:

- Right now the focus of the IDE probably is on the watch window. This means that when you press a key, the keystrokes you enter are sent to the watch window rather than to your program. But if you find a bug in your program and want to correct it, you first have to set the focus to the window that contains your program. Look for a number in the upper-right corner of the window that contains your program. There will be a number there. Hold down the Alt key and type the number in the upper-right corner of the program. Now the focus is on the edit window that contains your program. To move the focus to any other window, repeat this process, but use the number in the upper-right corner of the window you want to receive the focus. You can always tell which window has the focus, because it will have a double border.

- If you edit your program while stepping through it, the next time you press the F8 key, the IDE pops up a window stating that your program has changed. This is done as a courtesy to the programmer. If you want, you can restart your program so that the changes you have made will take effect. If you don't want to restart your program, you can simply continue stepping through the code.

Now that you have learned about the debugger, it is time for you to try to use it to find the errors in the following program. This program compiles fine, but it produces erroneous output. Try to find the errors in it by using the debugger:

```
program BugHunt;
var
  R1,R2,R3: Real;

begin
  Write('Enter a number between one and five: ');
  ReadLn(R1);
  R3 := Sqr(R2);
  WriteLn('The square of ', R1:0:2, ' is ', R3:0:2);
  WriteLn('To check our work, we will use a second ');
  WriteLn('method of achieving the same result.');
  R3 := R1 * R1;
  WriteLn('This time our answer is: ', R3);
  WriteLn;
  Write('Press the ENTER key to end this program.');
  ReadLn;
end.
```

# Summary

Well, here we are at the end of Lesson 3. This has been a big one that has introduced a lot of important concepts. Take the time to experiment with these concepts either by working through the following questions and exercises or by making up a few programs of your own which utilize the ideas outlined in the lesson.

Don't try to move through this material too quickly. The debugger is the best friend you can have when you need to correct a programming error. And don't worry; you will make plenty of errors. All programmers do. The thing that separates the professionals from the amateurs is that pros know how to fix their errors. When programming pros want to find a bug, the best tool in their arsenal is the debugger.

Remember to take your time. You are learning very important material in these early lessons, so make like a sponge and absorb!

# Review Questions

1. What key do you press to start stepping through a program? _____

2. What is the difference between a `Real` number and a `LongInt`? _____
   _____

3. Name three different ways to bring up the help system. _____
   _____

# Review Exercises

1. With the aid of the help system, create a small program that writes the mathematical constant πto the screen. Make sure your answer is accurate to ten decimal places.

2. Write a program that outputs the square root of πaccurate to five decimal places.

3. Write a program that displays the constant `MaxInt` on-screen, and then step through the program with the constant on display in the watch window.

4. Press Alt-F and then N (for New) five times in succession. Now five windows are visible on the screen. What menu option can you choose to tile these windows? How can you cascade them?

# Turbo Pascal
# CLASSROOM 2

# Basics

**Notes**

*L e s s o n*

# Variables and Types

*To learn about variables and types.*

After you have taken a look at some of the basics, it is time to consider the internals of Turbo Pascal. Specifically, this lesson covers memory issues and explores variables and types in some depth.

Don't be afraid of moving on to more advanced material. While you are exploring memory, you can watch the inner mysteries of computers start to unfold before your eyes. Nearly everything exciting that happens inside a computer occurs when pieces of information are moved from one place in memory to another. It is in these pages where you can start to explore how this process takes place.

**NOTE:** This lesson contains a considerable amount of pure, unadulterated theory. In other programming books, chapters on variables and types usually include very little theory. Instead, the reader is inundated with a tremendous number of facts he or she is expected to memorize. I don't want to do that to you, primarily because I don't like it when people do it to me. Instead, I'm going to show you what variables and types really are. I figure that once you grasp the concept, it will be easy for you to look up the details in the online help. For the majority of readers, this is the simplest and best way in which to proceed.

# A Model for Memory

What is a computer's memory? There is no simple answer to that question. A computer's memory is a volatile and complex set of interacting subsystems. To truly understand it correctly is a momentous task requiring months, if not years, of effort. It is possible, however, to get an overview of the subject if you are willing to put up with a few oversimplifications.

My goal in these pages is to develop an image, or a model, of a computer's memory. Even if this model is not perfect, it can still serve as a guide as you hack your way through the silicon jungle. Without some kind of mental image of what you are dealing with, you will soon find yourself groping in the dark, lost without any idea of where to turn for help. So even if the first image developed in this book is not particularly exact, it will form a starting point from which you can proceed. As you move forward, you can develop increasingly refined and accurate images of a computer's memory.

To begin forming this model in your mind's eye, you need to make a distinction between two types of memory that reside in a computer. The first type of memory is the more familiar: The memory found on a floppy disk or a hard drive. This is *persistent* memory; it exists even after you turn off a computer. If you save a file to a floppy disk or a hard drive, you can retrieve it later because its image *persists* on the disk where it is stored.

The other type of memory inside a computer can be thought of as existing primarily in random access memory (RAM). Anything stored in RAM disappears when you turn off the computer. This memory is often called *dynamic* memory.

As a rule, RAM is fast, whereas persistent memory is slow.

Anyone who has grown up in America will find it easy to conjure up a mental image of persistent memory. An LP, a cassette, a video tape, or a CD are all forms of persistent memory where information can be stored on a more or less permanent basis. As you undoubtedly know, cassettes and CDs are frequently attached to computers, and programs are stored on them or read from them.

So it is easy to understand, in general terms, what a floppy disk or a hard drive does.

But how do you picture RAM?

# The Endless Summer

To start, I'll draw an analogy between a computer and a theater. The parallels may seem a bit frivolous at times, but remember that the goal here is very serious. You need to form a working model of a computer's memory that is comprehensible to you. If you can hold this model in mind, you will begin to understand how a computer really works. So give yourself the liberty to use your imagination. It can prove to be a tool that unlocks the secrets of a computer for you.

Slow down for a moment and picture yourself opening a computer. Instead of finding the usual array of boards, drives, and silicon, you see a miniature theater.

At the front of this theater is a table labeled *CPU*. As you stare at this scene, you are amazed to find that, like Alice's, your body is shrinking. At last you find yourself so small that you can take a seat at this table. Lined up in front of you are many rows of seats. In fact, in this particular theater there happen to be 655,360 seats. Every seat in this movie theater is filled.

The really strange thing about this theater is that the people who fill its seats are each guaranteed to be able to remember a number between 0 and 255 with absolute certainty. Tell them any number in that range, and they will give it back to you any time you want. This is a very attentive audience, and they are all eager to remember any number you tell them, as long as it is one of the 256 numbers they know so well.

You know you are in charge of this theater, and you know it is up to you to organize it in such a way that it can execute the instructions that you find on the table in front of you. These instructions take the form of a Turbo Pascal Program that looks like this:

```
program Theater;

var
  N: Byte;

begin
  N := 126;
  WriteLn(N);
end.
```

This simple program writes the number 126 to the screen.

You look down at the sheet of paper containing these instructions, and then you look out at the seats in front of you. It occurs to you that because each of the people in the seats in front of you can remember a number between 0 and 255, it would be easy to ask one of them to remember the number in this program. So you ask one of the people in the front row to remember the number 126. You relay the number to him, and he nods back to let you know that he understands. Now you can rest easy; this guy's whole purpose in life is to remember numbers between 0 and 255. He's not going to forget.

On the table before you is a card labeled *N*. On the back of it is a place where you can write the row and seat number of the person who is remembering your number. There is also a place labeled *TYPE* where you can write down how many people are required to remember this fact for you. In this space you write the words *one byte,* because it takes only one person to remember your number. You place this card in a designated spot on the table in front of you.

Suddenly, a light on the table in front of you turns green. It is the signal to begin executing the program. The first thing you do is pick up the card in front of you labeled *N*. You hand it to an assistant, who reads the row number on the back. The assistant runs out to the correct seat and row, asks the person there to tell him the number he is remembering, and then runs back to you and tells you the number. Now you execute the next line in the program, which involves standing up and writing the number on a glass plate in front of you. The number is then projected on a big screen behind your head.

So why have I told you this quaint little story? My goal is to demystify the inner workings of a computer. Of course, there is no table labeled *CPU* in a computer, and there is no crowd of 655,360 people lined up in orderly seats waiting for you to ask them to remember numbers between 0 and 255.

But there are certain parallels between the imaginary scene just created and the way a real computer works. The most important point to remember is that there is a single place inside a computer that controls the way the machine operates. This is called the *central processing unit,* or CPU. It is where the majority of most programs are executed.

The CPU is very powerful and very fast, but it can remember only a few facts at a time. To overcome this weakness, the CPU uses a "theater" filled with 655,360 bytes of available low memory that reside in most DOS-controlled computers. Each of these bytes can hold a number between 0 and 255.

When a computer needs to remember something, it stores its information someplace in these 655,360 bytes of memory. These bytes of memory are called random access memory (RAM). The name reflects the CPU's capability to access these bytes of memory randomly. In other words, it can store a certain number between 0 and 255 in row 23, seat 15, and another piece of memory in some other randomly chosen location, such as row 12, seat 15. The CPU can access either piece of memory at will. You can think of it as having the capability to store information at random locations throughout these 655,360 bytes of memory.

The analogy being developed in this book equates a control "table" with the CPU and a "theater" full of people with RAM. When the CPU needs to remember something, it stores that information with one of the "people" in the theater. When it needs the information back, it requests the information from the person seated in the appropriate seat and row number. Its big limitation is that each member of the audience can remember only a number between 0 and 255.

# The Fly in the Ointment

I hope all this seems almost excessively simple and straightforward to you. That's the way it should be. Get a clear image in your mind of the relationship between the CPU and RAM, and you have a context in which you can fit many of the important facts you are told about computer programming. First you learn how the system works, then you begin to examine the details.

The details, in this case, start to mount quickly the moment you learn that computers don't always store information one byte at a time. In fact, DOS computers tend to work with at least two bytes at a time.

You know now that every person in the imaginary audience can remember any one of 256 numbers at a time. What hasn't yet been explained is that any two members of the audience can remember not one of 256 + 256 numbers at a time, but rather one of 256 * 256 numbers. In other words, a single byte in a computer can hold one of 256 numbers. But two bytes working together can hold one of 65,536 numbers.

Consider the following program which writes the number 53,345 to the screen:

```
program TwoBytes;

var
  W: Word;

begin
  W := 53345;
  WriteLn(W);
end.
```

In this case, when you are sitting at the CPU in front of the huge array of seats, you find that you need to work with a number larger than 256. Fortunately, the instructions before you tell you to work not with a variable of type Byte, but with one of type Word. This means you can use not one audience member, but two.

This is a very important concept. In other words, I'm not just whistling Dixie here. I've gone to great lengths to create this analogy primarily so that you can understand these next few paragraphs about types and how they fit into memory.

If you are working with a variable of type Byte, you have one audience member allocated to you; if you are working with a variable of type Word, you have two members available. This is always the case. Byte is one member of the audience; Word is two members.

Because you know your audience, you know that any two members of the audience working in concert can remember a number between 0 and 65,535. So you cheerfully execute the first instruction, which stores the number 53,345 with two members of the audience. After you've told them the number, you can rest easy. These two guys were born to do this. Nothing makes them happier than remembering a number between 0 and 65,535. They are in heaven out there, thinking about your number.

The program you are executing is very simple. Now that you have stored the number in memory, you immediately turn around and get the number back so that you can write it on the board.

Now you understand something about two different Pascal *types*. The first type is called a `Byte`, and it is good for storing numbers between 0 and 255. The second type is a `Word`, and it is good for storing numbers between 0 and 65,535. If these facts have sunk in, then great, you are doing very well. A bare memorization of the facts is all you really need. But I have created the little analogy to give you something more than "just the facts." You want to arrive at an understanding of the underlying processes involved.

Of course, the programs you have been working with in this chapter are extremely simple. But even very complex programs most of the time work in exactly this way. Memory is being moved into RAM and out of RAM, or memory is being shifted around in RAM.

Most of the acts a computer performs are simple at heart. The thing that is confusing is the rate at which computers work. In this sense, they are very much like magicians who perform sleight-of-hand tricks. When you watch the magicians do something, it seems amazing. But if you ask them to slow down and perform each movement at a rate you can follow with your eyes, all at once the mystery melts away.

# Negative Numbers

You might be wondering how computers work with negative numbers. It's great to be able to remember a number between 0 and 255. But what if you want to remember a number like –7?

It just so happens that bytes of memory are so dumb that they can remember only numbers between 0 and 255. There's nothing you can do about that. But you can interpret these numbers differently. In other words, even though a byte can hold only 256 numbers, you can imagine those numbers as ranging not from 0 to 255, but from –128 to 127.

Remember, however, that the byte itself cannot remember a number like –7. It can remember only numbers between 0 and 255. But you, sitting up there at the head of this huge audience, are definitely smart enough to interpret that number differently if only you are reminded to do so.

Here is how you "remind" a computer to regard the value stored in a byte as ranging not between 0 and 255, but between –128 and 127:

```
program Negatives;
var
  I: ShortInt;
```

```
begin
  I := -17;
  WriteLn(I);
end.
```

In this example, when you begin reading the program on the table in front of you, you see that the variable you're working with is of type ShortInt. So when you get to the statement I := -17, you know you can't tell a byte to store the number –17. Instead, you use a special method for translating that number into a number between 0 and 255; then you store it with a member of the audience. When you get the number back a moment later, you check the program and see that it is of type ShortInt, so you immediately translate the number with your secret formula and see that it is actually –17. You write this number on the board.

By now, I'm sure you can guess that there is a Pascal type for holding negative numbers larger than –17. It works by storing these numbers in two bytes of memory. This Pascal type is called an Integer, and its values range between –32,768 and 32,767.

I don't want to mislead you by introducing Integers so late in the game. Integers are anything but second-rate citizens. In fact, they are probably the most commonly used type of number in Pascal programs. This is true simply because most of the numbers you work with happen to fall neatly in their range.

Of course, in the first lesson you also worked with the LongInt type. Just like ShortInts and Integers, LongInts hold both positive and negative numbers. Numbers of this type are called *signed numbers,* in part because they need to be thought of as having either a positive sign or a negative sign in front of them.

I'm sure you probably thought it was strange that LongInts ranged between –2,147,483,648 and 2,147,483,647. But now it is easy for you to understand where those seemingly random huge numbers come from.

To understand how LongInts work, you first need to remember that ShortInts are held in one byte of memory and cover a range of 256 different numbers. Integers are held in two bytes of memory and cover a range of 256 * 256, or 65,536, possible numbers. And it so happens that LongInts are held in four bytes of memory. They can hold one of 65,536 * 65,536 or 4,294,967,296 numbers. Because these numbers can be either negative or positive, they range not from 0 to 4,294,967,296, but from –2,147,483,648 to 2,147,483,647.

You might be wondering why the Integer type is more popular than the LongInt type. This is partly a matter of convention and partly a matter of convenience.

The convention part comes from the fact that memory in computers used to be in extremely short supply. Many computers had considerably fewer than 655,360 bytes with which to work. In those days, the capability for programmers to conserve even two bytes of memory was considered vitally important. Integers were used more than LongInts simply because they took up less memory. The convenience of the wide range of a LongInt was shunned for the sake of saving memory.

Programmers still avoid LongInts today, partly out of habit, and partly because DOS computers can manipulate two bytes of memory with extraordinary speed, whereas they tend to spend a bit longer when working with four bytes. So in the interest of speed, programmers still often try to use Integers rather than LongInts.

Whenever you use Integers, you have to be very aware of their limited range. The following program does not perform as you might at first expect:

```
program IntError;

var
  I,J,K : Integer;

begin
  I := 20000;
  J := 20000;
  K := I + J;
  WriteLn(K);
end.
```

At first glance, you might think that this program would write the number 40,000 to the screen. However, this program writes garbage to the screen. The problem is that all the variables are declared as Integers. Integers range between –32,768 and 32,767. But 40,000 is larger than what Pascal programmers call MaxInt, which is equal to 32,767.

To get this program to perform as expected, you need to declare the variables as LongInts:

```
var
  I,J,K: LongInt;
```

The moral here is not to be controlled by tradition. Regardless of your target machine, if you find LongInts easier to work than Integers, go right ahead. The first goal in programming is to get the job done clearly and precisely. Working with LongInts rather than Integers does not compromise

this cardinal rule in any way. Programming is very much about "doing your own thing." Programmers should always have the freedom to make their own decisions—as long as they understand why they are doing things in a certain fashion.

# One Last Night—er, Type

You have had a chance to take a good look at the way numbers are treated on computers. But what about the letters of the alphabet, which we string together to form words? How do they fit into the scheme of things? If the members of the imaginary throng can remember only numbers between 0 and 255, how are you ever going to teach them to remember an English letter or word?

Well, the first step on this journey is fairly obvious: Don't try to cram a whole word into a byte; instead, work with just one letter at a time. In other words, ask each member of the audience to hold only one letter in his or her mind.

How is this going to work? Each byte can hold only numbers between 0 and 255. How can you get it to remember a letter of the alphabet? Again, after only a moment's thought, the answer becomes obvious: Why not assign a number to each letter of the alphabet?

Because there are only 26 letters in the alphabet, it should be easy to find a scheme that works. Suppose, for instance, you assign the letter *A* the number 1. Whenever you need to store the letter *A* in memory, you translate it into the number 1, and then store that number in a byte. When you need to get the letter back, first you get the number from the selected member of your audience, and then you translate that number back into a letter. What could be simpler?

Nothing could be much simpler. In fact, it's possible that the people who designed computers found this scheme altogether too simple. So instead of assigning the letter *A* to the number 1, they decided to assign it to the number 65.

Frankly, this is a somewhat embarrassing and even sobering moment in this book. This is one of the first times you have come up against the sad fact that the people who design computers have not always made the most rational decisions. In fact, sometimes they have made downright crazy decisions. One of those decisions was to assign the letter *A* to the number 65.

As it happens, another very dubious decision was to limit DOS to only 655,360 bytes of easily accessible RAM. But this is not the time to open that particular can of worms.

Instead, concentrate on the way computers store letters inside bytes of memory.

I have already sketched the basic outline of the plan. There are 26 letters of the alphabet, or really 52, if you count both lowercase and uppercase letters. As it happens, computers assign the numbers 65 through 90 to the letters *A* to *Z*, and the numbers 97 to 122 to the letters *a* through *z*.

Just to make sure this is all sinking in, step back into the memory theater for a moment. You are in front of the throng of 655,360. A program is placed in front of you. It looks like this:

```
program Letters;

var
  ALetter: Char;

begin
  ALetter := 'A';
  WriteLn(ALetter);
end.
```

When you start executing this program, you see that the variable ALetter is of type Char. Because Chars usually hold letters rather than numbers, you are not surprised when you see that the variable ALetter is assigned the value A. But you also know that you can't ask any of the Bytes in the audience to remember the letter *A* for you. So you translate it into the number 65, then send it into the audience. A moment later you ask for it back. You check your card and see that it is of type Char, so you translate the number 65 back into the letter *A* and write it to the screen.

What could be simpler? All in all, despite its flaws, this system is very reasonable and easy to use.

There is one last loose end to be tied up. Each byte can remember one of 256 numbers. But so far you have worked with only 52 different values, that is, the letters *Z* through *Z* and the letters *a* through *z*.

What about the other 204 possible values? What do you do with them?

This apparently random spew of numbers is called the ASCII table. Figure 4.1 shows the first half of this table, and Figure 4.2 shows the second half. The output visible in these two tables is produced by the program

`ASCII.PAS`, included on the disk that comes with this book. You don't know enough yet to understand how that program works, but you might want to take a look at it anyway. It can be a handy reference. (Please note that this is one of the few programs in this book which cannot be run from inside Turbo Pascal for Windows.) Appendix C contains a complete hardcopy of this table.

*Figure 4.1.*
*The first half of the ASCII table.*

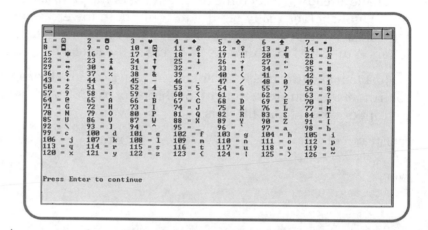

*Figure 4.2.*
*The second half of the ASCII table.*

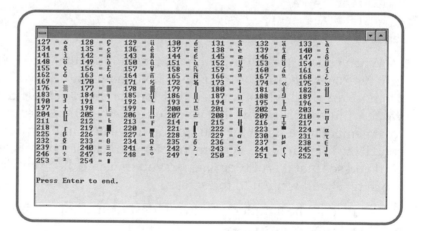

As you can see, each of the characters in the ASCII table is assigned to a number between 0 and 255. In DOS text mode programs, you can use most of these characters however you want, whenever you want to write words or draw pictures. The book you are reading right now was written on a computer that used these characters to form words. (If you look in the middle of the muddle just shown, you will see the letters of the alphabet hiding amid the other symbols. They begin, of course, with the 65th member of the ASCII character set.)

50

Okay, that's plenty for this lesson. It has been a very big one.

You have now explored all the major *ordinal types.* You can think of ordinal numbers as whole numbers, or values that can always be translated into whole numbers. For instance, in program IntError, I is an Integer, which means that by definition it must always be a whole number. The other numeric ordinal types are ShortInts, LongInts, Bytes, and Words, all of which are now familiar to you. The two non-numeric ordinal types are Booleans and Chars. Both of these types can be translated directly into whole numbers. For instance, Booleans have a value of either 0 if FALSE, or 1 if TRUE. Chars can be translated into ASCII numbers between 0 and 255. Examples of nonordinal types are real numbers and strings. Neither of these latter two types can be translated readily into whole numbers.

Another way to think of ordinal types is that they are sets of numbers that begin and end at certain defined values and that the interval between each member of the set is exactly one. For instance, Integers start at –32,768. The next number in the series is the *successor* of –32,768, which is –32,767. Functions called Succ and Pred yield the successor or predecessor of any ordinal value.

I leave you with one final thought: Study Table 4.1.

**Table 4.1. Data types and their values.**

| Data Type | Range | Value |
| --- | --- | --- |
| ShortInt | –128 to 127 | Signed 1-byte value |
| Integer | –32,768 to 32,767 | Signed 2-byte value |
| LongInt | –2,147,483,648 to 2,147,483,647 | Signed 4-byte value |
| Byte | 0 to 255 | Unsigned 1-byte value |
| Word | 0 to 65,535 | Unsigned 2-byte value |

Does this table make sense to you? If it doesn't, you might want to reread this chapter before continuing. If it does make sense to you, congratulations! You have taken a big step toward understanding how a computer works. By the way, don't bother trying to memorize this table. Any time you program in Turbo Pascal, the table is only a few keystrokes away in the online help service.

One last note is probably in order. The material in this lesson will be referred to often in this book. As you move on, its importance will grow and grow, until finally it will become clear that this is really the pivotal lesson around which the rest of the book is written. As a result, it definitely would not hurt to come back to these few pages from time to time and reread them. The whole thing is meant to be swallowed in one bite, and in one sitting. It shouldn't take more than 15 to 30 minutes to peruse. If you really want to understand computers, return here as often as you want, giving yourself a chance to absorb all the nuances in this discussion of variables and types.

# Review Questions

1. What is the difference between dynamic and persistent memory?
   _____

2. What do the letters *CPU* stand for? _____

3. The letters *RAM* stand for random access memory. What purpose does RAM serve in a computer? _____
   _____

4. What range of numbers can be stored inside a byte? _____

5. If you didn't know the answer to Question 4, how could you find out without ever opening a book? _____

6. How many bytes are in a word? _____

7. What's the difference between a signed and an unsigned number?
   _____

8. What type of variable is usually stored in a `Char`? _____

# Review Exercise

1. What's wrong with the following program?

```
program Whoops;
var
  i: Byte;

begin
  i := 256 * 256;
end.
```

# A Sprinkling of Syntactical Sugar

**OBJECTIVE**

*To understand operators, statements, and expressions.*

The stated objective for this lesson has a slightly ominous ring. In fact, if I read it and then close my eyes, I feel a bit like a grammarian who, for reasons no one can fully comprehend, is about to embark upon a truly soul-trying exploration of split infinitives and dangling participles.

Never fear: The situation is not nearly so dire.

In fact, the majority of this lesson is dedicated to a review of all the concepts introduced so far. In the process, you will add to your vocabulary through a discussion of operators, statements, and expressions.

Operators can be divided into three categories: *mathematical operators, logical operators,* and *relational operators.* Don't let these impressive-sounding names fool you. They are mostly sound and fury, signifying, if not nothing, then only very little.

In this lesson I concentrate primarily on mathematical operators, while taking the time to discuss relational operators, so that you can see how they relate to something called Boolean variables.

# Operators

Actually, you've already learned almost everything there is to know about mathematical operators. They are really nothing more than the little bits of syntax used to tie together simple mathematical statements. For instance, in the statement X := 2 + 2, the key operator is the plus symbol. (The assignment operator, :=, is also a part of this statement. But its function is so obvious that I will do little more than mention its existence.)

Three other important mathematical operators are the multiplication symbol, the division symbol, and the subtraction symbol. Because you've already worked with multiplication and addition, it shouldn't be hard for you to move on to a brief examination of subtraction and division.

Knowing what you know, nothing could be simpler than beginning an exploration of the subtraction operator:

```
program Subs1;

begin
  WriteLn('34 minus 28 = ', 34 - 28);
  ReadLn;
end.
```

As expected, this program produces the following output:

```
34 minus 28 = 6
```

Of course, if you subtract a negative number from another number, the result is the same as if you add a positive number to the first operand:

```
program Subs2;

begin
  WriteLn('34 minus -28 = ', 34 - (-28));
  ReadLn;
end.
```

A negative number minus another negative number produces equally obvious results:

```
program Subs3;

begin
  WriteLn('-34 minus 28 = ', (-34) - 28);
  ReadLn;
end.
```

In these two programs, the parentheses around -28 and -34 are only for clarity's sake. They could just as easily have been omitted.

Now that you know something about the subtraction operator, complete the following program:

```
program Subs4;
uses
  Crt;


var
  Result,
  N1, N2: LongInt;


begin
  ClrScr;
  WriteLn('This program subtracts one whole number from ');
  WriteLn('another, and writes the result to the screen.');
  WriteLn;
  Write('Enter the first whole number: ');
  ReadLn(N1);
  Write('Enter the second whole number: ');
  ReadLn(N2);
```

_____

_____

_____

_____

_____

_____

_____

# Division

Pascal division operators come replete with a nasty little curve that makes it necessary to have two separate symbols for this operation. It's not really that hard to understand why this little curve exists or what it's all about. You just have to remember that it's there. If you ever forget its existence, you can run into trouble.

The issue boils down to the fact that if you subtract, multiply, or add one whole number from or to another whole number, you always get another whole number. The same, however, cannot be said of division.

Think of the matter this way: 30 divided by 5 equals 6, which is a nice whole number. But 30 divided by 7 equals 4.2857143, which is not a whole number.

Sometimes when you divide 30 by 7, you want to know the result as closely as possible, whereas other times you just want to know the result to the nearest whole number. Because of these differing needs, Pascal has two division operators, one of which returns a whole number, and one of which returns a decimal value.

Consider the following program:

```
program Div1;
begin
  WriteLn(30 div 7);
  WriteLn(30 / 7);
end.
```

This program demonstrates the two types of division operators. The first returns a whole number, and the second returns a floating-point, or real, number.

As written, this program returns output that looks like this:

```
4
4.2857142857E+00
```

Rewrite the program so that it has the following output:

```
4

4.286
```

Here are the first few lines of the new program:

```
program Div2;

begin

  WriteLn(30 div 7);
```

_____

_____

The second form of division, which uses the slash (/) symbol, is often called floating-point division because the result returns a decimal.

When using standard Turbo Pascal, you usually declare decimal numbers as being of type Real. Real numbers are sometimes called floating-point numbers. The word _floating_ is appropriate because Real numbers are not always completely accurate. Instead, they tend to "float" very close to the exact result. These approximations occur not because of any flaw in Turbo Pascal, but because of the way computers are, of necessity, designed. As you progress as a programmer, you will learn ways of dealing with this problem. For now it is sufficient just to be aware that the problem exists.

When using floating-point division, you need to be especially conscious of the type of variables you are using.

Correct the following program so that it compiles and runs as it should.

```
program Div3;
var
  N1, N2: Integer;

begin
  N1 := 30 div 7;
  N2 := 30 / 7;

  WriteLn;
  WriteLn('Integer division returns: ', N1);
  WriteLn('Floating-point division returns: ', N2:0:2);

  WriteLn;
  WriteLn('Press the ENTER key to end this program');
  ReadLn;
end.
```

When this program is working correctly, it returns the following output:

```
Integer division returns: 4
Floating-point division returns: 4.29

Press the ENTER key to end this program
```

Before I leave the topic of mathematical operators, it is necessary to say a few words about something called *operator precedence*. This scary-sounding word comes close to living up to its name. It's not that operator precedence is all that confusing, but in practice it can turn out to be a bit tricky . You can better understand the basic issue by examining the following program:

```
program Prec1;

var
  N: LongInt;

begin
  N := 2 + 3 * 6;
  WriteLn(N);
end.
```

The output from this program is the number 20. If you take a moment, you can see how this result is produced. First the program adds 2 and 3 to produce 5. Then it multiplies 5 by 6 to get 30.

Wait a minute!

What did I just say? The output from this program is 20, and yet I just calculated that it should return 30! What went wrong?

The problem is that in situations like this, operator precedence takes over, producing results you might not expect. For now, all you need to know about operator precedence is that multiplication and division have a higher precedence than addition and subtraction. This means that when the program is executed, 3 is multiplied by 6 first, and then 2 is added to the result.

If you wanted the program to add 2 and 3 first, you would have to include parentheses to tell the computer the order in which you want it to perform its operations:

```
program Prec2;

var
  N: LongInt;
```

```
begin
  N := (2 + 3) * 6;
  WriteLn(N);
end.
```

This program writes the number 30 to the screen. The rule here is that expressions enclosed in parentheses have a higher order of precedence than multiplication. Thus, 2 is added to 3 before 3 is multiplied by 6 simply because of the way the parentheses are placed.

Clean up the following program so that it first performs both additions, then divides 46 by the result of the second addition, and then multiples the result of this division by the result of the first addition.

```
program Prec3;
{
  Lesson 5
  Operator precedence example
}

var
  N: LongInt;

begin
  N := 122 + 33 * 46 div 5 + 4;
  WriteLn(N);
end.
```

If you get it right, your result is 775. If you don't force the division to occur first, your program erroneously returns 792.

Whenever I have any confusion in my mind about operator precedence, I always turn to the on-line help screens for guidance. Figure 5.1 shows one important screen that you might want to refer to.

# True or False

Before you can understand relational operators, you need to come to terms with Boolean variables.

Despite the obscure-sounding name, Boolean variables are one of the simplest Pascal types. In fact, you can think of them as `Byte` variables that are limited in range to either 0 or 1. In these cases, the number 0 is associated with FALSE, and the number 1 is associated with TRUE.

**Figure 5.1.**
*Once you understand
operator precedence, the
online help can serve as
a handy reference.*

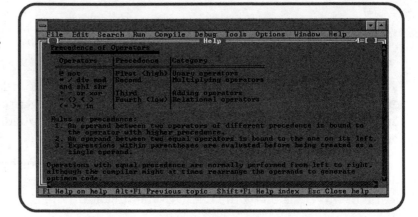

Consider the following program, which uses the *less than operator* (<):

```
program True1;

begin
  WriteLn(5 < 6);
end.
```

This program writes the word TRUE. The program could just as easily have been written as follows:

```
program True2;

var
  Result: Boolean;
begin
  Result := 5 < 6;
  WriteLn(Result);
end.
```

These programs return TRUE because 5 is indeed smaller than 6. The less than symbol used in this program is known as a *relational operator*. Relational operators always return either TRUE or FALSE.

The following program uses the *greater than* operator (>). Can you predict its output?

```
program True3;

var
  Result: Boolean;
begin
```

```
  Result := 5 > 6;
  WriteLn(Result);
end.
```

Table 5.1 displays the most commonly used relational operators. It is copied directly from the online help. If you ever want to see it, just go to the online help index and search for the word operators.

**Table 5.1. Commonly used relational operators.**

| Operator | Meaning | What Types It Compares |
|---|---|---|
| = | Equal to | Ordinal, real, string, set |
| <> | Not equal to | Ordinal, real, string, set |
| < | Less than | Ordinal, real, string |
| > | Greater than | Ordinal, real, string |
| <= | Less than or equal to | Ordinal, real, string, set |
| >= | Greater than or equal to | Ordinal, real, string, set |

Most of these operators work in an intuitive manner. The big exception to this rule is the equal (=) operator. It's not that it is difficult to use this operator. In fact, this operator does just what you would expect it to do, as the following short program shows:

```
program True4;

begin
  WriteLn(5 = 5);
  WriteLn(5 = 6);
end.
```

As expected, this program returns the following output:

```
TRUE
FALSE
```

But consider the following program:

```
program True2;

var
  Result: Boolean;
begin
```

```
c
  WriteLn('The expression 5 = 6 is ', Result);
  Result := 5 = 5;
  WriteLn('The expression 5 = 5 is ', Result);
end.
```

The first statement in this program might be somewhat clearer if it were written like this:

```
Result := (5 = 6);
```

The added parentheses give some additional clarity without changing the meaning of the statement. But they do not eliminate the basic confusion, which is that the equal sign can mean two different things in Pascal, depending on whether it is preceded by a colon.

On one side of the coin is the assignment operator (:=), and on the other side of the coin is the relational operator (=). In some languages, such as C, the confusion between these two operators can lead to some very nasty and hard-to-find bugs. But the Pascal language is structured in such a way that usually the compiler notices when you confuse the two and reports the error in bold red and yellow print.

Instead of boring you with an all-too-obvious discussion of the other operators, I'll leave them as an exercise for you to explore, either now or at your leisure. As a rule, their use is very straightforward, and they seldom act in a surprising or counterintuitive fashion. The best course to follow is simply to write a series of small programs that use the operators, so that you can get a feel for how they work.

# Statements and Expressions

What are statements and expressions? By now, you probably have noticed that I have used the words *statement* and *expression* several times without defining them.

This, of course, has been intentional. The problem is that most definitions of statements are very confusing, although the basic idea is simple. The *Turbo Pascal Programmer's Guide* that comes with your compiler spews forth the following jewel when it tries to define a *statement:*

```
Statements describe algorithmic actions that can be executed.
```

This definition is fine—as far as it goes. The only problem is that it doesn't go very far, because many people won't have a clue as to what it means.

Although I might be accused of going to the opposite extreme, I'll try to clarify the issue by stating the matter in somewhat oversimplified terms. My definition of a statement is that it is a chunk of code that ends with a semicolon or a period.

For instance, the following line is a statement:

```
i: Integer;
```

So is the following line:

```
i := 2 + 2;
```

In fact, these are both what are called *simple statements*. The following is a *compound statement:*

```
begin
  i  := 2 + 2;
  x := 2 * 2;
end;
```

Because the statement enclosed by the begin...end pair contains two statements, it is called a compound statement.

The closest the programmer's guide comes to defining an expression is simply to say:

```
Expressions are made up of operators and operands.
```

This statement obviously is not all that useful. So again I will oversimplify things a bit by saying that expressions are subsets of simple statements. For instance,

```
2 + 2
```

is an expression, whereas

```
x := 2 + 2;
```

is a statement. Notice that if you declare the variable x, and enclose the second statement in a begin...end pair, it will compile, whereas the second will confront you with the error message Unknown Identifier, and the cursor will blink under the first instance of the number 2. The issue here is that the latter bit of code is a full statement, whereas the former is merely a subset of a statement, which is called an *expression*.

I want to emphasize that I am intentionally shying away from giving you a technical definition of expressions and statements. This is because every technical definition I have seen is hopelessly confusing and unclear. All I need to do in this book is to use these two words in a way that is meaningful

to you. A more technical definition might satisfy the compulsive nitpickers, but it wouldn't do you much good. So I'll ride with this relatively easy-to-understand explanation, filling in any missing details only when, or if, I need to do so.

## Summary

Welcome to the end of Lesson 5. These last few pages have covered a wide range of syntactical issues that are elemental to the construction of many Pascal programs. Most of the time, you will not have to think consciously about much of the material presented in this lesson. A plus operator is a plus operator, and a statement is a statement; no amount of discussion about these subjects is going to change the way you think about them. There are times, however, when you need to understand the syntactical basis of a code fragment to analyze its function properly. This lesson provides you with the tools necessary to complete that task.

## Review Questions

1. What is an operator? _____

   _____

2. What is operator precedence? _____

   _____

3. What kind of variable do you use with relational operators? _____

   _____

# Taking a Branch in the Road

**To understand case *statements and* if *statements.***

Robert Frost ends one of his most famous poems with these lines:

> *Two roads diverged in a wood, and I—*
> *I took the one less traveled by,*
> *And that has made all the difference.*

Almost everyone who has sampled American literature knows these lines. They occur over and over in books or in our imagination because they represent something so elemental in human experience. They are about the process we undergo daily when we have to choose between alternatives.

Choosing between alternatives is also one of the central aspects of programming computers. When working in Pascal, we talk about these famous forks in the road as branches. We come to a point where we must branch either to the right or to the left.

This topic is so central to the way computers work that it is appropriate to devote an entire lesson to it. In these pages I focus primarily on if statements and case statements. These two branching techniques are used repeatedly every day by thousands of programmers. They are an elemental part of the language.

# If It's Not One Thing, It's the Other

Type and run this simple program that demonstrates how if statements work:

```
program Guess;
uses
  Crt;

var
  NumToGuess,
  UserGuess: Byte;

begin
  ClrScr;
  Randomize;
  NumToGuess := Random(3);
  WriteLn('I''m thinking of a number between 0 and 2');
  WriteLn('I will give you one chance to guess it.');
  Write('Pick a number between 0 and 2: ');
  ReadLn(UserGuess);
  if NumToGuess = UserGuess then
    WriteLn('You guessed it')
  else
    WriteLn('Bad luck! I was thinking of: ', NumToGuess);
  ReadLn;
end.
```

The opening lines of this program introduce the Pascal Random function, which is a *random number generator*. Random number generators, logically enough, produce random numbers.

The first time you call the Random function, you should begin by calling Randomize, which initializes the built-in random number generator. If you do not call `Randomize` first, the Pascal random number generator fails to produce truly random selections.

When you call `Random`, you pass it the number 3 as a parameter. This guarantees that it returns a number between 0 and 2. If you had passed `Random` the number 7, it would have returned a random number between 0 and 6. If you had passed Random 11, it would have returned a number between 0 and 10, and so on.

After prompting the user for his or her guess, you enter the `if` statement. An if statement often takes this form:

```
if certain conditions are met then
  do one thing
else
  do this other thing;
```

Compare this template with the code from program `Guess`:

```
if NumToGuess = UserGuess then
  WriteLn('You guessed it')
else
  WriteLn('Bad luck! I was thinking of: ', NumToGuess);
```

It is easy to see how this code follows the template. This is a classic pattern in computing, and one that should quickly become like an old familiar friend.

While you are considering these lines of code, it is important to note that `if` statements are one single thought in Pascal. Therefore, only one semicolon is used in the entire four lines of code presented.

In a moment I will illustrate this point. First I want to remind you that in Pascal, the < operator means less than and the > operator means greater than. The expression A > B reads: A is greater than B. This concept should be familiar to you, both from earlier lessons and from math courses.

Try typing and compiling the following small program:

```
program SemiError;


begin
  if 1 < 3 then
    WriteLn('One is less than three');
  else
    WriteLn('Three is less than one.');
end.
```

This code says that if 1 is less than 3, the computer should print one statement; otherwise, it should print a second statement.

The compiler will reject this code because the semicolon after the word three makes it think that the first two lines of code you have written form an entire statement. It then tries to parse your next statement and chokes on the word else. As a result, it puts up the message Error in Statement. In this case, it thinks you are making an error by trying to start a statement with the word else. In Pascal, it makes no sense to start a statement with the word else.

To fix the code, you can take one of two courses of action. The first would be to remove the lines.

```
else
   WriteLn('Three is smaller than one.');
```

The second course of action would be to remove the first semicolon.

Either action solves the problem. In this case, however, it is probably best to keep the semicolon and remove the fourth and fifth lines of code. The reason is that the else portion of the if statement will never be called because it is never true that 3 is less than 1.

# Man Versus Machine

One of the oddities of the Guess program is that it asks the user to guess a number between 0 and 2 rather than a number between 1 and 3. It does this because the random number generator chooses numbers between 0 and some arbitrary number less than 65,536. People don't tend to think of 0 as being the first number in a series. Instead, they usually think of 1, which begins the set of positive whole numbers.

To understand this issue better, take a moment to consider the random number generator. The following short program demonstrates the function in action:

```
program Rando;
uses
   Crt;

begin
   ClrScr;
   Randomize;
```

```
  repeat
    WriteLn(Random(5));
    Delay(250);
  until KeyPressed;
end.
```

When you run this program, a series of numbers ranging from 0 to 4 is printed down the left side of the screen. To stop the process, we merely have to press any key.

> **TIP:** To prevent the numbers from appearing so quickly that you can't read them, use the `Delay` procedure to slow the action to a comfortable speed. If you want, you can increase or decrease the period of the delay by changing the parameter passed to the `Delay` procedure. For instance, the program runs faster if `Delay(100)` is used, instead of `Delay(250)`.
>
> Regardless of the kind of machine you use, the `Delay` procedure always slows down the machine by the same amount of time. The period of the delay is measured in milliseconds, so `Delay(250)` represents a delay of 250 milliseconds.

After running this short program, you can see that the random number generator naturally turns out zeros. But as mentioned previously, people don't normally think of 0 as the first number. Instead, they think of the number line as starting with the number 1.

Here you face a common dilemma. The computer wants to behave one way, but your mind naturally behaves in a different manner. In situations like this, the human mind should always win out. A good programmer should teach the computer to bend to meet people's needs, rather than forcing the user to adopt unnatural patterns.

How can you change the program so that it produces output more natural to the human mind? One fairly obvious solution looks like this:

```
program Rando2;
uses
  Crt;

begin
  ClrScr;
  Randomize;
  repeat
```

```
        WriteLn(Random(5) + 1);
        Delay(250);
    until KeyPressed;
end.
```

Notice that in this example the WriteLn procedure prints the result of the Random function plus the number 1.

This is perhaps a good time to point out the difference between functions and procedures. The key thing to remember while considering this difference is that a function always returns a value. The expression Random(5) returns a value between 0 and 4. The Randomize and WriteLn procedures, on the other hand, don't return any values.

When the computer parses the statement WriteLn(Random(5) + 1), it gets the value returned by the Random function first. Suppose that value is 4. It then adds the number 1 to 4, yielding 5. Next, the computer passes this result to the WriteLn procedure, which prints the result to the screen.

Knowing this, you can easily see how to change the program to produce a more sophisticated result:

```
program Rando4;
uses
  Crt;

var
  i: Integer;
  j, Ones,
  Twos, Threes,
  Fours, Fives: LongInt;

begin
  ClrScr;
  Randomize;
  Ones := 0;
  Twos := 0;
  Threes := 0;
  Fours := 0;
  Fives := 0;

  for j := 1 to 500 do begin
    i := Random(5) + 1;
    WriteLn(i);
```

```
    case i of
      1: Inc(Ones);
      2: Inc(Twos);
      3: Inc(Threes);
      4: Inc(Fours);
      else Inc(Fives);
    end;

  end;

  ClrScr;
  WriteLn('One was returned: ', Ones, ' times.');
  WriteLn('Two was returned: ', Twos, ' times.');
  WriteLn('Three was returned: ', Threes, ' times.');
  WriteLn('Four was returned: ', Fours, ' times.');
  WriteLn('Five was returned: ', Fives, ' times.');
  WriteLn('Total = ', Ones + Twos + Threes + Fours + Fives);
  WriteLn;
  WriteLn('Press the Enter key to end this program.');
  ReadLn;
end.
```

This program is a bit longer than any presented so far in this text. It is not, though, necessarily any more complex.

The program begins by adding Crt to the uses clause so that the ClrScr procedure can be used. The next step is to declare some variables and then to initialize several of them to 0. Then a loop is begun that executes 500 times. The first part of the loop is taken from the example program examined previously. The second part of the loop introduces the Inc procedure and a new form of branching called a case statement.

The Inc procedure is simply a fast way of doing addition. For instance, Inc(i) has the same result as the statement i := i + 1. The former statement, however, executes more quickly than the latter.

To understand why one statement executes faster than another, you need to look not only at the Pascal code present in a program, but also at the machine code that the compiler generates. Because an examination of low-level assembly language code is beyond the scope of this book, you just have to take my word that there is a very simple way to translate Inc(i) into Assembler, whereas i := i + 1 can be translated into several rather convoluted lines. Sometimes, however, the Pascal compiler is clever enough to translate two different pieces of Pascal code into the same short, fast

machine code. So the ultimate arbiter of this type of thing is the machine code itself, rather than your best guess about what is likely to be generated. It is, however, safe to say that you will rarely go wrong if you use the Inc procedure.

A good way to think of case statements is that they provide a way to avoid multiple embedded if statements. For instance, the preceding case statement could have been written like this:

```
if i = 1 then
  Inc(Ones)
else if i = 2 then
  Inc(Twos)
else if i = 3 then
  Inc(Threes)
else if i = 4 then
  Inc(Fours)
else
  Inc(Fives);
```

This is much more awkward than writing it this way:

```
case i of
  1: Inc(Ones);
  2: Inc(Twos);
  3: Inc(Threes);
  4: Inc(Fours);
  else Inc(Fives);
end;
```

It's also important to remember that embedded if statements take longer to execute than case statements. Under normal circumstances, however, the speed at which code executes is not nearly so important as its readability. In other words, the fact that case statements execute faster than if statements is not nearly so important as the fact that case statements are easier to read than if statements.

case statements can be used only with ordinal values. (Ordinal values are discussed in Lesson 4, "Variables and Types.") Because case statements work with ordinal values, they usually are the best way to handle branching when you are working with Chars. Consider the following example:

```pascal
program Quiz;
uses
  Crt;

var
  Ch: Char;

begin
  ClrScr;
  WriteLn('The first president of the United States was: ');
  WriteLn('A) Karl Marx');
  WriteLn('B) Attila the Hun');
  WriteLn('C) Bill Gates');
  WriteLn('D) George Washington');
  WriteLn;
  Write('Enter A, B, C or D: ');
  Ch := ReadKey;
  WriteLn(Ch);

  case Ch of
    'A','a': begin
      WriteLn('Wrong. Karl Marx was a philosopher.');
      WriteLn('He lived from 1818 - 1883.');
    end;
    'B','b': begin
      WriteLn('Wrong. Attila the Hun was a warrior.');
      WriteLn('He lived from approximately 406 - 453.');
    end;
    'C','c': begin
      WriteLn('Wrong. Bill Gates is a capitalist.');
      WriteLn('He was born in 1955.');
    end;
    'D','d': WriteLn('Yes. Washington: 1732 - 1799.');
    else    WriteLn('Invalid input.');
  end;

  ReadLn;
end.
```

Notice that in this example ReadKey rather than ReadLn is used for getting input from the user. The ReadKey function returns a single character input when the user presses a key. Use the ReadKey function to get one character from the user and the ReadLn procedure to get multiple characters.

This example also shows two new aspects of case statements. First, it shows how to use begin...end pairs in case statements to set off blocks of code. Second, it shows how to use more than one constant for each option inside a case statement. Both of these techniques are illustrated in the following code excerpt:

```
'A','a': begin
  WriteLn('Wrong. Karl Marx was a philosopher.');
  WriteLn('He lived from 1818 - 1883.');
end;
```

This statement tells the compiler that if the user presses either the letter A or the letter B, the block of code after the colon and between the begin...end pair should be executed.

Besides multiple constants, you can also specify a range of constants in a case statement:

```
program Range;
uses
  Crt;

var
  Ch: Char;

begin
  Write('Enter a letter: ');
  Ch := ReadKey;
  WriteLn(Ch);

  case Ch of
    'a'..'z': WriteLn('You entered a small letter.');
    'A'..'B': WriteLn('You entered a capital letter.');
    else WriteLn('Invalid input');
  end;

end.
```

In this example, when you designate a range from the small letter a to the lowercase letter z, you are working with portions of the ASCII character set introduced in Lesson 4, "Variables and Types." (See Appendix C for the complete ASCII table.) Take another look at a subset of the ASCII characters, and notice how the lowercase and uppercase letters are represented by two ranges:

```
!  "  #  $  %  &  '  (  )  *  +  ,  -  .  /
0  1  2  3  4  5  6  7  8  9  :  ;  <  =  >
?  @  A  B  C  D  E  F  G  H  I  J  K  L  M
N  O  P  Q  R  S  T  U  V  W  X  Y  Z  [  \
]  ^  _  '  a  b  c  d  e  f  g  h  i  j  k
l  m  n  o  p  q  r  s  t  u  v  w  x  y  z
```

The fact that ASCII character A is followed by ASCII character B enables you to use ranges in case statements.

# case Versus if Statements

In the brief discussion of ordinal types, I mentioned that there are five numeric ordinal types: ShortInts, Integers, LongInts, Bytes, and Words. I also mentioned that there are two non-numeric ordinal types: Booleans and Chars. I have already shown that case statements are sometimes a good way to handle branching when working with Chars.

Booleans, on the other hand, are best handled by if...then...else statements because they can have only one of two values.

For instance:

```pascal
program Happy;

var
  GoodMood: Boolean;
  Ch: Char;

begin
  WriteLn('Answer with a ''Y'' for yes or an ''N'' for no.');
  Write('Are you happy: ');
  repeat
    Ch := ReadKey;
    Ch := UpCase(Ch);
  until (Ch = 'Y') or (Ch = 'N');

  if Ch = 'Y' then begin
    GoodMood := True;
    WriteLn('Y');
  end else begin
    GoodMood := False;
    WriteLn('N');
  end;
```

```
if GoodMood then
  WriteLn('Glad to hear you are doing so well.')
else
  WriteLn('Sorry to hear that.');
end.
```

This program contains several interesting programming examples. First, notice that it demonstrates a simple way of getting a yes-or-no answer from the user. It does this by taking advantage of the Pascal UpCase function. The UpCase function takes a single character as a parameter and then, if necessary, capitalizes that letter. For instance, both UpCase('A') and UpCase('a') return the capital letter A.

Notice that the first if...then...else statement chooses between two different characters, a capital Y and a capital N. Earlier in this lesson, the Quiz program used a case statement to differentiate between four different characters. The Range program, however, uses an if...then...else statement because there are only two possible characters to choose between. I point this out just to make it clear that it's not true that if...then statements must always be used with Boolean values and case statements with characters. Instead, weigh all the factors involved and choose the best possible option.

Program Happy also demonstrates two kinds of if...then...else statements. In the first kind, the two portions of the statement are set off by begin...end pairs, whereas in the second, there is no need to set off the two WriteLn statements with begin...end pairs. To understand why, take a careful look at the code. In the first if...then statement, two lines need to be executed before and after the word else; but in the second if...then statement, only one line needs to be executed.

# Summary

Well, here we are at the end of another lesson. This one introduced more complex concepts than any previous lesson. But don't worry; the next lesson is considerably simpler, and the chapter following it contains a good deal of review material.

Be sure not to move on too quickly. Take the time you need to absorb these ideas. They will come up again and again.

# Review Questions

1. What is an ordinal value? _____
   _____

2. Name two times when you would want to use `case` statements
   rather than `if...then` statements. _____
   _____

3. Name at least one case when you might want to use the `ReadKey`
   statement instead of a `ReadLn` statement. _____
   _____

## Lesson

# Looping

**To explore** for **loops,** while **loops, and** repeat...until **loops.**

I hope it is becoming clear that computer programming is not always as complicated as some people claim. Much of it is really rather straightforward—so straightforward, in fact, that some of you may be wondering how computers can do the many wonderful things they do.

Part of the answer to that question is simply that computers are very fast. The other part is that they are very good at repetition.

In fact, repetition—or looping, as it is sometimes called—is the subject of this lesson. In these pages, you are going to have a chance to learn how to make a computer perform an action over and over again. In the process, you will watch many amazing things happen.

This lesson explores three types of loops: for loops, while loops, and repeat...until loops. Pay careful attention, because looping is one of the keys to computer programming.

# for Statements

The classic looping statement is the *for loop*. The first example of a for loop serves as a platform for reviewing Pascal's multiplication symbol, an asterisk. Remember that in Pascal, if you want to write 2 times 2, you use the following syntax: 2 * 2.

Consider the following example:

```
program Doubler;
uses
  Crt;

var
  Count: Integer;
  Result: LongInt;

begin
  ClrScr;
  Result := 1;
  for Count := 1 to 16 do begin
    Result := Result * 2;
    WriteLn(Result);
  end;
end.
```

Take a moment to type this program and run it. Don't be concerned if you don't yet understand it. The point is merely to see what it does. When you are done, come back and examine the program in some detail.

If everything went smoothly, the first few lines of your program produced the following output:

```
2
4
8
16
32
```

These are the powers of 2. Note that many of the numbers discussed in the preceding lesson are powers of 2. For instance, 2 to the eighth power is 256. This number is associated with Bytes in the preceding lesson. Two to the fifteenth is 32,768. This number is associated with integers. And 2 to the sixteenth is 65,536, a number associated with type Word. It is not a coincidence that these Pascal types are so closely linked to the powers of 2.

At any rate, to understand how the program produces this output, examine the code in detail, noting first that it begins with a title and a *uses clause*. The uses clause brings in the Crt unit, which is needed to issue the ClrScr command.

Some variables are declared, and then the program begins with a bold sweep as it clears the screen. Afterward, Result is initialized to the value 1. It is now time to begin the for loop. Take a moment to really understand what it says.

Here is how the first line of the loop sounds when it is spoken aloud:

"For count equals 1 to 16 do begin..."

Say this statement in your mind a few times. Repeat it like a mantra or a line from a poem.

This bit of code states that the variable count will be incremented from 1 to 16. In other words, the program will keep adding 1 to the variable count until it equals 16.

Furthermore, each time this is done, a certain action will be repeated. In the example just given, the action repeated involves the following two lines:

```
Result := Result * 2;
WriteLn(Result);
```

The loop could have repeated any action. For instance, in the following example, all the program does is print the variable count each time it is incremented.

```
program ForLoop;
var
  Count: Integer;

begin
  for Count := 1 to 24 do begin
    WriteLn(Count);
  end;
end.
```

This simple loop does nothing more than count from 1 to 24. Because it executes only one line of code, you can omit the begin...end pair. For instance, you could have written:

```
for Count := 1 to 24 do
  WriteLn(Count);
```

Furthermore, in a case like this, it is entirely legitimate, and perhaps somewhat clearer, to write the statement on one line:

```
for Count := 1 to 24 do WriteLn(Count);
```

The question of which format is best is entirely a matter of taste. The computer does not care one way or the other. (However, some managers in the computer world, and some teachers, do care. If you run across one of these fellows, my strong advice to you is to humor them. Also, it might be worth mentioning that in matters of style, consistency is generally considered a virtue.)

If you want, you can have your loops count from virtually any whole number to any other whole number, so long as you stay within the scope of the variable's declaration. For instance, you can write:

```
for i := 123 to 135 do WriteLn(i);
```

This loops counts from 123 to 135. You also can count backward:

```
for i := 12 downto 1 do WriteLn(i);
```

Here the loop counts backward from 12 to 1. Take a moment to expand these examples into complete programs that compile and run correctly.

Now that you understand something about `for` loops, you can return to the original example and see whether you can make sense of it. The heart of it looks like this:

```
for Count := 1 to 24 do begin
  Result := Result * 2;
  WriteLn(Result);
end;
```

Think for a moment about what happens to the variable `Result` as this program runs. (If you want, follow this discussion by stepping through the program with the debugger. When you do this, be sure to place `Result` in the watch window.)

When the program begins, `Result` is equal to 1. Then the statement `Result := Result * 2` is executed. If `Result` equals 1 when this statement executes, the line reads `Result := 1 * 2`.

The big mistake that can be made here is to suppose that after substitutions are made the line should read `1 := 1 * 2`. This may seem to be the intuitively obvious interpretation, but it is incorrect. Remember that what you are really doing is assigning `Result` a new value. In this case, `Result` will equal its old value multiplied by 2:

```
(new) Result := (old) Result * 2;
```

After you have executed this line one time, `Result` equals 2, which is the first value the program writes to the screen. The second time this line executes, it reads as follows:

```
Result := 2 * 2
```

After this line is executed, `Result` equals 4. This means that the next time the line executes, it will look like this:

```
Result := 4 * 2
```

And so on. Over and over again. This mind-numbing repetition would be enough to drive anyone to utter distraction were it not for the fact that computers can execute these lines so incredibly fast and with such stupefying ease.

The result is that the program reels off the powers of 2 as if it were reciting its ABCs. In fact, computers love to do this sort of thing. It's their bread and butter.

# The Wily while Loop

The `for` loop is a real workhorse that all programmers use, appropriately enough, over and over again. But sometimes `for` loops aren't exactly the tool you need.

In the main example outlined previously, you performed an action 16 times. But suppose you didn't know how many times an action was to be performed? For instance, suppose you wanted to know how many times an action needed to be repeated before a certain condition was met. How could you handle that type of situation?

Consider the following example:

```
program Wily;
uses
  Crt;

var
  i: Integer;
begin
  ClrScr;
  i := 100;
```

```
     while i < 580 do begin
       Write(i, ' ');
       Inc(i, 2);
     end;
  end.
```

This program counts by 2s from 100 to 578.

When you look at this program, you can see immediately how different `while` loops are from `for` loops. `for` loops increment or decrement a number over a particular range. But `while` loops execute a statement or set of statements as long as a particular expression is true. This principle is illustrated in the following template:

```
while some expression is true do
  some particular action
```

Notice that this template is similar to the one followed by `if...then` statements:

```
if some expression is true then do
  some particular action
```

If you already understand `if...then` statements, obviously you are a good deal of the way down the road toward understanding `while` loops.

In the previous example, notice also that the variable `i` must be initialized at the beginning of the program and that the value must be incremented by 2 with the `Inc` procedure each time the loop is executed. In the past when the `Inc` procedure has been used, the variable has always been incremented by one number at a time. On this occasion, however, `Inc` is passed a second parameter, which instructs it to increment the variable by 2.

Just to be sure that you understand `while` loops, take a moment to complete the following program:

```
program WhilRoot;

var
  i: Integer;
  Result : Real;

begin
```

```
WriteLn('This program finds the square root ');
  WriteLn('of the first 16 whole numbers');
  WriteLn;
  i := 1;
  while Result < 4 do begin
    Result := Sqrt(i);
```

_____

_____

_____

_____

_____

When working with while loops, even good programmers can sometimes stumble into a classic error that lurks stealthily in the background, ever on the lookout for an opportunity to wreak havoc with even the most carefully laid plans. This error crops up when a programmer creates what is called an *infinite loop.* These loops appear when programmers accidentally write while loops that never end.

The following program demonstrates this error. The first time you run this program, it loops endlessly for as long as you let it continue, or at least until the next power failure. To end this impasse, hold down the Control key and press Break.

It is important to note that the Ctrl-Break trick usually works only if you are writing to the screen. Therefore, rebooting your machine might be the only way to break out of an infinite loop that, for instance, does nothing more than increment a number. Of course, every time you reboot your machine, you are going to lose any unsaved work. So the possibility that you might stumble into an infinite loop is yet one more excellent reason to save your work regularly.

See whether you can debug the infinite loop in this program:

Find
The

```
program WhileBug;
{
  Warning: This program contains an infinite loop!
  To end it, hold down the Control key and press the
  Break key once or twice.
```

```
}
var
  Factor,
  i: Integer;

begin
  Factor := 10;
  i := 3;

  while i <> 20 do
    WriteLn(i * Factor);

  WriteLn;
  WriteLn('Press ENTER to end this program');
  ReadLn;
end.
```

The previous examples have the virtue of being relatively simple and straightforward. They are not, however, very interesting. To rectify this situation, I present the following program, which draws a sine curve down the left side of the screen:

```
program Sin1;
uses
  Crt;

var
  x, y: Integer;
  r: Real;
begin
  ClrScr;
  y := 1;
  while y < 25 do begin
    r := Sin(y);
    x := Round(r);
    GotoXY(x + 10, y);
    Write('*');
    y := y + 1;
  end;
  ReadLn;
end.
```

This program is driven by the interaction of a while loop and the Pascal Sin function. The Sin function returns the sine of the number passed in its sole parameter. Figure 7.1 shows the output from this program:

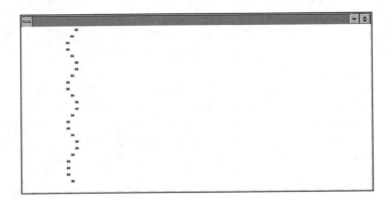

*Figure 7.1.*
*Sample output from the*
*Sin1 program.*

The big difference between this program and the Wily program is the following line:

```
r := Sin(y);
```

This line is really the heart of the program. It sets the variable r equal to the sine of the variable y.

If you look in the declaration, you will see that r is declared as a real number. As you no doubt recall, real numbers contain decimals. You need to use a real number here because the Sin function returns a decimal number. It returns a real because the Sin function would not be valuable to mathematicians if it did not have the capability to give answers accurate to several decimal places.

In the program, however, there is no need to work with a decimal number. In fact, you ultimately want to pass the result of the Sin function to the GotoXY procedure. Of course, the GotoXY procedure expects to be passed not a real number, but a whole number.

Given these circumstances, it is clear that you have to translate the result returned by the Sin function into a whole number. To do this, use the Pascal Round function. The Round function rounds off the decimal part of a real number so that only the integer remains.

Now you understand everything about the program except for why the number 10 is added to x when GotoXY is called. The reason for this is simple. When the sine curve is drawn, it needs to be moved in a few columns toward

the middle of the viewing area so that it does not bump into the left side of the screen. In this case, I arbitrarily moved the curve in toward the middle of the monitor by 10 columns:

```
GotoXY(x + 10, y);
```

It has taken me a few paragraphs to explain this program to you. The mechanisms involved, however, are not very complicated. If you want to see just how simple they are, then please take this occasion to fire up the debugger and step through this program with the F8 key. While doing so, place the variables r and x in the watch window. As you step through this program, take a glance at the previous paragraphs. What's hard to explain in words can be explained in just a few moments by the debugger. Let it be your teacher as you step through this program.

# More About Sine Curves

I've had you study this sine curve example not because I want to teach you about math, but because it is interesting to watch a Pascal program plot out the rudiments of a graph. The only problem with this program is that it stops just when things are getting interesting. In other words, it would be fun to have the code continue drawing the sine curve for more than 24 iterations of a loop. To do this, the program must scroll the screen. But you can't use GotoXY to scroll the screen. That's simply beyond its capability.

The following program shows a way to solve this dilemma:

```
program Sin2;
uses
  Crt;

var
  x,y,i: Integer;
  r: Real;

begin
  ClrScr;
  y := 1;
  while y < 100 do begin
    i := 1;
    r := sin(y);
    x := round(r) + 12;
```

```
    while i < x do begin
      Write(' ');
      inc(i);
    end;
    WriteLn('*');
    y := y + 1;
    Delay(100);   { Adjust the parameter to change speed }
  end;
end.
```

This program replaces the GotoXY statement with a second while loop. As a result, you end up with one while loop imbedded inside another while loop. Rather than wasting words trying to explain the relationship between the inner while loop and the outer while loop, I'll leave it to you to fire up the debugger and step through this program. When you do so, the mechanisms driving this program should become clear in only a few moments.

Notice also that the Delay procedure is used in this program to slow execution to a pace you can easily follow. Remember that you can adjust the speed at which this program executes simply by changing the parameter passed to Delay. For example, if you want this program to execute four times faster than it does now, write: Delay(25).

# The repeat...until Loop

The most recent version of the sine program is a considerable improvement over earlier versions. It is still limited, however, in that it ends after 100 iterations of the outer while loop. Some people (such as I) might find this program so much fun to watch that they might be a bit disappointed to have it end before they are ready for it to end. How can it be arranged so that this program will draw its little snake pattern for as long as the user wants, but not any longer?

Well, one good way to do this is with a repeat...until loop.

Here is a simple example of this type of loop:

```
program ComeBak1;
uses
  Crt;

var
  i: Integer;
```

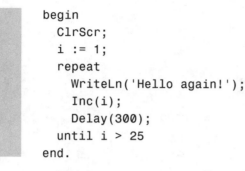

```
begin
  ClrScr;
  i := 1;
  repeat
    WriteLn('Hello again!');
    Inc(i);
    Delay(300);
  until i > 25
end.
```

This program repeatedly prints the words Hello again!, like an overly attentive salesman who keeps popping up just when you need to look after some other order of business.

You can see from this example that repeat...until loops execute until a particular expression becomes true:

```
repeat
  Some statements
until some expression is true.
```

Notice that repeat...until loops are structured so that they always execute at least once. while loops, on the other hand, are structured so that their bodies are not executed even once if certain conditions are not met.

A repeat...until loop can be particularly useful when combined with the Pascal KeyPressed function. The KeyPressed function is what is known as a Boolean function; that is, it returns either TRUE or FALSE. As you might suppose, the KeyPressed function returns FALSE until a key is pressed.

Suppose you apply this principle to the case of the overly ambitious salesman who keeps popping up to say hello at the wrong moment:

```
program ComeBak2;
{
 Lesson 5
 This program executes until a key is pressed.
}
uses
  Crt;

var
  i: Integer;
begin
  ClrScr;
  i := 1;
```

```
  repeat
    WriteLn('Hello again!');
    Inc(i);
    Delay(300);
  until KeyPressed;
end.
```

This time you have a little more control over our anxious friend. He'll continue to pop up repeatedly, but only as long as you allow. The moment you grow tired of his interruptions, you can simply press a key. If you do, he'll get the message.

Now you are ready to apply these principles to the sine wave program. Without further ado, here is the newly revamped code, called SIN3.PAS on your disk:

```
program Sin3;
uses
  Crt;

var
  x,y,i: Integer;
  r: Real;

begin
  ClrScr;
  y := 1;
  repeat
    i := 1;
    r := sin(y);
    x := round(r) + 12;
    while i < x do begin
      Write(' ');
      inc(i);
    end;
    WriteLn('*');
    y := y + 1;
    Delay(100);  { Adjust the parameter to change speed }
  until KeyPressed;
end.
```

If you are so inclined, you can watch the little snake wiggle across the screen for as long as you like. When you get tired of it, all you need to do is press a key.

# Review Exercises

1. In the first sine wave program, SIN1.PAS, the sine wave is very narrow. In fact, it is only three columns wide. If you modify the line that reads x := round(y), you can change the width of the sine curve. What modifications are necessary?

2. Make the same changes to SIN2.PAS.

3. Modify the Doubler program so that the output gets smaller each time rather than larger.

# urbo Pascal
# CLASSROOM 3

# Structured
# Programming

**Notes**

# Procedures

***To learn to create your own procedures.***

Creating procedures will move you to a whole different level of programming. So far, you have been learning the basic skills that every programmer needs and that nearly everyone approaches in a similar manner. However, there are many ways of creating procedures and functions. There are, in fact, whole schools of thought as to how to best go about this aspect of programming.

Most people agree that there probably are no "correct" or "right" answers to questions about how best to write a function or procedure. Instead, there are only opinions, theories, and aesthetics.

Some people, however, believe that programming is a science and that there is some objectively best way to write a particular piece of code. But I disagree with that view and, instead, believe that the issues involved are fundamentally a matter of taste.

In the long run, the only answer to this question that matters is what you yourself decide. So perk up your ears and focus your eyes. Look carefully at procedures in this lesson and functions in the next, using your own judgment to decide exactly what you want to make of them.

# Breaking Up the Monolith

Procedures and functions break up code into manageable chunks. They have the same function in programming that paragraphs have in writing. Without them, the code would be one long unmanageable mess. With them, the programs you produce can begin to become orderly, comprehensible, and manageable.

Consider the following program, which demonstrates how to perform simple animation:

```pascal
program Bounce;
uses
  Crt;

var
  i: Integer;

begin
  ClrScr;
  for i := 1 to 70 do begin
    GotoXY(i - 1, 5);
    WriteLn(' ');
    GotoXY(i, 5);
    WriteLn('*');
    Delay(140);
  end;

  for i := 70 downto 1 do begin
    GotoXY(i + 1, 5);
    WriteLn(' ');
    GotoXY(i, 5);
    WriteLn('*');
    Delay(140);
  end;
end.
```

This program moves an asterisk from the left side of the screen to the right side of the screen and back again. If the program moves too quickly or too slowly on your machine, you can change the speed at which it operates by tweaking the parameter passed to the Delay procedure. To make the program move more slowly, change the call to Delay so that it reads Delay(250). To make it move more quickly, make the call to delay read Delay(50). Or choose some other number, if you prefer.

This program is driven by the power of a `for` loop. I won't discuss how it works in detail, but if you want to explore it on your own, the best way to do so is with the debugger. As you learned earlier, the way to begin the process is to press the F8 key. This compiles the program and moves you to the `begin` statement at the start of the program. Each time you press F8, you move another instruction into the program. To view what is happening on-screen, open an *output window* or press Alt-F5 to toggle between the *output screen* and your code. If you get bored of stepping through the `for` loops, press Alt-R and then R for Run to execute the rest of the program in one step.

If you're like me, you probably will be fascinated by this type of program the first time you see it. Likely, you will want to play with it for a bit, testing its limits, tweaking it a little to see what you can make it do. Go ahead and try it out. When you are done, come back and join the discussion. After all, you're probably wondering why I showed you this program. Hadn't I just promised to show you how to write procedures and functions? What does this program have to do with those subjects?

In fact, there is a certain method to my madness.

Notice that this program can be broken into segments. For instance, the first `for` loop and the second `for` loop form their own discreet sections of the program. This arrangement makes it possible to remove the first `for` loop from the body of the program and place it in its own procedure:

```
program Bounce2;
uses
  Crt;

var
  i: Integer;

procedure MoveRight;
begin
  for i := 1 to 79 do begin
    GotoXY(i - 1, 5);
    WriteLn(' ');
    GotoXY(i, 5);
    WriteLn('*');
    Delay(140);
  end;
end;
```

```
begin
  ClrScr;

  MoveRight;

  for i := 79 downto 1 do begin
    GotoXY(i + 1, 5);
    WriteLn(' ');
    GotoXY(i, 5);
    WriteLn('*');
    Delay(140);
  end;
end.
```

Look at this program very carefully. In many ways, it is the most important program you have seen so far. Go ahead and run it, taking time to note that Bounce and Bounce2 look exactly the same when you run them.

What do you have here? What are the differences between Bounce and Bounce2?

Well, the essence of it is that the first for loop has been moved out of the main body of the program and put in its own procedure. This is what the procedure looks like:

```
procedure MoveRight;
begin
  for i := 1 to 79 do begin
    GotoXY(i - 1, 5);
    WriteLn(' ');
    GotoXY(i, 5);
    WriteLn('*');
    Delay(140);
  end;
end;
```

Logically enough, the procedure begins with the keyword procedure. This word tells the compiler that what is about to follow is a discreet chunk of code that can be analyzed separately from the rest of the code in the program. It forms a single autonomous, portable entity.

Notice that the declaration for a procedure is similar to the code written at the beginning of a program. For instance, at the start of this example, you write program Bounce2. At the start of the procedure, you write procedure MoveRight. Each statement ends with a semicolon. There is a certain parallel here that should not be ignored. In the first instance, you can see the reserved word `program` and then the program's title. Following this bit of syntax are the actual contents of a program. In the second case is the reserved word `procedure` and then the title of the procedure. Following this declaration are the contents of the procedure.

Similarly, the code that makes up each procedure is encapsulated inside a `begin...end` pair, just as the main body of a program is encapsulated inside a `begin...end` pair.

As you can see, there are several parallels between a procedure and a program. But the big difference is that a program is normally started from the DOS prompt, from a menu program, or from inside a compiler. But a procedure is never anything more than a subset of a program. Every procedure is called either from inside the main body of a program or from inside another procedure or function.

To understand this process, take another look at the main body of the program:

```
begin
  ClrScr;

  MoveRight;

  for i := 79 downto 1 do begin
    GotoXY(i + 1, 5);
    WriteLn(' ');
    GotoXY(i, 5);
    WriteLn('*');
    Delay(140);
  end;
end.
```

Notice that where the first `for` loop used to reside, there is now only the word `MoveRight`, followed by a semicolon. This word tells the compiler to call the procedure named `MoveRight`.

Now pay attention for a moment, because what I'm about to tell you is very important. Look at the line above the word `MoveRight` in the example. There, sitting innocently on the page, is the word `ClrScr`. The word `ClrScr` and the word `MoveRight` perform exactly parallel functions in this program. In other words, there is a place where the `ClrScr` procedure exists just as there is a place where the `MoveRight` procedure exists. In fact, the `ClrScr` procedure exists inside a module called `Crt`. That is why you always have to

add the line uses Crt whenever you want to call the ClrScr procedure. Later in this book, you'll learn how to create your own modules, or *units*. You'll use these units as places to store procedures and functions you want to use in the main program.

If you don't understand what I've written in the preceding paragraph, take a moment to reread it. This is a topic I am going to come back to again later, so don't worry if it doesn't make complete sense to you yet. But if the general idea begins to come into focus, the very essence of how modern computer programs are structured will begin to fall into place in your mind.

Nearly everything in programming boils down to the act of writing procedures and functions. The old workhorses GotoXY and WriteLn are themselves procedures not so very different from the MoveRight procedure created previously. Learn how to write well-structured procedures and functions and you will be well on your way to writing good programs.

# Hold on a Second!

You probably have questions for me at this point, but all I can say is to be patient. You will not get to the end of this book without learning a good deal about procedures and functions. I am going to keep coming back to these subjects, exploring them from a hundred different angles. By the time you are done, they will be utterly familiar.

To begin by addressing one obvious question, I'm sure some readers are wondering why I moved the first for loop, and not the second for loop, out of program Bounce. The answer is simply that I didn't want to confuse anyone by doing too much at once. So here, for your viewing pleasure, is a third version of this program with both for loops placed in their own procedures:

```
program Bounce3;
uses
  Crt;

var
  i: Integer;

procedure MoveRight;
begin
  for i := 1 to 79 do begin
```

```
      GotoXY(i - 1, 5);
      WriteLn(' ');
      GotoXY(i, 5);
      WriteLn('*');
      Delay(140);
    end;
end;

procedure MoveLeft;
begin
  for i := 79 downto 1 do begin
    GotoXY(i + 1, 5);
    WriteLn(' ');
    GotoXY(i, 5);
    WriteLn('*');
    Delay(140);
  end;
end;

begin
  ClrScr;
  MoveRight;
  MoveLeft;
end.
```

Notice the main block of this program. It can be distilled to a series of three very short, very easy-to-understand commands:

*Clear the screen.*
*Move right.*
*Move left.*

What could be simpler?

To appreciate the beauty of this approach, try stepping through this program with the debugger. Begin by pressing the F8 key once. Then press it three more times to execute each of the three sections of this program. The step is to clear the screen, then move to the right, then move to the left. Now press F8 once more to end the program.

Suppose, however, that you want to examine how one of the procedures works. How do you do that? You begin exactly the same way, by pressing F8. Then press F8 once more to step over the ClrScr procedure. Now, this time press F7 to step into the MoveRight procedure. Notice how the debugger

jumps you up to the proper place in the code. One moment you're looking at the main block of the program, and the next moment you're stepping through the MoveRight procedure.

This is a very powerful capability. Remember the way it works: F8 to step over a procedure, F7 to step into a procedure. When you get tired of stepping through the for loop, remember that you can run the program to the end by pressing Alt-R, R.

This is probably a good time to learn about an important variation on the breakpoint feature in the Turbo Pascal debugger.

Suppose you start stepping through the program by pressing F8 twice and then pressing F7. Now you are in the middle of the MoveRight procedure. You step through the for loop a few times, learn how it works, and then grow bored. You could run the program to the end from here, but suppose you didn't want the program to end, and merely wanted to skip ahead to the MoveLeft procedure so you could see how it worked.

This is an excellent time for you to learn a neat little trick involving the F4 key. Stop stepping through the MoveRight procedure. Instead, move the cursor down to the beginning of the MoveLeft procedure. Take the time to carefully place the cursor directly under the begin statement at the start of the procedure. Now press the F4 key.

The program immediately begins running again, enabling you to watch the asterisk move from the left to the right part of the screen. But the program stops execution when it reaches the begin statement at the start of the MoveLeft procedure. It stops here because this is where you were when you pressed the F4 key. Now you can again start stepping through your code with the F8 key. When you grow tired of this, run the program through to the end.

A second breakpoints technique is probably more important than the "run to cursor" capability of the F4 key. In fact, it is essential that you know how to set breakpoints. This is an excellent time for you to practice using them by setting one at the beginning of each of your procedures. To do this, move the cursor so that it is moving directly under the word begin at the start of the MoveRight procedure. Now do the same thing at the start of the MoveLeft procedure.

This time when you run your program, it will stop automatically at the beginning of the MoveRight procedure. Step through an instruction or two after this, and press Alt-R, and then R a second time. This time your program will run to the next breakpoint, which is at the start of the MoveLeft procedure. From here you can either step or run through the rest of your program.

102

Any breakpoints that you set will remain in effect until you turn them off. To do this, just move the cursor to where a breakpoint is, and then press Ctrl-F8 again. In other words, the Ctrl-F8 key combination is a toggle that turns your breakpoints on or off each time you use it. You should also know that breakpoints can be set or cleared from the Debug menu at the top of the IDE.

Overall, the point to understand is that breakpoints are a crucial feature of all good debuggers. Use them as often as you want.

Don't think of these discussions of how the debugger works as digressions from the main topic of functions and procedures. The debugger helps you explore procedures so that you can see how they work. All good programmers use the debugger to help them create good procedures and functions. Or, to state the matter somewhat differently, I have never known a good programmer who didn't know the debugger inside and out. The two ideas are virtually synonymous: Bad programmers don't use the debugger; good programmers use it all the time. There may be some exceptions to this rule, but I've never encountered them.

Learning to use the debugger is one of the crucial make-or-break issues when it comes to being a good programmer.

# More About Procedures

To make sure the examination of procedures is sinking in, why don't you take a few moments to finish the following program, which prints the words Good Day and Sunshine to the screen:

```
program Sunshine;

procedure WriteGoodDay;
begin
  WriteLn('Good day');
end;

procedure WriteSunShine;
begin
```

```
    WriteLn('Sunshine');
  end;
```

_____

_____

_____

# The Scope of a Variable

When writing procedures and functions, you need to carefully consider the _scope_ of the variables you use. The scope of a variable is the area over which you are allowed to use a variable.

In programs that contain only one module, the rule to follow is that a variable is valid from the place where it is declared until the end of a program. But it is not valid above the place where it is declared.

For instance, the following program will not compile:

```
program NoScope;

procedure WriteName;
begin
  WriteLn(Name);
end;

var
  Name: String;
begin
  Write('Enter your name: ');
  ReadLn(Name);
  WriteName;
end.
```

To correct the problem, you need to move the declaration of the variable to a location above procedure WriteName:

```
program NoScope;

var
  Name: String;

procedure WriteName;
begin
```

```
    WriteLn(Name);
end;

begin
  Write('Enter your name: ');
  ReadLn(Name);
  WriteName;
end.
```

This little introduction to the topic of scoping variables will have to serve as only an introduction to what can prove to be a complicated subject. For now, just absorb what I have presented so far, but be prepared to come back to this topic several times throughout the course of this book.

# Review Questions

1. During debugging, what key is associated with the command "run to cursor"? _____

2. During debugging, what key is associated with the command "step into"? _____

# Review Exercises

1. Point out two errors in the following lines of code:

```
procedure Samuel
begin
  WriteLn('Hello');
end.
```

2. Divide the following program into a main block and two procedures:

```
program Ages;
{ Lesson 8 }

var
  Born,
  Current: Integer;
```

```
begin
  Write('In what year were you born: ');
  ReadLn(Born);
  Write('What year is it now: ');
  ReadLn(Current);
  WriteLn('I see you are ', Current - Born, ' years old.');
  WriteLn;
  WriteLn('Press ENTER to end this program');
  ReadLn;
end.
```

3. The preceding program can give the wrong answer, depending on when in the year your birthday falls. Can you modify it so that it always gives the correct answer?

Lesson

9

# The Divide-and-Conquer Strategy

*To use procedures to create structured programs.*

The intelligent use of procedures and functions is part of what is called structured programming. Structured programming is the art of breaking up code into a series of small, easy-to-understand segments. The philosophy behind this mode of programming can be summed up in a single phrase: Divide and conquer.

In this lesson you learn how to use procedures to create structured programs. Your job is to break the code into its component parts, each a relatively simple, discreet task.

# Getting Down to the Nitty Gritty

You're going to start by plunging into a program that's a little larger than anything you've seen before. This shouldn't worry you because the program is divided into little segments, each as easy to comprehend as the code that appeared in the first three or four lessons. This is the essence of the divide-and-conquer structured programming philosophy: Take a seemingly complex task, and divide it into a series of relatively trivial procedures and functions.

Consider the following lines of code:

```
program Blake1;
uses
  Crt;

var
  Name: String;
  Ch: Char;

procedure Stars;
begin
  WriteLn;
  WriteLn('**********************************');
  WriteLn;
end;

procedure DoMale;
begin
  WriteLn('Hello ', Name, '.');
  WriteLn('Remember the words of the poet: ');
  Stars;
  WriteLn('What is it women do in men require?');
  WriteLn('The lineaments of gratified desire.');
  Stars;
end;

procedure DoFemale;
begin
  WriteLn('Hello ', Name, '.');
  WriteLn('Remember the words of the poet: ');
  Stars;
  WriteLn('What is it men do in women require?');
```

```
  WriteLn('The lineaments of gratified desire.');
  Stars;
end;

begin
  ClrScr;
  Write('Enter your first name: ');
  ReadLn(Name);

  Write('Enter your sex (M/F) : ');
  repeat
    Ch := UpCase(ReadKey);
    WriteLn(Ch);
    WriteLn;
  until (Ch = 'M') or (Ch = 'F');


  if Ch = 'M' then
    DoMale
  else
    DoFemale;

  WriteLn;
  WriteLn('Press <Enter> to end this program.');
  ReadLn;
end.
```

This program uses two quotations from the often-anthologized William Blake poem "The Question Answer'd." I throw it in here just to remind you that there is more to life than the logic circuits inside a computer.

At any rate, the key new element in this program is that it calls the procedure Stars from inside the procedures called DoMale and DoFemale. This means that the program really has three levels. It begins in the main block at level one. Then it jumps up to level two when it enters either the DoMale or the DoFemale procedure. From there it jumps twice to the third level, which contains the Stars procedure. (If you want, step through this program with the debugger so you can see how it works.)

This process of having procedures call other procedures is very common in real-world programs. In fact, it is the very heart of the process called structured programming.

One of the main challenges of this type of programming is to decide when it is necessary to break up a block of code into two or more procedures. There are no clear-cut answers here, but one guide to remember is that no single block of code should take up more than about 20 lines, or one screen, of text.

If you examine the program Blake1, you can see that its main block consists of 22 lines. Although this is a borderline case, you might decide that this code block is a little too long. Looking for a remedy, you might notice that the program could easily be divided into several procedures. For instance, you could move the middle section of the program into a procedure called GetGender.

Here is how this program might appear after you make this change:

```
program Blake2;
uses
  Crt;

var
  Name: String;
  Ch: Char;

procedure Stars;
begin
  WriteLn;
  WriteLn('**********************************');
  WriteLn;
end;

procedure SayHello;
begin
  WriteLn('Hello ', Name, '.');
  WriteLn('Remember the words of the poet: ');
end;

procedure DoMale;
begin
  SayHello;
  Stars;
  WriteLn('What is it women do in men require?');
  WriteLn('The lineaments of gratified desire.');
  Stars;
end;
```

```
procedure DoFemale;
begin
  SayHello;
  Stars;
  WriteLn('What is it men do in women require?');
  WriteLn('The lineaments of gratified desire.');
  Stars;
end;

procedure GetGender;
begin
  Write('Enter your sex (M/F) : ');
  repeat
    Ch := UpCase(ReadKey);
    WriteLn(Ch);
    WriteLn;
  until (Ch = 'M') or (Ch = 'F');

  if Ch = 'M' then
    DoMale
  else
    DoFemale;
end;

begin
  ClrScr;

  Write('Enter your first name: ');
  ReadLn(Name);

  GetGender;

  WriteLn;
  WriteLn('Press <Enter> to end this program.');
  ReadLn;
end.
```

Notice that now the main block is only 12 lines long. What was previously a fairly confusing fragment of code is now simplicity itself. This is the very essence of structured programming: Divide and conquer!

In the rewrite of the program, one other change was made. You will notice that near the top of the code there is now a procedure called SayHello. This

111

procedure consists of the two lines that used to be in the beginning of both the `DoMale` and the `DoFemale` procedures. The `SayHello` procedure eliminates this repetition. It's a waste of space to have the same two lines of code in two places in the program. So they are moved out of their respective procedures and placed in a new procedure.

Both of the changes made to the `Blake1` program would generally be considered good programming practice. However, any time you make decisions like this, you have to make judgment calls. Remember that there are very few hard and fast rules in this area of programming.

One other point is worth mentioning here. You might think that all the procedures created in `Blake2` make the program too complicated. Wouldn't it be easier to start at the beginning and run through to the end rather than jump all over the place with a convoluted series of nested procedures?

Indeed, I might agree with this criticism if it weren't for the fact that you have the debugger to call on in your time of need. Start the debugger, use the F8 key, the F7 key, the F4 key, the watch window, and breakpoints, and the secrets of this program reveal themselves in a matter of moments!

# The Length of a Procedure

You have read about the maximum number of lines you might want to include in a procedure. But what about the optimum number of lines? What is the best length for a procedure?

Obviously, the answer is a matter of opinion. Each programmer has a right to develop his or her own style of writing, and the length of the procedures should be a part of that style.

Nevertheless, it is probably best to keep your routines as short as possible. By this I mean three to five lines in length. The reason for keeping procedures so short is that it is relatively easy to debug short pieces of code.

Suppose you know that a program has a bug in it. You fire up the debugger and start stepping through the code. Everything is fine until you reach a certain procedure that immediately crashes and burns when you try to step through it. Obviously it is going to be easier to find the problem with that procedure if it is only 5 lines long than if it is 25 lines long.

Another rule of thumb here is to take only one action in each procedure. An easy way to help enforce this rule is to give each procedure a short name that sums up its purpose. For instance, a procedure called

GetName or even GetAddress makes sense, whereas a procedure called GetName_WriteItToScreen_SayGoodBye is a bit of a mouthful.

Before finishing this lesson, take a moment to complete the following program. While you are working with it, notice how the code includes two apostrophes to create the single apostrophe in the word *user*. This happens because you are already using single apostrophes to tell the compiler that you are about to begin or end a string. To distinguish a quotation mark from an apostrophe, you type two apostrophes in succession.

```pascal
program Confirm;
uses
  Crt;

var
  City,
  State: String;

_____

_____

_____

_____

_____

_____

_____

_____

_____

_____

_____

_____

_____

procedure WriteResults;
var
  Ch: Char;
begin
  WriteLn('You said you were born in ', City , ', ', State);
  Write('Is this information correct: ');
```

```
repeat
    Ch := UpCase(ReadKey);
    WriteLn(Ch);
  until (Ch = 'Y') or (Ch = 'N');
end;

begin
  { Give instructions to user }
  WriteLn('This program gets a user''s city of birth and ');
  WriteLn('state of birth and confirms the input. ');

  GetCity;
  GetState;
  WriteResults;

  WriteLn;
  WriteLn('Press the ENTER key to end this program');
  ReadLn;
end.
```

When you are done, the output from your program should look something like this:

```
This program gets a user's city of birth and
state of birth and confirms the input.

Enter the city where you were born: Olympia
Enter the state where you were born: WA
You said you were born in Olympia, WA
Is this information correct: Y

Press the ENTER key to end this program
```

# Summary

This is the end of Lesson 9. Think about what you have read. Work some of the review questions and exercises. Then when you're ready, move on to the next lesson, where you will study functions and learn how to pass parameters to both procedures and functions.

# Review Questions

1. The process of dividing programs into procedures and functions is called _____ programming.

2. Structured programmers split their programs into procedures and functions. Their motto is _____ and _____ .

3. What is the maximum number of lines you usually want to include in a single block of code? _____

4. Is structured programming an exact science, an art, or something else altogether? If it's something else, what would you call it? _____
   _____

# Review Exercise

1. Use procedures to eliminate repetition from this program:

```
program Sunflower;
begin
  WriteLn;
  WriteLn;
  WriteLn('Ah! Sun-flower');
  WriteLn;
  WriteLn;
  WriteLn('Ah, Sun-flower, weary of time,');
  WriteLn('Who countest the steps of the sun,');
  WriteLn('Seeking after that sweet golden clime');
  WriteLn('Where the traveler''s journey is done:');
  WriteLn;
  WriteLn;
  WriteLn('Where the youth pined away with desire');
  WriteLn('And the pale virgin shrouded in snow');
  WriteLn('Arise from their graves and aspire');
  WriteLn('Where my Sun-flower wishes to go.');
  WriteLn;
  WriteLn;
  WriteLn('Press ENTER to stop viewing this Blake poem');
  ReadLn;
end.
```

# The Other Side of the Coin

*To learn about functions.*

This lesson picks up pretty much where I left off in the last lesson. I was discussing procedures, showing how you can use them to create structured programs that are easy to comprehend and modify.

In this lesson you get a chance to take a careful look at functions and parameters. As you proceed, you will begin to see how you can use the information you have been soaking up to create useful programs.

## A Square Deal

Writing a function is like asking a question. You ask a friend, "Tell me, what is the square of the number 5?" She answers, "25."

Here is how the same exchange looks in Turbo Pascal:

```
program Squares;

function Square(NumToSquare: LongInt): LongInt;
begin
    Square :=  NumToSquare * NumToSquare;
end;

var
  Result: LongInt;

begin
  Result := Square(5);
  WriteLn(Result);
end.
```

This function returns the square of a number passed to it. In this case, I pass it the number 5 as a *parameter,* and it returns the number 25.

When looked at from a certain perspective, there is nothing new about this process. For instance, you have been passing parameters to procedures like GotoXY and WriteLn since the first lessons in this book. But this marks the first time you are on the receiving end of a passed parameter.

In this case, the function square receives one parameter, called NumToSquare, which is declared as a LongInt. After it receives the parameter, it multiplies NumToSquare by itself and then returns it.

After the function is completed, the variable Result in the main block of the program contains the result of the multiplication, which in this case is the number 25. The program then writes this number to the screen.

The Square function is flexible in that it returns the square of any number you pass it. For example, if you pass it 6, it returns 36; if you pass it 10, it returns 100. This useful program performs a real-world function.

A glance at the sample program reveals that functions are divided into two sections—the heading and the body. The body is the part between the begin...end pair. The heading of the function looks like this:

```
function Square(NumToSquare: LongInt): LongInt;
```

It begins with the word function, then declares the name of the function—in this case, Square.

> **NOTE:** This is a good time to point out one of those hairy pitfalls that newcomers can stumble into totally unawares. Notice that the name of the function is `Square`, and the name of the program is `Squares`. In this case, it is illegal to assign the same name to two identifiers. If you did, you would get the message `Error 4: Duplicate Identifier`. If you can, try to remember this method of coming up with the famous `Duplicate Identifier` error. For some reason, it can be a particularly nasty stumbling block for beginners. If you can remember this point, you won't end up wasting precious programming time trying to figure out where this error message came from.

Returning to the example, notice that the function name is followed by a parameter and its type in parentheses. Then there is a colon, followed by the type of variable the function returns. In other words, this function answers the question by returning a variable of type `LongInt`.

So far so good. However, the following simple example hides a frightening little beast that is always lurking about, on the lookout for unsuspecting programmers. The danger is concealed in the simple act of passing the parameter to a function.

If you try to run this program, the compiler chokes on the seemingly innocent parameter. Instead of seeing the cheerfully blinking `Success` message, you end up staring at the dreaded, well-known words `Error 26: Type Mismatch`. See whether you can find the problem on your own before reading the explanation that follows the program.

```
program Square;

function Square(NumToSquare: LongInt): LongInt;
begin
  Square :=  NumToSquare * NumToSquare;
end;

var
  Result: LongInt;

begin
  Result := Square('Sam');
  WriteLn(N);
end.
```

The problem is that the parameter passed to the function Square is the string 'Sam'. Square, of course, expects to be passed a LongInt as its sole parameter. After all, its job is to find the square of that number. It doesn't make any sense to talk about the square of the name 'Sam', so no wonder the compiler rejects this example!

It should be easy to grasp that there is something wrong with the idea of passing a string to a function that squares numbers. But putting the matter in those words can cause a certain amount of confusion. A better way to state the problem is to say that the function square expects to be passed a number.

The first way of stating the matter implies that the function square knows something about its purpose. Unfortunately, computers are rarely that bright. However, the function Square does know what sort of parameter it's going to be passed. It learns this information by referring to its own header:

```
function Square(NumToSquare: LongInt): LongInt;
```

The parameter declaration NumToSquare: LongInt tells the function that it is going to be passed a LongInt. That is why the compiler prints the dreaded message Error 26: Type Mismatch. A mismatch was created between the type of parameter passed to the function and the type of parameter it was expecting. The two didn't match, resulting in a type mismatch.

Some might think that I am making too much of a fairly obvious point. Well, that is my intention. Believe me, there will come a time when that error message will pop up in front of you and you will wonder what in the world is going on. In such moments, think back to this example, where you try to pass a string to a function that wants a number and the result is a type mismatch. I promise that there will be occasions where the reason for this error is not nearly so obvious. But you can return to this example when facing more confusing circumstances. Remember, you can't get the square of the name 'Sam': It's a type mismatch. Old Error 26, right? The type mismatch!

# Raising $x$ to the $y$ Power

Everyone is familiar with the idea of raising a number to a certain power. For instance, the square function you saw earlier raises numbers to the second power. But what if you want to raise a number to the third or fourth power?

One obvious solution would be to create functions named PowerOfThree, PowerOfFour, and so on, that would be variations on the Square function. For instance, a PowerOfThree function might look like this:

```
function PowerOfThree(Num: Integer): LongInt;
begin
  PowerOfThree := Num * Num * Num;
end;
```

This type of scheme works fine, but it has the drawback of forcing you to create a different function for each power to which you might want to raise a number. What you need is a more generalized function.

In the following program, the function XToTheY demonstrates a solution to this problem. Type this program and run it. Don't try to understand it yet, just see what it does.

```
program Powers;

function XToTheY(X: Integer; Y: Integer): Real;
var
  Count: Integer;
  Result: Real;
begin
  Result := 1;
  for Count := 1 to Y do
    Result := Result * X;
  XToTheY := Result;
end;

var
  i: Integer;
  Result: Real;
begin
  for i := 1 to 16 do begin
    Result := XToTheY(2,i);
    WriteLn(Result:12:0);
  end;

  WriteLn;
  WriteLn('Press ENTER to end this program');
  ReadLn;
end.
```

The output looks like this:

```
2
4
8
```

```
16
32
```

These results should look familiar. This is the same output that the `Doubler` program produced back in Lesson 7, "Looping." Go back and look at that program and compare it to the `XToTheY` procedure. The `Doubler` program has been encapsulated in a single function. In the process, we have increased its power greatly.

Take a moment to consider exactly what is happening here.

As is, this program prints the powers of 2 from 1 to 16. For instance, the first line of output is 2 to the first power, the second is 2 to the second power, the third is 2 to the third power, and so on.

If you want this program to produce the powers of 5 instead of the powers of 2, you need to change only one character. That character appears in the line that reads:

```
Result := XToTheY(2,i);
```

To see the program print the powers of 5, change the line so that it looks like this:

```
Result := XToTheY(5,i);
```

Notice that you pass two parameters to the function. The first parameter is a number that you want to raise to a certain power, and the second parameter is the power to which you want to raise the number. For instance, suppose you typed

```
Result := XToTheY(3,2)
```

In this case, `Result` would be set to the number 9. That is because 3 to the second power is 9:

```
9 = 3 * 3
```

If you typed

```
Result := XToTheY(4,3);
```

`Result` would be equal to 64:

```
64 = 4 * 4 * 4
```

The mechanism of the function itself is very simple. It multiplies the parameter x times itself y times.

As you can see, the `Powers` program is aptly named: It contains a robust routine that can produce extremely powerful results.

122

# Passing a Parameter to a Procedure

You now know how to pass parameters to functions. But you can just as easily pass a parameter to a procedure. For instance, the following program creates a procedure that can draw a line of a certain length. The length is specified in a parameter:

```
program Triangle;
uses
  Crt;

{ Draw the triangle }
procedure LineDraw(Length: Integer);
var
  i: Integer;
begin
  for i := 1 to Length do
    Write('>');
  WriteLn;
end;

var
  Count : Integer;
begin
  ClrScr;

  { Top half of triangle }
  for Count := 1 to 10 do
    LineDraw(Count);

  { Bottom half of triangle }
  for Count := 10 downto 1 do
    LineDraw(Count);

  WriteLn;
  WriteLn('Press ENTER to end this program');
  ReadLn;
end.
```

This program, powered by a series of for loops, draws a funny sort of sideways triangle on the screen, as Figure 10.1 shows.

*Figure 10.1.*
*The output from the triangle program.*

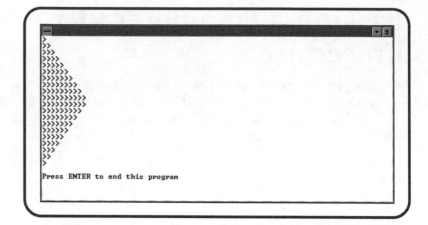

The heart of the program is the LineDraw procedure. This procedure can draw the greater than character multiple times across the screen in a straight line. It takes a single parameter, which specifies how many times the greater than character is drawn to the screen.

 If this program seems at all mysterious to you, take a moment to step through it with the debugger. While doing so, be sure to place the variable Count in the watch window. This variable becomes the parameter that is passed to procedure LineDraw. As Count is incremented and decremented, the number of greater than symbols drawn to the screen increases and decreases.

# Passing Two Parameters to a Procedure

Some modifications to the preceding program make it considerably more flexible:

```
program Triangl2;
{
  A program that draws a triangle. It enables
  the user to control the triangle's width.
}
uses
  Crt;
```

```pascal
{ Draw the triangle }
procedure LineDraw(Length: Integer; Width: Byte);
var
  i: Integer;
begin
  for i := 1 to Length * Width do
    Write('>');
  WriteLn;
end;

{ Get user input }
function GetWidth: Byte;
var
  Num: Integer;
begin
  WriteLn('This program draws a sideways triangle.');
  WriteLn('The width of the triangle can be controlled');
  WriteLn('by the user if he or she enters a number');
  WriteLn('between one and seven.');
  Write('Enter that number and press enter: ');
  repeat
    ReadLn(Num);
  until (Num > 0) and (Num < 8);
  ClrScr;
  GetWidth := Num;  { Return result }
end;

var
  Count: Integer;
  Width: Byte;
begin
  ClrScr;

  { Get input }
  Width := GetWidth;

  { Draw triangle }
  for Count := 1 to 10 do
    LineDraw(Count, Width);
  for Count := 10 downto 1 do
    LineDraw(Count, Width);
```

```
   WriteLn;
   WriteLn('Press ENTER to end this program');
   ReadLn;
end.
```

This program passes two parameters to the LineDraw procedure. Figure 10.2 shows the output from this program.

*Figure 10.2.*
*The output from the*
*TRIANGL2.PAS*
*program.*

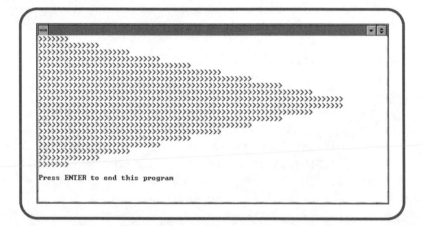

Notice the syntax of the procedure's header:

```
procedure LineDraw(Length: Integer; Width: Byte);
```

Both parameters are declared in parentheses after the procedure's name. The drill is as follows: Declare the name of the first parameter, follow it with a colon, then write the type. To add a second parameter, enter a semicolon, a name, a colon, and the correct type.

If both parameters have the same type, you can take a bit of a shortcut:

```
procedure LineDraw(Length, Width: Byte);
```

Here the names of the two parameters are declared and then separated with a comma. After declaring the names, enter a colon and declare their type.

It is also probably worth remembering why the variable Width is declared as a byte instead of an integer. Bytes, as you recall, have a range from 0 to 255. Because the variable Width can have only values between 1 and 7, there is no need to expend more than one byte on storage for this variable.

126

Find the two errors in the following program:

```pascal
program Taste;
uses
  Crt;

{ Get the user's favorite color }
function GetColor: String;
var
  S: String;
begin
  Write('What is your favorite color: ');
  ReadLn(S);
end;

var
  Ch: Char;
  Color: Integer;

begin
  Color := GetColor;
  WriteLn('So, your favorite color is ', Color, '.');
  WriteLn;
  WriteLn('Press any key to end.');
  Ch := ReadKey;
end.
```

Notice that the ReadKey procedure is used to pause the program so you can view the output before returning to the IDE. When this is done, you can press any key to end the program rather than just the Enter key.

# Summary

Well, look who's programming! You are!

It's taken ten lessons to get here, but finally you know enough about programming to begin to have some real control over what is taking place. Using procedures, functions, and parameters makes your programs considerably more interesting than the programs you were writing just a few lessons ago. That's because you're really learning how to program. This is where the real fun begins!

# Review Exercises

1. Change the `Triangle` program presented earlier so it draws a triangle with its base on the bottom rather than on the left edge of the screen. In other words, the triangle should look like this:

```
      **
     *****
    *******
   *********
  ************
 *************
```

2. Modify the program in Exercise 1 so that it looks like this:

```
      **
     *****
    *******
   *********
  ************
 **************
  ************
   *********
    *******
     ****
      **
```

# urbo Pascal
## CLASSROOM 4

# Arrays and
# Text Files

**Notes**

# 11

## Lesson

# Arrays

**OBJECTIVE**

*To learn about arrays.*

Building a program is a lot like building a house. You need to start from the foundation and lay each brick one at a time.

An architect designing a house does not always think in terms of working with one brick at a time or one board at a time. Instead, the architect often thinks in terms of whole rooms or an entire wall.

So far, when you have been programming, you have been working at the level of individual bricks. You have been picking up pieces of data usually one, two, or four bytes at a time and moving them around.

Taken as a whole, the types of data you have been working with are called *simple data types*. Simple data types include integers, words, bytes, `LongInts`, and real numbers.

You have progressed far enough to move from simple data types to *complex data types*, or *complex data structures* as they are sometimes called. If you think of a byte as an individual brick in a structure, then you can think of complex data structures as larger units such as walls.

Pascal has four very commonly used complex data types—strings, arrays, records, and objects. Most programmers use these four complex data types in nearly every program they write.

This lesson begins the discussion of complex data types by examining arrays.

# What Is an Array?

When reading the first part of this lesson, you may have been surprised to learn that strings are part of the family of complex data types. After all, there's nothing complex about strings. You have been dealing with them since the first lesson, and they have proven to be exceptionally easy to handle.

As it turns out, complex data types get their name not because they are difficult to use but because they are made up of a *complex* of smaller pieces.

Strings, for instance, are made of a series of individual chars linked by what might seem like mysterious, even sinister, forces. But regardless of the mechanism that holds strings together, in essence they are really nothing more than a long row, or array, of chars linked by a common purpose. The letter *T* that begins this sentence is just a one-byte char glorified by the fact that it plays a leading role in the string that makes up this sentence.

In fact, strings and arrays are conceptually very closely linked. An array is just a series of individual data types, such as chars, bytes, integers, or even other arrays, linked by the compiler.

This program demonstrates a very simple array:

```
program SimpleArray;
uses
  Crt;

type
  TArray = Array[1..10] of Byte;

var
  MyArray: TArray;
  Count: Integer;
  Num: Integer;

begin
  ClrScr;

  for Count := 1 to 10 do
    MyArray[Count] := Count;
```

```
  for Count := 1 to 10 do begin
    Num := MyArray[Count];
    WriteLn(Num);
  end;

  Readln;
end.
```

When you run this program, be sure to fire up the debugger and put the variable MyArray in the watch window. Then press Alt-W-A to cascade the windows so that no important lines of data get hidden.

When you begin by pressing F8 once, the variable MyArray in the watch window should look something like this:

```
MyArray: (0,0,0,0,0,0,0,0,0,0)
```

Of course, this representation is not the way MyArray actually looks in memory. Instead, it is a model or symbolic diagram.

If you think back to the analogy of memory's being like a very large array of seats spread out in an auditorium, then what you see here is like a close-up of one section of one particular row. For instance, these could be a close-up of row 25, seats 12 through 21.

Right now each person in those ten seats is remembering the number 0. (If you are running an older version of Turbo Pascal, this array might be filled with random data at this time, but in most cases it should be filled with zeros.

The first thing you have to understand about this program is why the array is 10 bytes long. Look near the beginning of the program to find these two lines:

```
type
  TArray = Array[1..10] of Byte;
```

This is the *type declaration.* In the past, all the types were predefined. But now that you are starting to deal with complex data structures, you will find that you have at least a limited ability to create your own types. For instance, if you had written:

```
type
  TArray = Array[1..25] of Byte;
```

you would have created a data structure that looks like this in the watch window:

```
MyArray: (0,0,0,0,0,0,0,0,0,0,0,0,0,0,0,0,0,0,0,0,0,0,0,0,0)
```

133

If you compare this with the first array, you can see that they clearly are two different types. One holds 10 bytes, the other 25. Now you can begin to appreciate why these declarations are made in a separate section of the program that begins with the word `type`.

Below the type section is the var section. Here you declare a variable of type TArray:

```
var
    MyArray: TArray;
```

This declaration tells the compiler that the variable `MyArray` is of type `TArray`.

It is important to understand the difference between a variable declaration and a type declaration. A *type declaration* states how a particular kind of data structure is shaped. For instance:

```
type
    TMyArray: array[0..10] of Char;
```

As soon as this definition is declared, you can have many instances of this type of variable in your program.

A *variable declaration* usually tells the type of a particular identifier. For instance:

```
var
    MyArray1: TMyArray;
    MyArray2: TMyArray;
```

 This sometimes confusing distinction between type and var declarations is very important. The sooner you can grasp it, the better. If the difference between the two is not yet obvious to you, make a note in your mind that there is a distinction here that must be respected.

> **NOTE:** To add to the confusion, it happens that it is possible to declare the dimensions of an array in a var statement. For instance, this is legal:
>
> ```
> var
>     MyArray: array[0..10] of Char;
> ```
>
> But you should remember that you are not declaring a reusable type, but only the dimensions of a particular variable. In other words, given the preceding declaration, you can't now declare three or four variables of type `MyArray`.

Now you are ready to continue stepping through the program with the F8 key. Clear the screen, and then enter the first `for` loop. Before stepping through this section of code, be sure to add the variable `Count` to the watch window.

Now step into the `for` loop. `Count` is first initialized to the value 1. If you make mental substitutions, you can see that the body of the `for` loop now looks like this:

```
MyArray[1] := 1;
```

This statement says that the first element of `MyArray` will be set to the value 1. If you wanted to say the line aloud, you would say:

"MyArray sub one colon equals one."

> **NOTE:** It's worth noting that some people would read this line, "MyArray sub one gets one." In some ways, this language is more self-explanatory than the method I prefer. But I remain faithful to the way I originally stated this line because it is, by a narrow margin, a lesser aesthetic and grammatical evil. Another option would be to say, "MyArray sub one is assigned the value one." This certainly is the best alternative from an aesthetic standpoint, but I find it potentially confusing because it doesn't sound at all like the code looks.

If you look in the watch window, you will see that executing the first iteration of the loop has set the first member of the array to the value held in the variable count, which is 1.

When you press F8 again, the loop is incremented by 1. After making mental substitutions, you know that the body of the loop now reads:

```
MyArray[2] := 2;
```

Sure enough, you can see in the watch window that the second member of the array has been set to the value 2. If you continue in this fashion, you can watch the remaining members of the array being filled out one by one.

Exit the first `for` loop and enter the second. This time all the program is doing is reading the values placed in the array and passing them to `WriteLn`, which prints them to the screen. This is a simple procedure. The program gets the first item, sees that it is equal to 1, and prints it to the screen. Then it gets the second item, sees that it is equal to 2, and prints it to the screen.

Just to be sure that you understand how arrays work, note the changes to this program, and then run it. You will get more insight into the nature of arrays.

```pascal
program SimpleArray2;
uses
  Crt;

type
  TArray = Array[10..20] of Integer;

var
  MyArray: TArray;
  Count: Integer;

begin
  ClrScr;

  for Count := 10 to 20 do
    MyArray[Count] := Sqr(Count);

  for Count := 10 to 20 do
    WriteLn(Count, ' squared = ', MyArray[Count]);

  Readln;
end.
```

Notice that each member of the array is set to the square of the variable count. As a result, the numbers printed in the output range from 100 to 400:

```
10 squared = 100
11 squared = 121
12 squared = 144
13 squared = 169
14 squared = 196
15 squared = 225
16 squared = 256
17 squared = 289
18 squared = 324
19 squared = 361
20 squared = 400
```

The first time you step through the first `for` loop, the assignment statement looks like this:

```
MyArray[10] := Sqr(10);
```

The square of 10 is 100, so the first element of the array is equal to 100. The second time, the body of the loop looks like this:

```
MyArray[11] := Sqr(11);
```

The square of eleven is 121, so the second element of the array is equal to 121, and so on, throughout the entire `for` loop.

One thing I haven't discussed yet is the fact that in the type declaration for the array, you declared its elements to be integers. After running the program, you can see that all the elements of the array are well within the range of the integer type. The range of the elements in the array is a factor you must always consider.

Take a look at the following program, and see if you can find the bug in it:

```
program SimpAry3;
uses
  Crt;

type
  TArray = Array[10..20] of Integer;

var
  MyArray: TArray;
  Count: Integer;

begin
  ClrScr;

  for Count := 10 to 20
do
    MyArray[Count] := Sqr(Count) * 100;

  for Count := 10 to 20 do
    WriteLn(Count, ' squared = ', MyArray[Count]);

  Readln;
end.
```

# More About Arrays

So far, all the arrays you have examined have contained numbers. But these data structures are also commonly used to hold chars and strings.

The following is a simple program that demonstrates how to use an array of strings. Finish this program so that it displays these strings to the screen. The output from this program should look like this:

```
One
Two
Three
Press the ENTER key to exit
```

And here's how the program begins:

```
program StrArys;
{
    A demonstration of an array of strings.
}

type
  TStrAry = array [0..2] of String;

var
  StrAry: TStrAry;
  i: Integer;

begin
  StrAry[0] := 'One';
  StrAry[1] := 'Two';
  StrAry[2] := 'Three';

  for i := 0 to 2 do
  _____

  _____

  _____

  _____

  _____
```

Another common use for an array of strings is to declare them as constants. There are two different types of constants—typed constants and untyped constants. As soon as they are defined, untyped constants can never be changed, but typed constants can be changed.

Look at the following example of a typed constant:

```
program MonthAry;
uses
  Crt;

const
  Months: Array [1..12] of String = ('Jan', 'Feb', 'Mar', +
                                     'April', 'May', 'June', +
                                     'July', 'Aug', 'Sept', +
                                     'Oct', 'Nov', 'Dec');
var
 i, j, k: Integer;
begin
  ClrScr;
  k := 1;
  j := 1;
  for i := 1 to 12 do begin
    GotoXY(k * 10, j);
    Inc(k);
    WriteLn(i, ') ', Months[i]);
    if i mod 4 = 0 then begin
      Inc(j);
      k := 1;
    end;
  end;
end.
```

This program has several interesting aspects worth commenting on. First, the program shows a convenient way of keeping track of the names of the months of the year. Notice how the numbers 1 through 12 are associated with a corresponding month of the year. For instance, 1 is associated with January, and 6 is associated with June. As a result, it is easy to print the name of each month simply by iterating through an ordinary for loop.

It is important to understand that this method of declaring an array of strings is used here simply because it is convenient. There is no radical difference between this method of declaring the array and the method used in the StrArys program. In other words, the variable StrAry in the StrArys

program is functionally equivalent to the variable Months in the preceding program.

A second aspect of the program that needs to be addressed is the use of the modulus operator in the following line:

```
if i mod 4 = 0 then begin
```

The modulus operator can be thought of as the inverse of the div operator. div always returns the result of a division, stripped of any remainder, and mod always returns the remainder. For instance, 10 modulus 10 is 0, 10 modulus 9 is 1, and 10 modulus 7 is 3.

In the MonthAry program, the variable i is incremented from 1 to 12. This means that when it is set to 4, 8, and 12, the body of the if statement will be executed, because 4 modulus 4, 8 modulus 4, and 12 modulus 4 all equal 0.

If the preceding sentence doesn't make sense to you, step through the program with the debugger. When you do, place the variable i in the watch window, and notice its value every time the body of the if statement is executed.

Finally, notice that the MonthAry program has an if statement imbedded in a for loop. This is completely acceptable, but it can be a bit confusing at times. In order to keep situations like this under control, it is absolutely essential that you indent your code properly.

Notice also that in this example you can draw a straight vertical line between the if that opens the if statement and the end that closes it:

```
if i mod 4 = 0 then begin
  Inc(j);
  k := 1;
end;
```

The same thing is true of the for statement:

```
for i := 1 to 12 do begin
  GotoXY(k * 10, j);
  Inc(k);
  WriteLn(i, ') ', Months[i]);
  if i mod 4 = 0 then begin
    Inc(j);
    k := 1;
  end;
end;
```

Systematically blocking the code is essential if you don't want to waste time tracking down the correct order of the `begin...end` pairs. If you do this correctly from the beginning, you will never have to waste a minute on this silly error. If you are careless about formatting your text, you will end up wasting untold hours trying to track down trivial errors.

While I'm on this topic, it is worth noting that I'm not suggesting that there is one particular way of formatting text that is superior to another. For instance, the following common method of formatting the `if` statement is totally legitimate:

```
if i mod 4 = 0 then
begin
  Inc(j);
  k := 1;
end;
```

I avoid this method simply because I feel it wastes a line of code, because it hides the place where a block of code actually begins, and because I think it looks inelegant. But those are matters of opinion. It's silly to waste time arguing which method of formatting text is better. All that matters is that you have a clearly defined method and that you stick to it.

---

Despite the careful indentation, some people might find the nested `begin...end` pairs somewhat confusing. In fact, there are some instances where, for the sake of clarity, it is absolutely necessary to avoid nesting too many different compound statements. The following rewrite of the program demonstrates a way to avoid this situation. Take a moment to complete it.

```
program MonthAry;
uses
  Crt;

const
  Months: Array [1..12] of String = ('Jan', 'Feb', 'Mar', +
                                     'April', 'May', 'June', +
                                     'July', 'Aug', 'Sept', +
                                     'Oct', 'Nov', 'Dec');

procedure TestForNewLine(var i, j, k: Integer);
```

FINISH THE PROGRAM

```
_____

_____

_____

_____

_____

_____

var
 i, j, k: Integer;
begin
  ClrScr;
  k := 1;
  j := 1;
  for i := 1 to 12 do begin
    GotoXY(k * 10, j);
    Inc(k);
    WriteLn(i, ') ', Months[i]);
    TestForNewLine(i,j,k);
  end;
end.
```

In this program you remove the `if` statement from inside the `for` loop and place it inside a procedure called `TestForNewLine`. As a result, the `for` loop becomes much easier to read.

Notice the header for the procedure:

```
procedure TestForNewLine(var i, j, k: Integer);
```

It contains the keyword `var` right before the variables `i`, `j`, and `k`. It is very important to understand this is not the same thing as the word `var` that appears before the other variable declaration. In this case, `var` means that you are passing these parameters to this procedure by reference rather than by value. As a result, any changes made to these values inside the procedure will be reflected after you exit the procedure.

It is unfortunate that the word `var` takes on a second meaning in this case, and that the two phrases `by reference` and `by value` are used to describe two such vital concepts. For all the good the two phrases do, the people who chose them could just as easily have picked `MoonBeam` instead of `by reference`, and `StarLight` instead of by `value`. In other words, the two phrases offer only minimal mnemonic clues to their true meaning.

Nevertheless, it is very important to understand the difference between parameters that are passed by value and parameters that are passed by reference.

The following program is designed to illustrate the difference:

```
program MoonBeam;
uses
  Crt;

procedure ByValue(Num1, Num2: Integer);
begin
  Num1 := Num1 + Num2;
end;

procedure ByReference(var Num1, Num2: Integer);
begin
  Num1 := Num1 + Num2;
end;

var
  Num1, Num2: Integer;

begin
  ClrScr;
  Num1 := 5;
  Num2 := 2;
  WriteLn('At start, Num1 = ', Num1);
  ByValue(Num1, Num2);
  WriteLn('After ByValue Num1 is unchanged: ', Num1);
  ByReference(Num1, Num2);
  WriteLn('After ByReference, Num1 is changed: ', Num1);
end.
```

To test your understanding of how the preceding program works, take a moment to find the bug in this short program:

```
program ValueBug;

procedure Square(R: Real);
begin
  R := R * R;
end;
```

```
var
  Num2Sqr: Real;
begin
  Num2Sqr := 2.44;
  Square(Num2Sqr);
  WriteLn('2.44 squared = ', Num2Sqr:0:4);
end.
```

# Summary

This completes your introduction to arrays. In the next two lessons, you will get a chance to begin working with files, and to see how arrays can be used to simplify this process.

# Review Questions

1. What is the difference between a type statement and a var statement? _____
   _____

2. What is the meaning of the word var in the following two code fragments? _____
   _____

```
var
  MyArray: TMyArray;
procedure GoForIt(var MyArray: TMyArray);
```

3. How many elements are in the following array? _____

```
type
  TMyArray = array[0..10] of Char;
```

# Review Exercise

1. Using either a consistent style of your own or the style adopted in this book, format the following program:

```
program format1;
var i: integer;
begin
for i := 1 to 11 do begin
i := i + 1;
if i mod 2 = 0 then begin
dec(i);
writeLn('i has been decremented');
end;end;end.
```

12

*L e s s o n*

# Creating Persistent Data

*To learn about basic file I/O and to further your understanding of arrays.*

The results of all the programs you have run so far have disappeared as soon as you have run them. From a philosophical point of view, this may be somewhat satisfying, because it emphasizes Heraclitus's point about life and change: You can't step in the same river twice. Still, there are times when you want the results of your programs to persist in memory, even after the programs have ended. You may also want to be able to call this data up again later.

This whole process of saving information to disk is called *file I/O*. The origin of the first part of this phrase is obvious: We are concerned with files because we store our information in entities called files. The second part of the phrase, I/O, stands for input/output. This concept is important because we are constantly moving data *in* to and *out* of files. Hence the name file I/O.

The process of saving data to a hard drive or a floppy disk is a technically complex process. But Pascal simplifies this innately confusing task to the point where it can, under certain circumstances, be almost ludicrously simple. In fact, Nicholas Wirth, the inventor of Pascal, deserves special praise for the way he designed the parts of the language dealing with file I/O. His accomplishments in this area are a real masterpiece in terms of simplicity and cleanliness of design.

# Saving Information

The most basic form of file I/O involves saving strings or numbers inside text files. The following is a simple program that saves two strings and a number to disk so that they can be called up later:

```
program FileIO;

var
  F: Text;
  Name,
  Book: String;
  Rating: Integer;

begin
  Write('What is your name: ');
  ReadLn(Name);
  Write('What is your favorite book: ');
  ReadLn(Book);
  Write('Rate this book on a scale of 1 to 10: ');
  ReadLn(Rating);

  Assign(F, 'Books.Dta');
  ReWrite(F);

  WriteLn(F, Name);
  WriteLn(F, Book);
  WriteLn(F, Rating);

  Close(F);
end.
```

The output from this program might look like this:

```
What is your name: Charlie
What is your favorite book: The Tao Te Ching
Rate your favorite book on a scale of 1 to 10: 10
```

At any rate, this is what half of the output from this program looks like. The other half of the output from this program is included in the file BOOKS.DTA, which this program creates. You may view this file inside the IDE. To do this, press F3 to pop up the Open a File dialog box. Now type the filename BOOKS.DTA into the input line at the top of the dialog. After completing these steps, you will see the file you created.

After I ran the program, BOOKS.DTA contained the following:

```
Charlie
The Tao Te Ching
10
```

Of course, your file may contain different data, depending on what you typed when you ran the program.

Now turn your attention to the actual code in program `FileIO`.

Notice that at the beginning of this program I declared a variable `F` as being of type `Text`. This is the *file variable.* When you open a file, you need some way of keeping track of it. You do this with the file variable. If you had three files open at the same time, you would want to have three file variables, one for each file.

Think of a file variable the same way you would think of a receiver on a phone. You pick up the receiver and make a call. If you are connected, you can communicate with the person on the other end through your phone's receiver. If you lose the receiver, you lose your connection with the person on the other end of the line. A file variable works the same way. You are making a call between your program and a remote place on a floppy disk or hard drive. If you establish a connection with this distant entity, you use the file variable as a means of communicating with the floppy disk or hard drive. If you lose track of the file variable or if you damage it, the connection is broken.

In this case, I happened to assign the variable the identifier `F`. But I could just as easily have assigned it the letter `Z` or a name such as `MyFile` or `AFile`. I chose the identifier `F` simply because it is a traditional name for a Pascal file variable.

The next step is to declare a few more variables, and then engage in what should by now be a familiar type of conversation using `Write` and `ReadLn`. After using this technique to get some information from the user, you are ready to save this data to disk.

The first step in this process is to Assign a filename to the file variable. Think of this as the same thing as "assigning" a phone number to a phone call by entering it on a number pad. Once we have made the association between a filename and a file variable, you open the file with the Pascal command ReWrite. Think of this as being roughly equivalent to the moment when a phone call is "put through" by the phone company and a connection is established. Now you are ready to talk to the person at the other end of the line; that is, you are ready to write or read information to a file.

You do this by dragging out the old workhorse WriteLn—a very powerful and clever little equine vehicle. Not the least of its virtues is its capability to serve as a conduit between a program and a file. When you want it to serve this purpose, first pass it the file variable, and then pass it the information you want written to the file:

```
WriteLn(FileVariable, 'Put this sentence in the file.');
```

For instance, in the first instance of file I/O in the program, you pass WriteLn the file variable and the name you got from the user:

```
WriteLn(F, Name);
```

In the second instance, you pass it the file variable and the name of the user's favorite book:

```
WriteLn(F, Book);
```

The third instance gives you a chance to pass WriteLn your old friend the file variable and then the book's rating:

```
WriteLn(F, Rating);
```

The next and last step is to close the file. This is equivalent to hanging up the phone. Just as you would never end a phone conversation without hanging up the phone, you should never end a file I/O session without closing a file. If you just leave the line open, with the receiver sitting around in the middle of the room, then you are likely to have big trouble sometime in the future. (Specifically, you often find that your file is cut off somewhere in the middle and left incomplete.)

Take a moment to find the bug in the following program:

```
program SimpleIO;

var
  F: Text;
begin
  Assign(F, 'TheFile.Dta');
```

```
  WriteLn(F, 'This is the contents of the file.');
  Close(F);
end.
```

The following program is incomplete. What's missing?

```
program NotDone;

var
  MyFile: Text;

begin
  Assign(MyFile, 'MyFile.Dta');
  ReWrite(MyFile);
  WriteLn(MyFile, 'This sentence is incomplete because');

  _____

  _____
```

These last few pages have given you a basic overview of how to write to text files. The great virtue of this technique is its simplicity. But as you will see later on, it does have some limitations.

# Reading Arrays from Text Files

As you saw in the Lesson 11, "Arrays," arrays are a very convenient way to store data. Their usefulness, however, is much diminished if you don't have a way to store their contents on disk. There happens to be a number of ways to do this, some of which are more useful than others.

The following program shows one fairly safe way to store an array in a text file, and then to read the contents back out again:

```
program NumWrite;
uses
  Crt;

type
  TNumbers= array [0..9] of Integer;
```

```pascal
procedure WriteArray(TheArray: array of Integer;
                     NumItems: Integer);
var
  i: Integer;
begin
  Dec(NumItems);

  for i := 0 to NumItems do
    WriteLn(TheArray[i]);

  WriteLn;
  WriteLn('Press ENTER to end this program');
  ReadLn;
end;

var
  Numbers: TNumbers;
  F: Text;
  i: Integer;

begin
  ClrScr;
  Randomize;

  Assign(F, 'Numbers.Dta');
  ReWrite(F);

  for i := 0 to 9 do
    WriteLn(F, Random(10));

  Close(F);

  Reset(F);

  for i := 0 to 9 do
    ReadLn(F, Numbers[i]);

  WriteArray(Numbers, 10);
end.
```

The contents of the file NUMBERS.DTA, which is produced by the program, will vary, depending on the results returned by the random function. However, the output should look something like this:

```
8
9
5
6
8
5
3
8
7
3
```

The program begins by clearing the screen and initializing the random number generator. It then writes 10 random numbers between 0 and 9 to a text file and closes the file.

In order to reopen this file for reading, you call the Pascal function Reset. It is important to note that you ReWrite files when you want to start a file from scratch and that you Reset files when you want to read from existing files. If you ReWrite an existing file, you erase it. I discuss this matter again later in this lesson, but for now you need only remember that there is an important distinction here.

After reopening the file, you read its contents into an array and send this array to a procedure, which writes it to the screen. Notice the header for the procedure:

```
procedure WriteArray(TheArray: array of Integer;
                     NumItems: Integer);
```

First off, notice that the header is split into two lines because it is too long to place on a single line. The compiler has no trouble interpreting this type of formatting and therefore it is only important that you always format procedures in a clear and consistent manner that other programmers can readily understand.

A more important aspect of this header is the declaration:

```
TheArray: array of Integer;
```

This is a new syntax that you could not have used prior to version 7.0. In the past, you would have had to write something like this:

```
procedure WriteArray(TheArray: TNumber; NumItems: Integer);
```

This syntax is very clear, but it is somewhat limiting because it forces you to pass only a single type of array to the procedure—arrays of type TNumber. Now, however, you can pass any array of integers to a procedure, even one declared like this:

```
type
    TMyArray = array[0..20000] of Integer;
```

As a result, the procedure WriteArray is much more flexible than it would have been under the old system.

> **NOTE:** This is a good time to introduce a concept that will become fairly important if you become more experienced in programming. Under the current version of Pascal, no array can be larger than 64K. If you attempt to declare a larger array, you get a frustrating error message stating: Structure too large. The only consolation I can offer is to say that soon there should be a 32-bit version of Turbo Pascal that will obliterate this mind-numbing barrier. For now, you have to struggle along as best you can. Just be glad that you are coming aboard when the end is in sight. Others have had to struggle with this limitation for years.

You have learned a simple way to create a file that contains an array of numbers. Sometimes, however, you want to read and write multiple arrays of numbers to a file. The following program gives an example of how to proceed:

```
program NumWrit2;
{
  Lesson 12
  Write and read arrays of numbers from a text file
}
uses
  Crt;

type
  TNumbers= array [0..9] of Integer;

var
  F: Text;

{ Write the array to the screen }
procedure WriteArray(TheArray: array of Integer;
                     NumItems: Integer);
var
  i: Integer;
begin
  Dec(NumItems);
```

```
  for i := 0 to NumItems do
    Write(TheArray[i], ' ');

  WriteLn; { End the line in the file }
end;


{ Create a file containing three rows of numbers }
procedure WriteFile;
var
  i,j: Integer;

begin
  Assign(F, 'Numbers2.Dta');
  ReWrite(F);

  for j := 0 to 2 do begin
    for i := 0 to 9 do
      Write(F, Random(10), ' ');
    WriteLn(F);
  end;

  Close(F);
end;


var
  Numbers: TNumbers;
  i,j: Integer;

begin
  ClrScr;
  Randomize;

  WriteFile;

  { Read the contents of the file and
    write each row to the screen }
  Reset(F);
  for j := 0 to 2 do begin
    for i := 0 to 9 do
      Read(F, Numbers[i]);
    ReadLn(F);
```

```
    WriteArray(Numbers, 10);
  end;

  WriteLn;
  WriteLn('Press ENTER to end this program');
  ReadLn;
end.
```

The file created by this program might look something like this:

```
4 4 9 7 6 2 7 3 8 6
0 3 3 6 3 6 1 7 5 4
7 8 3 6 9 7 6 7 3 3
```

Naturally enough, the output printed to the screen by this program will look very much the same.

The code for this program is a little more complicated than some of the other examples, but on the other hand, it performs an extremely useful function. In fact, scientists and mathematicians who need to keep track of arrays of numbers (also called *vectors*) may find this type of file I/O to be exactly what they have been hoping to find. If this is the case for you, you might want to fire up the debugger and step through this program until you are sure you understand how it works.

One very important point to note about this program is that you declare the file variable only once:

```
var
   F: Text;
```

Because this variable is declared at the very beginning of the program, its *scope* extends over the entire program. This means that the main body of the program and each of its procedures have access to this variable.

I discuss the topic of *scope* in greater depth later in Lessons 20–24 of this book. For now, it's essential that you remember not to declare file variables in a program multiple times unless you're sure you know what you're doing. For instance, it would be a mistake to declare the variable F: Text once directly above the main body of the program and a second time inside the procedure WriteFile, which also needs access to this variable. If you did this, you would then Assign the filename NUMBERS2.DTA to one copy of that variable and not to the other.

 Why won't the following program work?

```
program FileBug;
```

```
procedure WriteFile;
var
  F: Text;
begin
  Assign(F, 'AFile.Dta');
  ReWrite(F);
  WriteLn(F, 'Ah, for the days of Phaetons and Buggys');
  Close(F);
end;

var
  F: Text;
  S: String;
begin
  WriteFile;
  Reset(F);
  ReadLn(F, S);
  WriteLn(S);
  Close(F);
end.
```

# A Little Bubble Sort

In the days when programming was still young, many beginning programming books concentrated heavily on the laborious and extremely technical
task of sorting data. I'm not going to waste much time on this subject because
I feel that sort routines should be treated as a black box. You have no more
need to understand how a sort procedure performs its magic than you do to
understand how to create your own WriteLn procedure.

It's important, however, that you have a few sorting mechanisms
available to you when you need them. The following program reads the
NUMBERS.DTA file that you created earlier in this lesson and sorts its
contents:

```
program NumSort;

type
  TNumbers= array [0..9] of Integer;
```

```pascal
procedure Switch(var i,j: Integer);
var
  k: Integer;
begin
  k := i;
  i := j;
  j := k;
end;

procedure BubbleSort(var TheArray: array of Integer;
                     NumItems: Integer);
var
  i,j: Integer;
begin
  Dec(NumItems);
  for i := 1 to NumItems do
    for j := NumItems DownTo i do
      if TheArray[j - 1] > TheArray[j] then
        Switch(TheArray[j], TheArray[j - 1]);
end;

var
  Numbers: TNumbers;
  F: Text;
  i: Integer;

begin
  Assign(F, 'Numbers.Dta');
  Reset(F);

  for i := 0 to 9 do
    ReadLn(F, Numbers[i]);

  BubbleSort(Numbers, 10);

  for i := 9 downto 0 do
    WriteLn(Numbers[i]);

  Close(F);
end.
```

This program demonstrates what is called a *bubble sort*. This is by far the simplest type of sort, and also one of the slowest. However, for many tasks, the bubble sort works just fine. The one just presented is quite flexible in that it sorts any array of integers.

# Summary

Here we are at the end of another lesson. This one is again full of important information. Before closing, I thought I'd best make a little public service announcement that might save you a great deal of work.

The fact I want to bring once again to your attention is the important distinction between Reset and ReWrite. Reset is used to open a file that already exists, and ReWrite is used to open a file that does not exist. If you try to Reset a nonexistent file, you create a runtime error. If you ReWrite an existing file, you erase its contents.

Suppose that a text file called LIFEWORK.DTA already exists, and suppose also that it contains the only copy of the results of a five-year long research project. Given these circumstances, what is wrong with the following program?

```
program LongData;

var
  F: Text;
  S: String;
begin
  Assign(F, 'LifeWork.Dta');
  ReWrite(F);
  ReadLn(F, S);
  Close(F);
end.
```

If you do not understand what is wrong with the preceding program, you are courting disaster! Don't precipitously rush ahead without comprehending what you have already read!

# Review Question

1.  What is the difference between Reset and ReWrite? _____
    _____

# Review Exercises

1. Rewrite the BubbleSort program so that it works with LongInts.

2. In this lesson, I make a point of the dangers inherent in declaring a single file's file variable in two different locations. Yet there are ways to do this without encountering any errors. Write a program that has one procedure that writes the phrase, "In Scotts Valley did Philippe Khan a stately pleasure-dome decree," and has another procedure that reads this phrase. Each procedure should have its own file variable. The main body of the program should contain only these lines:

```
begin
  WriteFile;
  ReadFile;
end.
```

3. Write a program that sorts the following numbers: 4, 2, 3, 5, 1, 6, 7, 9, and 8.

# Reading and Displaying Longer Files

***To learn how to show large chunks of text to the user.***

In this lesson you get a chance to look at several other aspects of arrays and text files. I present these two subjects in concert because they fit together hand in glove, as it were.

The reason for this affinity is easy to understand. A text file can hold disparate facts together under a single umbrella. That is, many numbers or sentences can be written to a single file, and then this conglomerate of different pieces can be treated as a single entity called a file. When you read these facts back from the file, however, there needs to be a way to hold them

together. In some cases, arrays form a simple solution to this problem. In other words, arrays hold disparate pieces of information together just as files do. Therefore, it seems appropriate to explore simultaneously two subjects that might not at first seem very closely related.

In this lesson you will see ways to work with files that contain not numbers but text. The methods shown here work on most midsize files. But you should be aware that none of the techniques presented here work on very large text files.

# Alice in Logic-Land

On the disk that came with this book is the following poem from Lewis Carroll's *Through the Looking Glass:*

> "Jabberwocky"
>
> 'Twas brillig, and the slithy toves
>  Did gyre and gimble in the wabe;
> All mimsy were the borogroves,
>  And the mome raths outgrabe.
>
> "Beware the Jabberwock, my son!
>  The jaws that bite, the claws that catch!
> Beware the Jubjub bird, and shun
>  The frumious Bandersnatch!"
>
> He took his vorpal sword in hand:
>  Long time the manxome foe he sought—
> So rested he by the TumTum tree,
>  And stood a while in thought.
>
> And as in uffish thought he stood,
>  The Jabberwock, with eyes of flame,
> Came whiffling through the tulgey wood,
>  And burbled as it came!
>
> One, two! One, two! And through and through
>  The vorpal blade went snicker-snack!
> He left it dead, and with its head
>  He went galumphing back.

"And hast thou slain the Jabberwock?
  Come to my arms, my beamish boy!
O frabjous day! Callooh! Callay!"
  He chortled in his joy.


'Twas brillig, and the slithy toves
  Did gyre and gimble in the wabe;
All mimsy were the borogroves,
  And the mome raths outgrabe.

Programmers have traditionally been fond of this poem in part because it can be viewed as both syntactically correct and utterly meaningless at the same time. This is a state of affairs well known to most programmers. Frequently we write programs to which the compiler assigns a clean bill of health. Syntactically they are pure. But when we try to run them, they produce no results at all, or results that are meaningless.

Besides being a gifted writer of children's stories such as *Alice in Wonderland,* Carroll was also a talented logician. His studies in this field, combined with his extraordinary imagination, made it possible for him to see some important truths about computers long before the machines actually came into being. As just described, he successfully captured one of these truths in "Jabberwocky." (Lovers of this poem, and computer students who have studied Carroll in depth, should forgive me for this cursory overview of a wonderful piece of literature. I do not mean to imply that my analysis is even partially complete, but I did want to open up one possible interpretation of this much talked-about poem for those who are new to the subject.)

Here is a program that, to a limited degree, enables you to view Carroll's famous poem on-screen. It contains the first use of color while performing screen I/O:

```
program Jabber;

uses
  Crt;

type
  TPoemAry = array [0..100] of String;

var
  F: Text;
  PoemAry: TPoemAry;
  i, NumLines: Integer;
```

```
procedure Init;
begin
  TextColor(14);
  TextBackGround(1);
  ClrScr;
  NumLines := 0;
end;

begin
  Init;

  Assign(F, 'Jabber.Txt');
  Reset(F);

  while not Eof(F) do begin
    ReadLn(F, PoemAry[NumLines]);
    Inc(NumLines);
  end;

  Close(F);

  for i := 0 to NumLines do begin
    WriteLn(PoemAry[i]);
    Delay(100);
  end;

  ReadLn;
end.
```

This program's output is the poem "Jabberwocky" as it appears earlier in this lesson. Remember that the file JABBER.TXT is on this book's disk. Make sure that JABBER.TXT is in the same directory as the program, or you will probably receive an error message. This program prints the lines of this poem rather slowly because of the Delay procedure in the last loop. You can, of course, change this effect by eliminating the Delay procedure or by changing the parameter you pass to it.

Overall, the program couldn't be simpler. It starts by calling the initialization procedure, it then opens the file called JABBER.TXT, and finally proceeds to read its contents into an array of strings. Notice that I take time to close the file. Never forget this crucial step!

After closing the file, the lines of the poem are written to the screen in a less-than-totally-useful fashion. Even if you don't have time to read each line, however, you still can see that the lines are at least being printed to the screen. For now, be content with that much.

If you are running on a color system, this program prints its output in gold letters on a blue background. This is the result of the following two lines located in the Init procedure:

```
TextColor(Yellow);
TextBackGround(Blue);
```

The first of these procedures, naturally enough, sets the text color of the display, and the second sets the background color.

The parameters passed to these procedures are declared in the Crt unit. They look like this:

```
const
    Black        = 0;
    Blue         = 1;
    Green        = 2;
    Cyan         = 3;
    Red          = 4;
    Magenta      = 5;
    Brown        = 6;
    LightGray    = 7;
    DarkGray     = 8;
    LightBlue    = 9;
    LightGreen   = 10;
    LightCyan    = 11;
    LightRed     = 12;
    LightMagenta = 13;
    Yellow       = 14;
    White        = 15;
```

This means that the previous two code lines are equivalent to these two lines:

```
TextColor(14);
TextBackGround(1);
```

In fact, if you do not include Crt in your uses clause, it's probably simplest to pass raw numbers to these procedures because you would not have access to the constants just listed. (I long ago memorized these numbers and almost always use them instead of their equivalent constants because they are shorter and easier to type.)

Two other important points are worth noting. It is legal to pass only the first eight constants to the TextBackGround procedure, and if you declare a TextBackGround color before calling ClrScr, the entire screen will be cleared to that color.

If you have a color monitor you may have done this already, but if you haven't, please take a moment to go back and run this program with variant parameters passed to TextColor and TextBackGround. For instance, the following combination should be enough to daze the senses of even the most ferocious Jabberwock:

```
TextColor(LightGreen);
TextBackGround(Magenta);
```

Take a moment to finish the following program so that it writes the word Look across the screen 16 times per row, seven rows deep. Each row should have a different background color, and each column a different foreground color. Refer to Figure 13.1, if you want.

```
program Colors;
uses
  Crt;
var
  i,j: Integer;
begin
  ClrScr;
  for i := 0 to 7 do
    for j := 0 to 15 do begin
      GotoXY((j + 1) * 4, i + 1);
      Write('Look');
```

_____

_____

_____

_____

*Figure 13.1.*
*The Colors program.*

166

# A More Useful Text Viewer

The following code is an improvement of the pervious version of the Jabber program:

```
program Jabber2;
{
  This program implements a simple text viewer
  custom-made for viewing the file jabber.txt
}
uses
  Crt;

const
  UpArrow = #72;
  DownArrow = #80;
  Escape = #27;

type
  TPoemAry = array [0..100] of String;

var
  F: Text;
  PoemAry: TPoemAry;
  i, NumLines: Integer;

procedure Init;
begin
  TextColor(Yellow);
  TextBackGround(Blue);
  ClrScr;
  NumLines := 0;
end;

{
  Create a status line to tell the user
  how to run the program and print a
  portion of the poem to the screen.
}
procedure ShowPoem(StartLine: Integer);
```

```
var
  i: Integer;
begin
  ClrScr;

  GotoXY(1, 24);
  Write('-------------------------------------------------');

  TextColor(Black);
  TextBackGround(Green);
  GotoXY(1, 25);
  Write('Escape Key Exits, PageUp, PageDown to navigate');
  TextColor(Yellow);
  TextBackGround(Blue);
  GotoXY(1,1);

  for i := StartLine to StartLine + 22 do
    WriteLn(PoemAry[i]);
end;

{
  Handle the user input, in particular the up-arrow,
  down-arrow, and Escape keys. The main loop that
  drives the program is in this procedure.
}
procedure GetInPut;
var
  Start: Integer;
  Ch: Char;
begin
  Ch := #0;
  Start := 0;

  while Ch <> Escape do begin
    ShowPoem(Start);

    repeat
      Ch := ReadKey;
```

```
        if Ch = #0 then
            Ch := ReadKey;
      until (Ch = UpArrow) or
              (Ch = DownArrow) or (Ch = Escape);

      if Ch = UpArrow then Dec(Start);
      if Ch = DownArrow then Inc(Start);
      if Start < 0 then Start := 0;
    end; { End while loop }
end;

begin
  Init;

  Assign(F, 'Jabber.Txt');
  Reset(F);

  { Read the poem from disk }
  while not Eof(F) do begin
    ReadLn(F, PoemAry[NumLines]);
    Inc(NumLines);
  end;

  Close(F);

  GetInPut;
end.
```

When you run this program, the first thing you probably will notice is that it contains a menu or status line that tells the user how to control the text output to the screen. The code that controls this aspect of the program comprises about 10 lines in the procedure called ShowPoem:

```
GotoXY(1, 24);
Write('----------------------------------------------');

TextColor(Black);
TextBackGround(Green);
GotoXY(1, 25);
Write('Escape Key Exits, PageUp, PageDown to navigate');
TextColor(Yellow);
TextBackGround(Blue);
GotoXY(1,1);
```

169

Compare these lines with the two lines of code located in the same procedure that actually write the poem to the screen:

```
for i := StartLine to StartLine + 22 do
   WriteLn(PoemAry[i]);
```

If you think about this for a moment, you can see that five times as much code is expended to write the status line as is used to perform the main function of the program. This is a very common situation in computer programming. Programmers constantly expend enormous amounts of energy on the interface of a program, while often the core of the program is relatively simple to write.

In some ways, it's as if programming were the opposite of real life. In our day-to-day existence, most of us devote only a relatively small amount of our attention to surface details. We constantly try to look beneath the facade to see what a person, company, or tool is really like. With programming, however, the core or center of our work is often a relatively simple or commonly known algorithm, while the interface is crucial. This is, of course, something of an oversimplification, but you should at least try to come to grips with this important concept.

After that digression, again turn your attention to the simple statement that prints the poem to the screen:

```
for i := StartLine to (StartLine + 22) do
   WriteLn(PoemAry[i]);
```

Notice that these lines of code print at most 23 lines of text to the screen. The other two lines of the screen are reserved for the status line. Whenever you create a text screen, you must take time to think in these terms. Say to yourself: "I have 80 columns and 25 rows to work with. How shall I arrange things to fit in that space?"

The crucial factor, of course, is which 23 lines of text the program will print to the screen. (This might be a good time to fire up the debugger and step through the program as I explain the mechanisms that make it work.)

You want to begin with the very first member of the array, which is the poem's title. The simple for loop proceeds to write the next 22 lines of text to the screen, and then comes to a screeching halt.

After a user has viewed the first 23 lines of text, he or she pushes the down-arrow key, thereby requesting to view more of the poem. Look at the section of the program that handles the keypress:

```
while Ch <> Escape do begin
  ShowPoem(Start);

  repeat
    Ch := ReadKey;
    if Ch = #0 then
      Ch := ReadKey;
  until (Ch = UpArrow) or
        (Ch = DownArrow) or (Ch = Escape);

  if Ch = UpArrow then Dec(Start);
  if Ch = DownArrow then Inc(Start);
  if Start < 0 then Start := 0;
end; { End while loop }
```

Ignore the `repeat...until` loop for a moment and concentrate on the `while` loop that encloses it. For now, all you need to know about the `repeat...until` loop is that it sets the value of Ch to `UpArrow`, `DownArrow`, or `Escape`, depending on what key the user presses.

If the user presses the down-arrow key, the program increments the variable `Start`, as shown in the following line of code:

```
if Ch = DownArrow then Inc(Start);
```

After this, the program reaches the bottom of the `while` loop and swoops back up to its top, where it finds the line `ShowPoem(Start);`.

Now enter the `ShowPoem` procedure a second time. This time when the simple `for` loop at the bottom of the procedure is entered, the variable `StartLine` equals 1 rather than 0:

```
for i := one to (one + 22) do
  WriteLn(PoemAry[i]);
```

On this iteration, the poem's title is skipped, and an extra line from the main body of the poem is picked up instead. That is, because the title of the poem is not written this time, there is room for one more line from the body of the poem.

When the `GetInput` procedure is reentered, the user might again choose to press the down-arrow key, and the value of the variable `Start` is incremented from 1 to 2. As a result, this time the first two lines of the text file are skipped and two more lines from its middle are shown. This process can continue until you finally see the end of the poem.

If at any point the user wants to move back up toward the top of the poem, all he or she has to do is press the up-arrow key. As a result, the value of the variable Start is decremented, and a line is lost from the end of the poem and one is picked up from its opening portion.

These lines of code represent a very simple but effective mechanism that includes only one minor bit of error checking, which looks like this:

```
if Start < 0 then Start := 0;
```

This line ensures that the variable Start will never be smaller than 0. As a result, never attempt to execute a line that would in effect look like this:

```
WriteLn(PoemAry[-1]);
```

Executing such a line would, of course, cause an error to occur in the program, because there is no line numbered –1 in the file.

# The Mysteries of the Scan Code

Now it's time to explore the very heart of the matter. Specifically, what does the following chunk of code mean?

```
repeat
  Ch := ReadKey;
  if Ch = #0 then
    Ch := ReadKey;
until (Ch = UpArrow) or (Ch = DownArrow) or (Ch = Escape);
```

Portions of it should be familiar to you. You've seen repeat...until loops before and you know how to read a single character from the keyboard. What is distinctly odd, however, is the bit that says:

```
if Ch = #0 then
  Ch := ReadKey;
```

What in the world is that supposed to mean?

Well, it happens that whenever a key is pressed, not one, but two bytes of information are loaded into memory. Often programmers have to deal with only the first of these two bytes. For instance, if the user presses the A key, ReadKey returns the 97th ASCII character. This, of course, is the letter A. The same holds true for all the letters of the alphabet. That is, when a program reads the basic alphanumeric characters, you never have to worry about the second byte loaded into memory whenever a key is pressed.

The time to worry about that second byte is whenever the peripheral keys—such as the up-arrow, down-arrow, and function keys—are pressed. Whenever these keys are pressed, the first byte they return is always ASCII character 0. If you then call ReadKey again, however, you pick up on what is called the scan code, whose value usually identifies the key that has been pressed.

The following program demonstrates how this works.

```
program ScanCode;
{
  Demonstration of how to read scan codes.
  Press the Escape key to end this program.
}
uses
  Crt;

function GetInput(var FunKey: Boolean): Char;
var
  Ch: Char;
begin
  FunKey := False;
  Ch := ReadKey;
  if Ch = #0 then begin  { Is it a function key? }
    Ch := ReadKey;
    FunKey := True;
  end;
  GetInput := Ch;
end;

var
  IsFunKey: Boolean;
  Ch: Char;

begin
  WriteLn(' Press any key to see its value.');
  WriteLn(' Press Escape to end this program.');
  repeat
    Ch := GetInput(IsFunKey);
```

```
  if IsFunKey then
    WriteLn('You pressed a function key. Code: ', Ord(Ch))
  else
    WriteLn('You pressed a normal key. Value: ', Ch);
  until Ch = #27;
end.
```

This is a classic program that appears in one form or another in nearly every beginning programming book that has ever been written. So accept no substitutes. This is the real thing. Study it, play with it, step through it with the debugger if necessary. Come to terms with this program. Comprehend it, and you will be well on your way to mastering the art of getting input from the user!

Here is a sample of what the output from the program might look like:

```
You pressed a normal key. Value: a
You pressed a normal key. Value: b
You pressed a normal key. Value: c
You pressed a normal key. Value: ♦
You pressed a normal key. Value: ♥
You pressed a normal key. Value: ♠
You pressed a function key. Code: 72
You pressed a function key. Code: 80
```

The diamond, heart, and spade are achieved by holding down the Control key and pressing the D, C, and F keys.

The values 72 and 78 are achieved by pressing the up-arrow and down-arrow keys. If you look near the top of the Jabber2 program, you will see that the identifiers UpArrow and DownArrow are associated with these two numbers:

```
const
  UpArrow = #72;
  DownArrow = #80;
```

Of course, you could simply have used the raw numbers without ever creating the constants. Then the code would look like this:

```
repeat
  Ch := ReadKey;
  if Ch = #0 then
    Ch := ReadKey;
until (Ch = #72) or (Ch = #80) or (Ch = #27);
```

174

rather than this:

```
repeat
  Ch := ReadKey;
  if Ch = #0 then
    Ch := ReadKey;
until (Ch = UpArrow) or (Ch = DownArrow) or (Ch = Escape);
```

Most programmers find it more meaningful to work with constants than with raw ASCII values, but you are free to proceed however you think is best.

What's wrong with the following program? (*Hint:* You might want to find the bug before you actually run this program. At worst, step through the program with the debugger rather than trying to run it outright.)

```
program NoEscape;
uses
  Crt;
var
  Ch: Char;

begin
  repeat
    Ch := ReadKey;
    if Ch = #0 then
      Ch := ReadKey;
  until (Ch = #0);
end.
```

I guess its only fair for me to say at this point that if you run the above program without first using the debugger, you enter an *infinite loop.* Do you understand why this program's loop will never end?

Sometimes you can break out of infinite loops by holding down the Control key and pressing the Break key several times in quick succession. If this does not work, you may have to reboot your machine by pressing Ctrl-Alt-Del.

> **NOTE:** There are three ways to restart your computer when it has stopped responding to input. They are, in order of preference:
>
> 1. Use Ctrl-Alt-Del to perform a *warm boot.*
>
> 2. Press the Reset button to perform a *cold boot.* A few computer manufacturers, such as DELL, do not provide a Reset switch.
>
> *continues*

*continued*

3. Turn the computer off, wait until it is **completely** quiet, and then turn it back on again. Never switch a computer on and off several times in quick succession.

# Summary

This lesson has been a bit unusual in that you have spent most of your time studying the inner workings of one program—namely, the simple text viewer.

# Review Questions

1. The first byte returned by ReadKey is called the Character Code. What is the second byte? _____

2. What range of colors are safe to assign to the procedure TextBackGround?_____

# Review Exercises

1. In Jabber2 the user can never attempt to scroll back past the beginning of the poem. Modify the program so the user can never scroll past its end.

2. Create a program that writes the words LeftArrow, RightArrow, UpArrow, DownArrow, PageUp, PageDown, Home, and End to the screen whenever the user presses the appropriate keys.

14

*L e s s o n*

# Arrays of More than One Dimension

*To examine multidimensional arrays.*

The next data structure you will examine is a perennial favorite of college computer-language instructors—the multidimensional array. I've never understood why there is a such a big to-do about this subject, because these arrays aren't used very often in real-world programming, except perhaps by graphics programmers and certain types of mathematicians.

Nevertheless, I wouldn't feel as though I were writing a real programming book unless I dragged you into this particular Sargasso Sea of the mind at least once. Consider working with multidimensional arrays a rite of passage that helps initiate you into the ways of the true programming cognoscenti.

Just because this little back eddy of the computer programming world is a bit confusing, that doesn't mean that grasping the subject means much in terms of your overall ability to become a good programmer. Multidimensional arrays exercise a certain part of your brain, but they aren't the final test of your ability to put together robust, powerful programs that perform useful or entertaining functions in the real world.

To put the best light possible on the situation, think of two-dimensional arrays as a kind of very clever intellectual puzzle. They are, when seen from a certain perspective, a brief, hardy exercise for the brain.

# From Vorpal to Vertex

Because this lesson is heavily math-oriented, I suppose it would be appropriate to stop talking and get down to business. So without further ado, here is an example of a two-dimensional array:

```pascal
program TwoAry;
uses
  Crt;

type
  TArray = Array[1..12, 1..12] of Integer;

var
  MyArray: TArray;
  i,j: Integer;

begin
  ClrScr;

  for i := 1 to 12 do
    for j := 1 to 12 do
      MyArray[i][j] := i * j;

  for i := 1 to 12 do begin
    for j := 1 to 12 do
      Write(MyArray[i][j]:5);
    WriteLn;
  end;

  ReadLn;
end.
```

For your viewing pleasure, here is the output from this program:

| 1 | 2 | 3 | 4 | 5 | 6 | 7 | 8 | 9 | 10 | 11 | 12 |
|---|---|---|---|---|---|---|---|---|----|----|----|
| 2 | 4 | 6 | 8 | 10 | 12 | 14 | 16 | 18 | 20 | 22 | 24 |
| 3 | 6 | 9 | 12 | 15 | 18 | 21 | 24 | 27 | 30 | 33 | 36 |
| 4 | 8 | 12 | 16 | 20 | 24 | 28 | 32 | 36 | 40 | 44 | 48 |
| 5 | 10 | 15 | 20 | 25 | 30 | 35 | 40 | 45 | 50 | 55 | 60 |
| 6 | 12 | 18 | 24 | 30 | 36 | 42 | 48 | 54 | 60 | 66 | 72 |
| 7 | 14 | 21 | 28 | 35 | 42 | 49 | 56 | 63 | 70 | 77 | 84 |
| 8 | 16 | 24 | 32 | 40 | 48 | 56 | 64 | 72 | 80 | 88 | 96 |
| 9 | 18 | 27 | 36 | 45 | 54 | 63 | 72 | 81 | 90 | 99 | 108 |
| 10 | 20 | 30 | 40 | 50 | 60 | 70 | 80 | 90 | 100 | 110 | 120 |
| 11 | 22 | 33 | 44 | 55 | 66 | 77 | 88 | 99 | 110 | 121 | 132 |
| 12 | 24 | 36 | 48 | 60 | 72 | 84 | 96 | 108 | 120 | 132 | 144 |

You probably recognize this as the multiplication table you were forced to memorize in elementary school. The key to using it is to think in terms of columns and rows. For instance, to find the result of multiplying 7 times 12, simply look at column 7, row 12. Or, likewise, to find the result of multiplying 4 times 8, look at row 8, column 4.

Here you can clearly see how two-dimensional arrays got their name. The printout literally has two dimensions—rows and columns.

Now you understand how to use this table, but not how it was created. To begin to get a feeling for how the code works, you should, of course, fire up the debugger. If you place MyArray in the watch window, you end up with a display that looks like Figure 14.1.

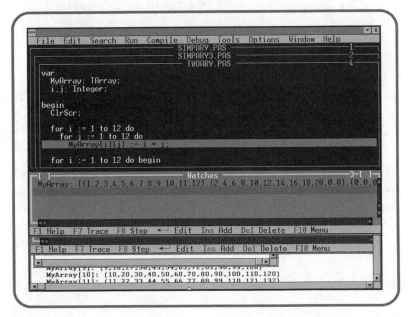

*Figure 14.1.*
*The IDE with MyArray in the watch window.*

This representation of MyArray in the watch window is not very helpful. You are looking at the first two-and-one-quarter elements of what might be called the "first dimension" of the array. In order to see each of these elements in full, you need to rearrange the elements in the watch window properly.

Here is one fairly useful way to look at a two-dimensional array in the watch window:

```
MyArray[1]:  (1,2,3,4,5,6,7,8,9,10,11,12)
MyArray[2]:  (2,4,6,8,10,12,14,16,18,20,22,24)
MyArray[3]:  (3,6,9,12,15,18,21,24,27,30,33,36)
MyArray[4]:  (4,8,12,16,20,24,28,32,36,40,44,48)
MyArray[5]:  (5,10,15,20,25,30,35,40,45,50,55,60)
MyArray[6]:  (6,12,18,24,30,36,42,48,54,60,66,72)
MyArray[7]:  (7,14,21,28,35,42,49,56,63,70,77,84)
MyArray[8]:  (8,16,24,32,40,48,56,64,72,80,88,96)
MyArray[9]:  (9,18,27,36,45,54,63,72,81,90,99,108)
MyArray[10]:  (10,20,30,40,50,60,70,80,90,100,110,120)
MyArray[11]:  (11,22,33,44,55,66,77,88,99,110,121,132)
MyArray[12]:  (12,24,36,48,60,72,84,96,108,120,132,144)
```

You can see that MyArray[1] actually consists of not just one integer but a whole array of integers.

As you step through the program, the elements of MyArray[1] are filled in one by one. Then the elements of the second array are filled in one at a time. Then MyArray[3] is filled in, and so on.

If you want to view an individual member of the array in the watch window, you might type something like this:

```
MyArray[2][2]: 4
```

Taking the time to think for a moment about these two views of the array in the watch window, you can begin to see what two-dimensional arrays are all about, and at the same time begin to get a more profound view of the way computer memory really works. Please try to pay attention as I attempt to dissect a fairly complex subject.

Memory has been compared to seats in an auditorium many times in this book, and it is an apt analogy. Another way to view memory, however, is to think of it as a long, straight road that starts at mile one and continues all the way to mile 655,360. Viewing it this way, you can think of memory as strictly linear; that is, it starts at one point and ends at another, with no real divisions in between except for the steady ticking off of bytes, one relentlessly following the next.

Imagine for a moment that long road, stretching out across an empty, clean, desert landscape. Suppose you placed the first byte of the array at mile 300,000 of this road. Then the second byte would be at mile 300,001, the third at mile 300,002, and so on. If you think about memory this way for a moment, you can stress its linear, one-dimensional nature. In fact, when seen from a certain perspective, the real memory inside your computer is indeed laid out like this. As a result, it is impossible for it to present you with a literal representation of a two- or three-dimensional object. All it can do is place things somewhere along this simple one-dimensional desert road.

That's why two-dimensional arrays can seem a bit confusing at times. A one-dimensional object, namely a computer's memory, can't represent a two-dimensional concept such as the multiplication table. Instead, it is forced to create a representation of that object that looks something like this in memory:

```
1,2,3,4,5,6,7,8,9,10,11,12,2,4,6,8,10,12,14,etc...
```

In reality, the two-dimensional array is really just a long string of numbers. The whole idea of treating this one-dimensional string of numbers as a two-dimensional object is really just a syntactical convention, a flight of fancy.

This little leap into an imaginary world can be confusing at times. It requires a certain inner vision on the part of the programmer. So do the best you can with this task. If you are good at it, some very interesting aspects of computing can open up before you. But if the whole concept boggles your mind, don't sweat it. There are more important things to worry about.

I think that most people can find ways to work with two-dimensional arrays even if they do not understand everything about them. In other words, just playing with them for a bit usually turns out to be a worthwhile exercise.

# Pascal's Triangle

To keep on hammering away at these clever little two-dimensional arrays, consider one of Blaise Pascal's most famous productions—an interesting little triangle that looks like this:

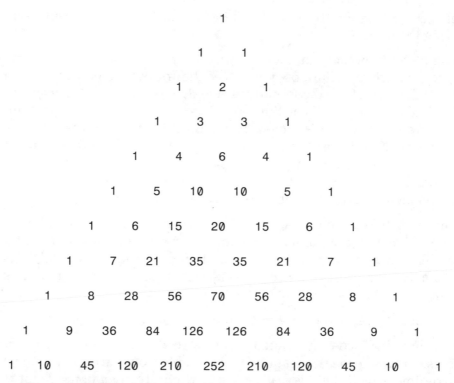

```
                            1
                        1       1
                    1       2       1
                1       3       3       1
            1       4       6       4       1
        1       5       10      10      5       1
        1       6       15      20      15      6       1
    1       7       21      35      35      21      7       1
  1       8       28      56      70      56      28      8       1
1       9       36      84      126     126     84      36      9       1
1   10      45      120     210     252     210     120     45      10      1
```

If you study this little fellow for a few minutes, you will notice that it has some interesting properties, not the least of which is the way the sum of two numbers on one row is represented by a single number on the next row. For instance, the sum of the two 1s in row two is 2, which appears directly below them on the third row. Likewise, the sum of the two 10s on the sixth row is represented by the number 20 on row seven, and so on.

This, however, is only the beginning. If you continue to study this fascinating triangle, you will find that it has many other interesting properties.

It probably comes as no surprise that you can represent Pascal's triangle as a two-dimensional array. The following program gets you started on a path toward one of the many possible ways of creating Pascal's triangle with a computer. See whether you can finish this program:

```
program PasTri;
{
  Prints Pascal's triangle.
  First, set all members of the array to 0 as an
  aid when it is time to print. Then fill
```

```
    the array with the members of Pascal's triangle.
    Print the array, ignoring all members still set to 0.
}

uses
  Crt;

const
  Max = 11;

type
  Matrix = Array[1..Max, 1..Max] of Integer;

var
  Triangle: Matrix;  { Array that holds Pascal's Triangle }
  Row, Col: Integer; { Locate place on screen }

{----- SetZero ------}
{ Set all members of the array to zero }
procedure SetZero;
begin
  for Col:= 1 to Max do
    for Row := 1 to Max do
      Triangle[Row,Col] := 0;
end;

{ ------ FillTri ------ }
{
  You hard-code the answers for the first two rows, then
  use nested loops to fill out the rest of the array.
}
procedure FillTri;
begin
  Triangle[1,1] := 1;
  Triangle[2,1] := 1;
  Triangle[2,2] := 1;
```

_____

_____

_____

_____

```
end; { FillTri }

{ ------ FillTri ------ }
{
  A nested loop is used to print the triangle
  to the screen
}
procedure PrintTri;
var
  x : Integer;
begin
  ClrScr;

  _____

  _____

  _____

  _____

  _____

  _____

end; { PrintTri }

{ ------ Program Body ------ }
begin
  SetZero;
  FillTri;
  PrintTri;
  ReadLn;
end.
```

# Two-Dimensional Arrays Swoop Near the Real World

Before you move on to the next lesson, it might be fun to take a quick look at a useful and fascinating application of two-dimensional arrays. The next few paragraphs are considerably more fun if you have a color screen. If you don't have this luxury, you will just have to follow along as best as you can in black-and-white.

Consider the following program:

```
program Screen10;
{
  Create a two-dimensional array with the same dimensions
  as a typical text mode screen, then print its contents
  to the screen.
  The result looks a bit like the patterns on Native-
  American rugs.
}
uses
  Crt;

type
  TScreen = array[1..25, 1..80] of Integer;

var
  Screen: TScreen;
  i,j: Integer;

begin
  TextAttr := 0;
  ClrScr;

  for i := 1 to 25 do
    for j := 1 to 80 do
      Screen[i][j] := (Round(Sqrt(i * Sqrt(j))));


  for i := 1 to 24 do
    for j := 1 to 80 do begin
      GotoXY(j,i);
      TextColor(Screen[i][j]);
      Write(#219);
    end;

  ReadLn;
end.
```

The output from this program looks like Figure 14.2.

*Figure 14.2.*
*The output from*
*SCREEN10.PAS.*

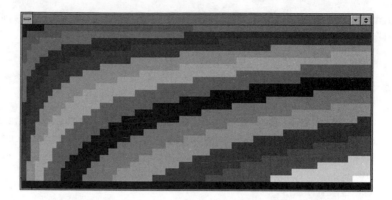

This visually captivating program takes advantage of the fact that a computer screen can easily be represented as a two-dimensional array with dimensions of 1 through 25 for the rows and 1 through 80 for the columns. The mathematical formula fills in the contents of this array with an orderly set of numbers:

```
for i := 1 to 25 do
  for j := 1 to 80 do
    Screen[i][j] := (Round(Sqrt(i * Sqrt(j))));
```

This section of code creates a logical screen in memory that duplicates the computer's physical screen. The contents of the logical screen can be thought of in a number of ways, but in this case, it is useful to consider the logical screen as merely a set of color attributes:

```
TextColor(Screen[i][j]);
```

This line sets the colors of the output to values defined inside the array.

You could, however, just as easily view the array as a series of numbers. To do so, change the line in this program that reads:

```
Write(#219);
```

so that it reads:

```
Write(Screen[i][j]);
```

Figure 14.3 shows the program's output after you make these changes.

When the program runs with this new code, the numbers produced by the formula fill the upper-left corner of the screen neatly. The bottom-right corner of the screen, however, is filled with a series of 1s. Of course, this portion of the array does not really contain 1s, but rather numbers in the low and middle teens. The problem is that only one space is allocated for each member of the array, and as a result, only the first digit of each number appears in full. The second digit of each number is overwritten by the next number in the array, and hence does not appear on-screen. But even with this limitation, viewing the data this way enables you to see how the program, in its original form, produces such a remarkable array of colors.

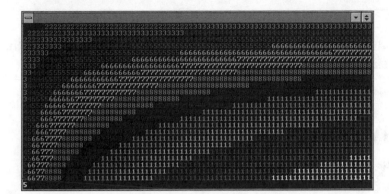

*Figure 14.3.*
*The output from SCREEN9.PAS.*

# Summary

This brings us to the end of Lesson 14. In the next lesson, "Strings are Just a Special Kind of Array," you will look again at one-dimensional arrays as you study the way strings are put together. Lesson 16, "Records: An Important Advanced Data Structure," looks at an entirely new type of data structure called a record.

Before wrapping this lesson up, I should mention that there is such a thing as a three- or even a four-dimensional array. To declare a three-dimensional array, you might write something like this:

```
array[0..12, 0..12, 0..12] of integer;
```

Arrays of this type can be very useful when you want to represent a three-dimensional object on-screen. If you've ever played a computer game that allowed you to enter a world that had not only width and height, but also depth, then it's likely that its makers spent a lot of time thinking about three-dimensional arrays like the one presented here.

This is a fascinating area of mathematics but not one that should be pursued in an introductory programming book. I should add, however, that if by chance your interest in computers takes you into a more in-depth study of these data structures, your best guide at that time will be a keen mind, a clear head, a steady hand, and someone who knows a whole lot more about math than I do.

# Review Questions

1. Besides a computer screen, what are some other two-dimensional objects? _____

   _____

2. Are two-dimensional arrays also subject to the 64K limitation on the size of a single data structure? _____

# Review Exercises

1. Finish this program so that it writes the contents of the `array of Char` on a single line:

```
program Napoleon;
uses
  Crt;

type
  TMyArray = array[1..5,1..5] of Char;

const
  MyArray: TMyArray = (('A','B','L','E',' '),
                       ('W','A','S',' ','I'),
                       (' ','E','R','E',' '),
                       ('I',' ','S','A','W'),
                       (' ','E','L','B','A'));

var
  i,j: Integer;
begin
  ClrScr;
```

2. Write a second version of the preceding program that writes the array both backward and forward.

# Strings: A Special Kind of Array

**OBJECTIVE**

*To learn about the relationship between strings and arrays.*

You're almost done learning about arrays, but before leaving this topic, you should look at one last very important aspect of arrays that hasn't been covered yet.

As I pointed out at the beginning of the discussion of arrays, it happens that strings are really only a special type of array. In fact, they are only an array of char with a few special traits (which I examine in a moment).

The point of this lesson is to show how strings are really put together and to demonstrate how to manipulate them. In particular, I examine how to

treat strings as arrays, how to concatenate strings, how to change the length of strings, and how to insert characters into a string. These are all operations you will have occasion to use many times if you continue to program seriously.

This is probably also a good time to make a brief note about pchar, a new type of string introduced in Turbo Pascal for Windows and now implemented for DOS in Turbo Pascal 7.0. This type of string is a very powerful and very fast extension to the Turbo Pascal language. However, pchars are more difficult to use than normal Pascal strings, and, unfortunately, I don't get a chance to discuss them in this book.

In this lesson, you get a chance to take a careful look at Pascal strings, and then in the next lesson you will look at an entirely different, and very powerful, type of data structure called a *record*.

# The Length Byte

Perhaps the biggest difference between an array and a string is that the first character of every string consists of a single byte that tells you the length of the string.

Consider the following program:

```pascal
program LookStr;
{
  A view of a string both as a series of Chars
  and as a series of ASCII numbers.
}
uses
  Crt;
var
  S: String;
  i: Integer;
begin
  ClrScr;
  S := 'One Two Three Four';

  for i := 0 to Length(S) do
    WriteLn('Character ', i:2, ' as Char: ', S[i],
                        ' as integer ', Ord(S[i]));
end.
```

Figure 15.1 shows the output from this program:

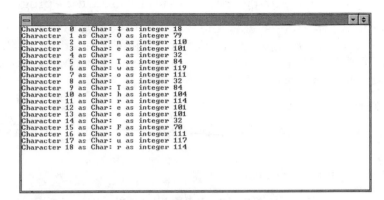

*Figure 15.1.*
*The output from*
*LOOKSTR.PAS.*

If you ignore the first line of this program's output for a moment, you see that it simply prints each letter of a string, one at a time, and also shows that character's ASCII value. Doing this demonstrates that it is possible to treat a string almost exactly as an array of char is treated.

Though it contains a few new ideas, this program really is very simple. The heart of it is a for loop, which writes each individual character in the string first as a char, and then as an integer, or rather as an ASCII value. (Because I refer to the ASCII table often throughout this lesson, you might want to look at the first half of the table, shown in Figure 15.2, or if you want, take a look at the ASCII table in Appendix C.)

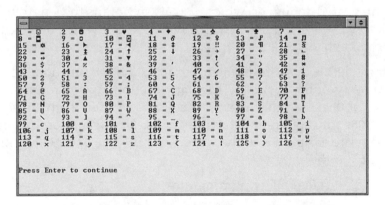

*Figure 15.2.*
*The output from the*
*program ASCII.PAS,*
*included on disk.*

The second line output by this program looks like this:

```
Character 1 as Char: O as integer 79
```

It states that a capital letter *O* can be thought of as ASCII character number 79. The third line states that a small *n* is ASCII character 110, and the fourth

lines says that a small *e* is ASCII character 101. Put these three letters together and you get the word *One,* the first word in the string S used in the program.

Notice that the `for` loop ends when the variable `i` is equal to `Length(S)`. The `Length` function returns the number of characters in a string. In this particular case, there are 18 characters in the string, so the `for` loop looks like this after substitutions are made:

```
for i := 0 to 18 do begin
```

Now, if you look at the first line of output from the program, you can see that it says:

```
Character  0 as Char: ô as integer 18
```

Here you can see that the first character in the string is equal to the ASCII value 18, which, when printed, looks like this: ô.

Now you can see clearly what it means to say that the first character of every string contains a character called the *length byte,* which designates the length of a string. For instance, if you wrote the string `One` to the screen, its first character would have an ASCII value of 3 because there are three letters in that word. If you wrote the word `Pascal` to the screen, its first character would be equal to the ASCII value 6.

Obviously, when `WriteLn` prints strings to the screen, it always omits this first byte. However, it should come as no surprise to learn that `WriteLn` uses this byte to determine how many characters it writes to the screen. The same is true of the integrated debugger, which also always omits the length byte when you ask to view a string in the watch window, but which makes use of the byte for its own purposes.

The only thing left to describe in the program is the `Ord` function, which appears in the body of the `for` loop. The `Ord` function always returns the ordinal value of a `Char`. In other words, it converts a `Char` to an `Integer`. Conversely, the `Chr` function converts an integer to a `Char`. Therefore, the line `Chr(65)` would write a capital *A* to the screen and the line `Ord('A')` would write the value 65 to the screen.

 Find The

What's wrong with the following program?

```
program LenBug;
{
  String length bug solution
}
var
  S: String;
```

```
begin
  S := 'This string has 34 characters in it';
  WriteLn('The string: "', S, '" has ', S[0],
          'characters in it.');
end.
```

# Shortening Strings

With your new knowledge of strings, it is fairly simple to see how to shorten a string.

Consider the following program:

```
program LookStr2;
{
  A demonstration of how to change the length of a string.
}
uses
  Crt;
var
  S: String;
  i: Integer;
begin
  ClrScr;
  S := 'One Two Three Four';
  S[0] := #3;
  WriteLn(S);    { Write One }
  S[0] := #7;
  WriteLn(S);    { Write One Two }
  S[0] := #13;
  WriteLn(S);    { Write One Two Three }
  S[0] := #18;
  WriteLn(S);    { Write One Two Three Four }
  ReadLn;
end.
```

The program's output looks like this:

```
One
One Two
One Two Three
One Two Three Four
```

As you can see, the program enables you to change the length of the string you write to the screen simply by changing the *length byte*.

Notice that in this program, you use the pound sign (#) as a shorthand way of writing the Chr function with literal constants. This means that the program would have exactly the same output if you wrote:

```
S[0] := Chr(3);
```

instead of

```
S[0] := #3;
```

In the first case, the Chr function is called; in the second, a literal character is imbedded into the program's code. In both cases, the results are identical.

To make sure you understand how to change the length of a string, take a moment to finish this program:

```
program LookStr3;
{
  This program writes five lines, the first containing
  the first word of a string, the second containing the
  first two words of a string, and so on.
}
uses
  Crt;
var
  S: String;
  i: Integer;
begin
  ClrScr;
  S := 'One Two Three Four Five';
  S[0] := #3;
  WriteLn(S);
  S[0] := #7;
  WriteLn(S);
  S[0] := #13;
  WriteLn(S);
  S[0] := #18;
  WriteLn(S);
  S[0] :=
```

_____
_____
_____
_____
_____

This is all very nice, as far as it goes, but the problem with the last two programs is that they assume the programmer knows ahead of time the length of each word in the string. In other words, you know that the first word in the string is three characters long, and that the first two words are seven characters long, and so on.

But suppose you wanted to write a procedure that automatically broke a string into individual words, without your knowing ahead of time the length of each word in the string. You handle this situation by searching through each string for the _space_ character, which has an ASCII value of 32.

```
program LookStr2;
{
  A demonstration of how to change the length of a string.
}
uses
  Crt;

procedure WriteWords(S: String);
var
  i: Integer;
begin
  for i := 1 to Length(S) do begin
    if S[i] <> ' ' then
      Write(S[i])
    else
      WriteLn;
  end;
end;

var
  S: String;
```

```
begin
  ClrScr;
  S := 'One Two Three Four';
  WriteWords(S);
end.
```

If you have any questions about how this program works, take a moment to step through it with the debugger. When you do, you will see that the program prints each letter of the string until it comes to ASCII character 32, the space character. At that point it calls WriteLn with no parameters, which automatically takes you to a new line. Then it continues printing each letter until it reaches the next space character.

The answers to many mysteries are at last being revealed to you in this lesson.

For instance, now the true story behind the mysterious and hitherto unexplained differences between WriteLn and Write can be unveiled. Until now it has been assumed that if WriteLn is called, you will be taken to the next line automatically, and that if Write is called, this will not happen. But until now I have never explained why.

The explanation is really very simple. The ASCII characters numbered 10 and 13, when taken together, always print a carriage-return/line-feed pair (CR/LF) to the screen. As it turns out, the ASCII character number 10 is the line-feed character, and the ASCII character number 13 is the carriage-return character. This distinction hardly matters, because on DOS machines the two characters are almost always printed together.

What this means is that the statement

```
Write(#10#13);
```

is, for all intents and purposes, identical to the statement:

```
WriteLn;
```

In order to see more clearly how this works, look at the Pascal string concatenation symbol. This piece of syntax, which is identical to the mathematical plus symbol, is very easy to use. The following program uses the concatenation symbol to join two strings.

```
program Concat;
const
  S1: String = 'Jump ';
  S2: String = 'for joy.';
```

```
begin
  S1 := S1 + S2;
  WriteLn(S1);
end.
```

Notice that in this program, we declare both strings as typed constants. If we did not include the type in the declaration, we could not change their values.

This program takes two strings and joins them so that they print on the same line. But sometimes you want to create a very different effect in which a single string prints on several different lines. The following program shows how to create that effect by using the ASCII CR/LF pair:

```
program Concat2;
const
  CRLF = #10#13;
var
  S1: String;
begin
  S1 := 'Jump for joy -- ' + CRLF + 'my beamish boy.';
  WriteLn(S1);
end.
```

Obviously enough, this program presents us with the following output:

```
Jump for joy --
my beamish boy.
```

Even though the concatenation symbol is very easy to use, you should keep two important caveats in mind. You must match quotation marks correctly to avoid compiler errors, and you must be sure never to create a string larger than 255 characters, which is the maximum number of characters that can be in a string.

Why doesn't this program perform as expected?

```
program Concat3;
{
  An exercise in using the concatenation symbol.
}
uses
  Crt;
const
  CRLF = #10#13;
```

```
S1: String =
    '''The time has come'', the Walrus said, ' + CRLF +
    ' ''To talk of many things: ' + CRLF +
    'Of shoes - and ships - and sealing wax - ' + CRLF +
    ' Of cabbages -- and kings -- ' + CRLF +
    'And why the sea is boiling hot -- ' + CRLF +
    ' And whether pigs have wings.''' + CRLF +
    CRLF +
    '''But wait a bit, '' the Oysters cried,' + CRLF +
    ' Before we have our chat; ' + CRLF +
    'For some of us are out of breath,' + CRLF +
    ' And all of us are fat!' + CRLF +
    '''No hurry!'' said the Carpenter.' + CRLF +
    ' They thanked him much for that.';
```

```
begin
  ClrScr;
  WriteLn('from The Walrus and the Carpenter by Lewis Carroll: ');
  WriteLn;
  WriteLn(S1);
end.
```

When you are working with this program, take time to note that two sets of quotation marks are used to print a single quotation mark to the screen. Remember that this syntax is used to differentiate quotation marks that you want to print from quotation marks that are part of the syntax of the Pascal expression.

# Summary

As you finish reading this lesson, keep in mind that there is much more you can learn about strings. I'm stopping at this point only because I think that this is probably enough for now. The key points you should remember are how strings are put together and how closely related they are to arrays.

Overall, strings should be regarded as an enormously powerful aspect of the Turbo Pascal language. Other languages seem to either make strings so complicated that they are difficult to use, or so simple that they are not powerful enough to meet all your needs. Turbo Pascal excels because it hits exactly the right balance between functionality and ease of use.

# Review Questions

1. Given a variable of type string called `MyString`, what is the difference between these statements? _____

   _____

   ```
   WriteLn(Ord(S[0]));
   ```

   and

   ```
   WriteLn(Length(S));
   ```

2. Considering what you know about how to keep track of the length of strings, can you figure out why no string can be longer than 255 characters? _____

   _____

# Review Exercise

1. Write a short program that shows what happens if you write a single line-feed character, rather than a CR/LF pair, to the screen.

# urbo Pascal
# CLASSROOM 5

# Records and Typed Files

# Notes

# Records: An Important Advanced Data Structure

*To examine records, a type of complex data structure that can contain several different data types.*

As you begin the examination of records, you near the end of the introduction to the fundamental aspects of the Pascal language. From here you will soon move on to some intermediate-level programming concepts, such as units and pointers.

You still, however, have a little work to do on the basics, and certainly records are one type of data structure that you don't want to overlook. They are, in fact, one of the most often used aspects of the language, as well as one

of the most powerful tools in any programmer's arsenal. Also, they form the foundation on which objects are built. Objects, which unfortunately I don't have room to cover in this book, are one of the key elements in the architecture of many sophisticated contemporary programs.

Let's get down to work. This is crucial material.

# Record Basics

When people build databases that contain, for instance, many names and addresses, they refer to each entry in the database as a *record.* When you go to the hospital, doctors keep a *record* of your visits and store them in a filing cabinet.

These uses of the word *record* should help turn your thoughts in the right direction as you begin to come to terms with the Pascal data structure of the same name. Records usually are used as the "glue" that holds together a set of related pieces of information such as names and addresses.

Consider the following program:

```
program Address1;
{
 This program introduces the reader to Records.
 You create a small record containing three fields.
 First you ask the user to fill in the fields,
 then you display the input to the screen.
}
uses
  Crt;

type
  TAddress = Record
    Name: String;
    Age: Integer;
    Phone: String;
  end;

{ Ask the user to enter his or her name, age, and phone }
procedure GetAddress(var Address: TAddress);
begin
```

```
  ClrScr;
  Write('Enter Name: ');
  ReadLn(Address.Name);    { Name is a field of the record }
  Write('Enter Age: ');
  ReadLn(Address.Age);     { Field Age is part of TAddress }
  Write('Enter Phone: ');
  ReadLn(Address.Phone);   { Phone is also part of TAddress }
end;

{ Write the user's input to the screen }
procedure WriteAddress(Address: TAddress);
begin
  ClrScr;
  WriteLn('Name: ', Address.Name);
  WriteLn('Age: ', Address.Age);
  WriteLn('Phone: ', Address.Phone);
end;

var
  Address: TAddress; { Declare a variable of type TAddress }
begin
  GetAddress(Address);
  WriteAddress(Address);
  WriteLn;
  Write('Press ENTER to end this program');
  ReadLn;
end.
```

The output from a typical run of this program might look like this:

```
Enter Name: Sam
Enter Age: 23
Enter Phone: 234-2345



Name: Sam
Age: 23
Phone: 234-2345

Press ENTER to end this program
```

The first three lines of output are produced by the procedure called GetAddress, and the second group of three lines is produced by the procedure called WriteAddress.

205

Let's contemplate the record's type declaration for a moment:

```
type
  TAddress = Record
    Name: String;
    Age: Integer;
    Phone: String;
  end;
```

What is actually being said here? The type of a record is being declared, just as the type of various arrays was declared in the last few lessons. Instead of consisting of a range of elements of one type like an array does, this record consists of three *fields,* which are definitely not all of the same type.

Specifically, the first field is declared to be of type String, the second to be of type Integer, and the third to be of type String. There is nothing special about the order of types in the declaration. In other words, if you wanted to, you could just as easily write

```
type
  TAddress = Record
    Age: Integer;
    Name: String;
    Phone: String;
  end;
```

or

```
type
  TAddress = Record
    Phone,
    Name: String;
    Age: Integer;
  end;
```

or any other combination that strikes your fancy. In fact, as I will show you later in this lesson, you can even include an array or another record as one of the fields of the record.

The point is that records are very flexible. They can have one field, two fields, 10 fields—even 20 or 30 fields if you so desire.

Coming back to specifics, in this case the record contains three fields. In the program each field is filled out one at a time. Then the record is passed to a procedure that writes its contents to the screen.

Take a moment to consider procedure GetAddress:

```
procedure GetAddress(var Address: TAddress);
```

```
begin
  ClrScr;
  Write('Enter Name: ');
  ReadLn(Address.Name);
  Write('Enter Age: ');
  ReadLn(Address.Age);
  Write('Enter Phone: ');
  ReadLn(Address.Phone);
end;
```

The first thing to notice is that the variable Address is passed by reference. That is, the keyword var is used to tell the compiler that you want to save the changes made to the record. If you didn't include this keyword, you would lose the user's input as soon as this procedure ended.

Now you can begin mentally stepping through this procedure. Imagine the program clearing the screen, and then writing Enter Name:. The next line reads the user's name. In the past, you might have written something like this:

```
ReadLn(Name);
```

This time, however, what is sometimes called *dot notation* is used:

```
ReadLn(Address.Name);
```

The *qualifier* Address is used to tell the compiler that the variable Name is part of a particular record. This process is repeated three times until the user has provided input for all the fields of the record.

The next step is to write the contents of this record to the screen. Again, notice how dot notation is used to reference a particular field in a record:

```
WriteLn('Name: ', Address.Name);
```

In this case, you are referencing the first field in the record, which is of type String. The WriteLn procedure prints this field to the screen for you, just as it faithfully does whenever you pass it a valid variable. That's WriteLn for you: an incredible, flexible, and stalwart vehicle.

This might be a good time for me to answer a frequently asked question: How do you write a procedure like WriteLn that can be passed a variable number of parameters or variable types of parameters? To give a somewhat oversimplified answer, my reply is that you can't. The compiler works in conjunction with some very low-level assembler code to create flexible procedures such as WriteLn. Ordinary Pascal programmers like you and me, however, do not have the opportunity to accomplish the same wonders.

Here's a chance for you to practice working with records:

```pascal
program RecWrite;
{
 Finish this program.
}

type
  TBirthPlace = Record
    City,
    State: String;
  end;


{ Write the user's place of birth }
procedure WriteResults(BirthPlace: TBirthPlace);
begin
  Write('So you were born in: ');
  WriteLn(BirthPlace.City, ', ', BirthPlace.State);
end;

var
  BirthPlace: TBirthPlace;
begin
  { Ask user where he or she was born and then call
WriteResults }
```

_____

_____

_____

_____

_____

_____

_____

_____

# An Array of Records

Now that you have worked through an introduction to records, it is time to see them in some different settings so you can get a better feel for how they work. In particular, you will examine a method for creating an array of records that shows a convenient way to organize a number of these data structures in memory at the same time.

The following program gives the user a chance to rate a few famous movies:

```
program movies;
{
  An example of an array of records
  The program asks the user to rate five movies
}

uses
  Crt;

type
  TMovie = Record
    Name: String;
    Rating: Integer;
  end;

  TMovieArray = Array[1..5] of TMovie;


{ Ask the user to rate five movies }
procedure GetMovieRatings(var MovieAry: TMovieArray);
var
  i: Integer;
begin
  WriteLn('This program will give you a chance to rate ');
  WriteLn('five famous movies on a scale of 1 to 10. ');
  WriteLn('Try to rate each of the movies you have seen. ');
  WriteLn('Give the movies you have not seen a rating of -1.');
  WriteLn;
  for i := 1 to 5 do begin
    WriteLn('Movie Title: ', MovieAry[i].Name);
    Write('Your Rating: ');
```

```
      ReadLn(MovieAry[i].Rating);
    end;
end;


{ Assess the user's answers }
procedure CalcResults(MovieAry: TMovieArray; var Total, NotSeen:
                      Integer);
var
  i: Integer;
begin
  NotSeen := 0;
  Total := 0;
  { Add total ratings score, keep track of movies not seen }
  for i := 1 to 5 do
    if MovieAry[i].Rating <> -1 then
      Total := Total + MovieAry[i].Rating
    else
      Inc(NotSeen);
end;


procedure ReportResults(MovieAry: TMovieArray; Total, NotSeen:
                        Integer);
var
  Average: Integer;
begin
  WriteLn;

  WriteLn('Total of scores: ', Total);
  { Check to make sure we don't divide by zero }
  if NotSeen <> 5 then Average := Total div (5 - NotSeen)
  else Average := 0;
  WriteLn('The average score you gave to these movies was: ',
          Average);
  { Rate user's enthusiasm for movies }
  WriteLn('Since you have seen ', 5 - NotSeen,
          ' of these 5 movies');
  Write('I suppose you ');

  case NotSeen of
    4,5: WriteLn('are not much of a movie lover.');
    2,3: WriteLn('know something about film.');
    0,1: WriteLn('are a true movie lover.');
```

```
    end;
  end;

var
  MovieAry: TMovieArray;
  Total, NotSeen: Integer;
begin
  ClrScr;

  MovieAry[1].Name := 'Gone With the Wind';
  MovieAry[2].Name := 'The Seven Samurai';
  MovieAry[3].Name := 'The Sound of Music';
  MovieAry[4].Name := 'Metropolis';
  MovieAry[5].Name := 'Star Wars';

  GetMovieRatings(MovieAry);
  CalcResults(MovieAry, Total, NotSeen);
  ReportResults(MovieAry, Total, NotSeen);

  WriteLn;
  WriteLn('Press ENTER to end this program');
  ReadLn;
end.
```

When I ran this program, I got the results visible in Figure 16.1. Your results probably will differ from these, but this should give you a general feel for how the program will look on the screen.

```
This program will give you a chance to rate
five famous movies on a scale of 1 to 10.
Try to rate each of the movies you have seen.
Give the movies you have not seen a rating of -1.

Movie Title: Gone With the Wind
Your Rating: 6
Movie Title: The Seven Samurai
Your Rating: 10
Movie Title: The Sound of Music
Your Rating: 5
Movie Title: Metropolis
Your Rating: 9
Movie Title: Star Wars
Your Rating: 7

Total of scores: 37
The average score you gave to these movies was: 7
Since you have seen 5 of these 5 movies
I suppose you are a true movie lover.

Press ENTER to end this program
```

*Figure 16.1.*
*Possible output from the program* MOVIES.PAS.

Now turn your attention to the source code.

This time you are dealing with a fairly large chunk of code, but don't let that intimidate you. This program is broken into three relatively small procedures, none of which is more than 20 lines in length, so let "divide and

211

conquer" be your motto. Study this program one step at a time, moving on only when you're sure you've mastered each procedure.

The record used in this program is very simple:

```
type
  TMovie = Record
    Name: String;
    Rating: Integer;
  end;
```

The first field is a string, which by default holds 256 bytes, and the second field is an integer, which is two bytes in size.

If you think for a moment about the memory theater containing 655,360 seats, you can quickly calculate that it would take 258 people to remember the contents of one record.

Notice, however, that I also declare an array containing five of these records:

```
TMovieArray = Array[1..5] of TMovie;
```

This means that back in the memory theater you have five sets of 258 people all lined up in a row and all wholeheartedly dedicated to remembering the contents of the array of records. To query the people who are remembering the first record, you use the syntax `MovieAry[1]`. When you want to talk to the people who are keeping track of the fifth record, you use `MovieAry[5]`.

Take a moment to remember that no one array you declare can contain more than 64K, which is 65,535 bytes. This particular array can have only five records, which means its total size is 5 * 258, or 1,290 bytes. If you divide 65,535 by 258, you can see that the most records of type `TMovieArray` that you can have in a single array is 254. If you try to declare the array with 255 or more elements, you will get the error message `Structure too large`. You get this message because you have run smack into the 64K barrier. To place more than this number of records in a single data structure, you need to use something besides an array, such as a linked list. Linked lists are a special kind of data structure, which will be covered in Lessons 28 and 29 of this book.

Focusing your attention back on the current program, you should find that you now know enough to understand the first procedure you call:

```
{ Ask the user to rate five movies }
procedure GetMovieRatings(var MovieAry: TMovieArray);
var
  i: Integer;
```

```
begin
  WriteLn('This program will give you a chance to rate ');
  WriteLn('five famous movies on a scale of 1 to 10. ');
  WriteLn('Try to rate each of the movies you have seen. ');
  WriteLn('Give the movies not seen a rating of -1.');
  WriteLn;
  for i := 1 to 5 do begin
    WriteLn('Movie Title: ', MovieAry[i].Name);
    Write('Your Rating: ');
    ReadLn(MovieAry[i].Rating);
  end;
end;
```

This procedure first writes some words of explanation, and then enters a for loop. The first statement in the for loop writes the words Movie Title and then the name of the movie associated with the first record in the array. That is, you ask the people in the memory theater who are remembering the first record about the contents of the first 256 bytes that they are remembering. They cheerfully return the associated bytes, which you fortunately know how to translate into a string that contains the name of the movie.

Then the user is asked to tell how he or she rates that movie. That result is passed to the last two people in the memory theater, who are remembering the first record in the array. They are told the rating, and they promise not to forget it.

**NOTE:** Actually, they will remember this information only as long as they are being supplied with energy in the form of electricity. The second you turn off the electricity in most computers, the information being held in RAM disappears. You can push the metaphor to an extreme by saying that the members of the memory theater will remember things for you only as long as you keep them supplied with their drug of choice—electricity.

Now that the first record is taken care of, the entire loop is repeated four more times, until the rating field for all the records is filled in. Then the results are tabulated in procedure CalcResults. Notice the lines that make up the heart of this procedure:

```
for i := 1 to 5 do
  if MovieAry[i].Rating <> -1 then
    Total := Total + MovieAry[i].Rating
```

```
else
   Inc(NotSeen);
```

As you iterate through the results of the poll, you keep track of the total number of points given to the movies and the number of movies the user hasn't seen.

Although this is meant to be an entertaining poll and not a scientific one, you should look carefully at the technique used. Each time you iterate through the loop, you face a little fork in the road. In effect, it says, "If the user saw the movie, add his or her score of the film to the total score. If the user did not see the movie, increment the total number of movies not seen."

Don't underestimate the power of this kind of logic. Certainly it is not much when compared to the feats the human mind can perform, but still you should have some respect for a machine that can be so discerning.

Finally, let me make two more important comments about this program. First, notice again how this program is divided into three procedures, the longest of which still can fit comfortably into a single viewing screen, as you can see in Figure 16.2. As I pointed out earlier, there is nothing innately wrong with making procedures longer than 20 lines or so, but still you should strive to keep your procedures as short as possible. The big benefit comes when you need to track down bugs: You can find a bug in a 10-line procedure much faster than you can in 45-line procedure.

*Figure 16.2.*
*The procedure*
`ReportResults` *fits*
*neatly inside the IDE's*
*screen.*

```
  File  Edit  Search  Run  Compile  Debug  Tools  Options  Window  Help
═[■]══════════════════════ MOVIES.PAS ═══════════════════════1═[↑]═
procedure ReportResults(MovieAry: TMovieArray; Total, NotSeen: Integer);
var
  Average: Integer;
begin
  WriteLn;

  WriteLn('Total of scores: ', Total);
  { Check to make sure we don't divide by zero }
  if NotSeen <> 5 then Average := Total div (5 - NotSeen)
  else Average := 0;
  WriteLn('The average score you gave to these movies was: ', Average);
  { Rate users enthusiasm for movies }
  WriteLn('Since you have seen ', 5 - NotSeen, ' of these 5 movies');
  Write('I suppose you ');

  case NotSeen of
    4,5: WriteLn('are not much of a movie lover.');
    2,3: WriteLn('know something about film.');
    0,1: WriteLn('are a true movie lover.');
  end;
end;
═══ 57:1 ═══◄▌
 F1 Help  F2 Save  F3 Open  Alt+F9 Compile  F9 Make  Alt+F10 Local menu
```

Also, notice that you pass local copies of the program's main variables to all the procedures that need them. For instance, the procedure `CalcResults` is passed an array and two integers as local variables:

```
procedure CalcResults(MovieAry: TMovieArray;
                      var Total, NotSeen: Integer);
```

You could declare the variables once at the top of the program and then allow each procedure to use these global variables whenever they need them. But that kind of approach almost always leads to serious trouble.

A classic pitfall users of global variables encounter is to mistake a local variable that was coincidentally assigned the same name as a global variable for that global variable. For example, suppose you have a global variable called Total. In a procedure in the middle of the program, you have declared a second variable also called Total. You might accidentally perform a calculation using the local variable, thinking that you were actually using the global variable, or vice versa. It can be very hard to track down this kind of mistake, but this error can completely undermine all the calculations in a program.

The general rule is to avoid using global variables, and instead pass local copies of those variables to every procedure that needs them. This does not mean that you should never declare a global variable, although some very dogmatic people might insist on the value of such an approach. But still, at least 99 percent of the time, it is best to work with local rather than global variables.

This is particularly true when a procedure is going to modify a variable. In that case, you should always pass the variable to the procedure by reference, *even if the variable has been declared globally.* The big benefit is that you can look at the procedure's heading and check for the keyword var. If it is present, you can assume that the procedure is likely to change the value of that variable. Keeping such important pieces of information plainly visible in a procedure's heading can make your programs considerably easier to understand.

The following program contains a classic bug. Can you find it?

```
program RecBug;

type
  TName = Record
    First: String;
    Last: String;
  end;

var
  Name: TName;
  i,
  Start,
  Last: Integer;
```

```
begin
  Start := 2;
  Last := 3;
  for i := Start to Last do begin
    Write('Enter a first name: ');
    ReadLn(Name.First);
    Write('Enter a last name: ');
    ReadLn(Last);
    WriteLn('You entered: ', Name.First, ' ', Name.Last);
  end;
end.
```

# Summary

As you have seen, records are extremely important but not particularly difficult to understand. There is a kind of innate logic to the way they are structured which to me, at least, is intuitively obvious. It's as if records were preordained: They simply had to exist. They are an obvious extension of the language, and they are real workhorses that programmers turn to often.

The next lesson examines records in a little more depth and teaches you how to store records and arrays in a file.

# Review Questions

1. Consider the following statement

   ```
   WriteLn(Address.Name)
   ```

   In the parameter passed to WriteLn, you could call the word Address a _____ because it _____ the variable Name.

2. In the preceding example, the variable Name is the first _____ of the record called address.

3. If you declare a variable inside a procedure, it is called a _____ variable. A variable listed at the top of a program, or directly above the program's main block, is called a _____ variable.

216

e s s o n

# Beyond Text Files

*To learn how to write arrays and records to files without using text files.*

Despite the fact that they are called *text* files, you saw in Lesson 12, "Creating Persistent Data," that you can read and write `Integers` and `Reals` from files of type `Text`. This means that you can store large amounts of numeric data in text files. However, this aspect of text files has some severe limitations.

Think for a moment about the term *text file*. These files are meant to be read as text, and you can pull them into editors like the IDE's and view or change them. These traits make text files easy to work with, but text files do not adapt well to the needs of programmers who want to store numeric data or some mixture of numeric and alphanumeric data.

To understand why this is so, several different aspects of text files must first be examined. To begin with, text file I/O is slow, which often doesn't matter much if you want to display written information. Because you want

the calculations you perform on numbers to go as quickly as possible, however, you should try to choose a faster form of I/O, such as the one outlined in this lesson.

Also, numeric data must be extremely precise. When you place a text file in an editor, it is easy to erase or change a portion of that file accidentally. This can be inconvenient when dealing with a file containing text, but not necessarily fatal. The same cannot be said of numeric files.

For instance, if the word *necessarily* were stored in a text file and then accidentally changed in a text editor to *nebessarily*, your knowledge of the English language would make it easy for you to spot the error and repair the damage. However, if the number 345 were accidentally changed to 343, it would be very difficult to notice the error, and quite likely impossible to repair it. Therefore, it is best when storing numeric data not to choose a form of file that can be easily read or edited in a standard text editor.

The subject of this lesson is how to avoid the pitfalls just mentioned. You will start by learning an easy way to write records to a file.

# A File of Record

There is nothing random about the way the Pascal language evolved. Every stone in the language was carefully laid by people who gave the matter considerable thought. One of the most carefully hewed rocks in the foundation was the keystone called a *typed file.*

Consider the following humorous program that stores records associated with each of the last four generations of Americans:

```
program Gens;
{
 Lesson 17
 An exercise in creating a file of record.

 This program, which is meant to be taken with a grain
 of salt, is about the last four generations of Americans.
 Thanks to Neil Howe and William Strauss's article
 "The New Generation Gap" published in Atlantic magazine.
}
```

```
uses
  Crt;

type
  TGeneration = Record
    Name: String;
    Dates: String;
    Trait: String;
  end;

  TGenFile = File of TGeneration;

{ Read the file }
procedure ReadFile(var F: TGenFile);
var
  i: Integer;
  Gen: TGeneration;
begin
  Reset(F);
  while not Eof(F) do begin
    Read(F, Gen);
    with Gen do begin
      WriteLn(Name);
      WriteLn(Dates);
      WriteLn(Trait);
      WriteLn;
    end;
  end;
  Close(F);
end;

{ Write each generation's description to the file }
procedure WriteGen(var F: TGenFile;
                   GName,GDates,GTrait: String);
var
  Gen: TGeneration;
begin
  with Gen do begin
    Name := GName;
    Dates := GDates;
    Trait := GTrait;
  end;
```

```
    Write(F, Gen);
end;

{ Open the file }
procedure OpenFile(var F: TGenFile);
begin
  Assign(F, 'Gens.Dta');
  ReWrite(F);
end;

var
  F: TGenFile;
  Gen: TGeneration;
begin
  ClrScr;

  OpenFile(F);

  { Fill in the records and write them to the file }
  WriteGen(F, 'GI Generation', 'Pre 1925',
              'Ambitious - Avaricious');
  WriteGen(F, 'Silent Generation', '1925 - 1942' ,
              'Stalwart - Mediators');
  WriteGen(F, 'Boomers', '1943 - 1960',
              'Moralists - Fickle');
  WriteGen(F, 'Thirteeners', '1961 - 1981',
              'Practical - Superficial - Unlucky');

  Close(F);

  ReadFile(F);

  WriteLn;
  WriteLn('Press ENTER to end this program');
  ReadLn;
end.
```

The output from this program is shown in Figure 17.1.

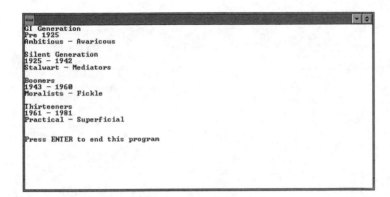

*Figure 17.1.*
*The output from*
*GEN.PAS.*

I suppose I should say a few words about this output before I discuss the program. The basic idea for the four generations came from an article in the *Atlantic* magazine that caught my fancy. The authors of the article, Neil Howe and William Strauss, came up with the names and dates for each generation. (Thirteeners are the thirteenth American generation.) The traits associated with each generation are my own subjective creations. I have no idea whether it is even remotely meaningful to try to divide the American public into generations like this. I just found the idea humorous and intriguing, if not necessarily totally convincing.

With that explanation out of the way, the analysis of GENS.PAS can begin. The first portion of the program that contains something of real interest is the declaration of the file type:

```
TGenFile = File of TGeneration;
```

This code fragment states that a file will be created whose purpose is to read and write records of type TGeneration.

Until now, all the files used in this book have been text files, which could be read in the IDE or various other editors. Now, however, you are creating a highly specialized type of file whose sole purpose is to work with the type of records defined inside this program.

GENS.DTA is known as a *binary file.* If you look at the record structure, you see that it is made up entirely of strings. Therefore, you might think that you could view GENS.DTA in a text editor just the way you would look at a text file, but you can't.

As it happens, binary files are meant for storing data or code, not for being viewed in text editors. If you insisted on looking at the inside of GENS.DTA in a text editor, however, you would be greeted with the unholy mess you see in Figure 17.2. Clearly this is not the optimal way to view this file.

*Figure 17.2.*
*A binary file viewed*
*in a text editor.*

> **CAUTION:** You should be aware that trying to view a typed file in a text editor can damage the file. It's a good idea never to try to view these files this way. I supplied a figure for the curious, but you probably shouldn't try this at home. If you do try it, however, you should be careful not to save the file while it is in the text editor.

If you can't view these files in text editors, how do you find out what's inside them? To understand the answer to that question, you'll need to take a closer look at the program.

First, you should note that it begins by calling a procedure that opens the file:

```
procedure OpenFile(var F: TGenFile);
begin
  Assign(F, 'Gens.Dta');
  ReWrite(F);
end;
```

Note that the file variable used in this procedure is passed by reference, that is, it is preceded with the var keyword. This is necessary because the internal status of that variable is going to be changed from being a closed and unassigned file variable to an open and assigned file variable.

Making sure that file variables are passed by reference instead of by value is so important that the Pascal compiler tends to get a bit dogmatic about the whole process. In fact, it never lets you pass a file variable to a procedure by value; it always insists that you include the keyword var. Some people object to such restrictive type checking, but I find this kind of paternalistic oversight endearing. I think it's nice that the compiler wants to keep me from making a stupid mistake, but I understand why some people get a bit stressed about this sort of thing, and I have some sympathy with their professed desire to be able to decide for themselves about such matters. Certainly this is where other, less strongly typed languages such as C tend to be a bit more open-minded.

At any rate, the next step in the program is to start writing records to this file:

```
procedure WriteGen(var F: TGenFile;
                   GName,GDates,GTrait: String);
var
  Gen: TGeneration;
begin
  with Gen do begin
    Name := GName;
    Dates := GDates;
    Trait := GTrait;
  end;
  Write(F, Gen);
end;
```

This procedure demonstrates a new way of dealing with the fields of a record. In the past you would have written

```
Gen.Name := GName;
Gen.Dates := GDates;
Gen.Trait := GTrait;
```

Pascal enables you, however, to use with statements to avoid having to laboriously qualify each of the field identifiers:

```
with Gen do begin
  Name := GName;
  Dates := GDates;
  Trait := GTrait;
end;
```

This is a handy, and optional, type of notation that can save programmers considerable effort. If you find it appealing, go ahead and use it.

procedure WriteGen has one other interesting aspect. Writing the record to the file is done with one very simple statement:

```
Write(F, Gen);
```

Contrast this with the effort you would expend writing these three strings to a text file:

```
WriteLn(F, Gen.Name);
WriteLn(F, Gen.Dates);
WriteLn(F, Gen.Traits);
```

Not only are typed files much faster than text files, but also, as you can see, they are much easier to use. The ease of use associated with typed files is evident, too, when it comes time to read the file off the disk:

```
procedure ReadFile(var F: TGenFile);
var
  Gen: TGeneration;
begin
  Reset(F);
  while not Eof(F) do begin
    Read(F, Gen);
    with Gen do begin
      WriteLn(Name);
      WriteLn(Dates);
      WriteLn(Trait);
      WriteLn;
    end;
  end;
  Close(F);
end;
```

Here you can see that the single statement:

```
Read(F, Gen);
```

is sufficient to retrieve the record from the file. The next step is to write the record to the screen, and then to shoot back up to the top of the loop to suck in another record from the disk. This process is repeated until all the records in the file have been processed. What could be easier?

Find what is wrong with the following two programs.

```
Program 1:

program BugIO1;

type
  TGeneration = Record
    Name: String;
```

```
    Dates: String;
    Trait: String;
  end;

var
  F: Text;
  Gen: TGeneration;

begin
  Assign(F, 'Gens.Dta');
  Reset(F);
  Read(F, Gen);
  WriteLn(Gen.Name);
  WriteLn(Gen.Dates);
  WriteLn(Gen.Trait);
  Close(F);
end.
```

- - - - - - - - - - - - - - - - - - - - - - - - - - -
Program 2:

```
program BugIO2;

type
  TGeneration = Record
    Name: String;
    Dates: String;
    Trait: Integer;
  end;

var
  F: File of TGeneration;
  Gen: TGeneration;

begin
  Assign(F, 'Gens.Dta');
  Reset(F);
  Read(F, Gen);
  WriteLn(Gen.Name);
  WriteLn(Gen.Dates);
  WriteLn(Gen.Trait);
  Close(F);
end.
```

# File I/O and Error Checking

Now that you have had a chance to get a more in-depth look at file I/O, it is time to introduce the subject of *error checking*.

Suppose you had a program called UseGens that depended on the file GENS.DTA. What would happen if you accidentally ran UseGens when GENS.DTA was not available on disk? Well, by now you should know eough to realize that a run-time error would occur, and the program would inevitably crash in mid-flight.

Problems like this happen all the time. If you don't plan for them, your programs will ignominiously crash, and you will become the butt of inconsiderate and derisive jokes. If you do plan ahead, however, you might be able to recover from the error or at least put up an appropriate error message. Surprisingly enough, the mere presence of a well-worded error message is often enough to deflect the ire of even the most presumptuous user.

To avoid becoming the butt of jokes, you should learn how to perform some minimal file I/O error checking. The following program attempts to open a file called NOFILE.DTA, which should not exist the first time you run the program. (If it does exist, you might want to delete it, so that you can see how this example works.) At any rate, once the program is loaded into memory, it searches for the file, finds that it does not exist, then recovers from the error by automatically creating the file.

Before running the program, be sure that NOFILE.DTA does not already exist. If such a file does exist, you should erase it and then run the program; otherwise, you won't get a chance to see the technique this program uses to recover from an error.

Often a program absolutely must create a file that does not exist. But on other occasions, this would not be the appropriate response. In these cases, an alternative is to simply display an error message and then terminate. This technique is also demonstrated in the following program.

Make sure NOFILE.DTA does not exist on disk, then step through NOFILE.PAS with the debugger:

```
program NoFile;
{

  File I/O error checking example. If File.Dta does not
  exist, it is created. If other I/O errors occur, the
  program displays an error message and terminates.
```

```
}
uses
  Dos;

const
  FileName = 'NoFile.Dta';

type
  TMyArray = array [1..3] of String;
  TAryFile= file of TMyArray;

{ Respond to a fatal error }
procedure Error(S: String);
begin
  WriteLn('Error: ', S);
  Halt(1);    { Stop the program! }
end;

{ Attempt to open file; return True only if all is okay }
function OpenFile(var F: TAryFile): Boolean;
var
  n: Integer;
begin
  OpenFile := True;
  {$I-}                     { Turn I/O checking off }
  Assign(F, 'NoFile.Dta');
  Reset(F);
  {$I+}                     { Turn I/O checking back on  }
  if (IOResult <> 0) or (FileSize(F) <> 1) then
    OpenFile := False;
end;

{ Attempt to create file; return True only if all is okay }
function CreateFile(var F: TAryFile): Boolean;
begin
  CreateFile := True;
  {$I-}                     { Turn I/O checking off }
  Assign(F, FileName);
  Rewrite(F);
  {$I+}                     { Turn I/O checking back on }
  if IoResult <> 0 then CreateFile := False;
end;
```

227

```
{ Convert a Word value to a string }
function Word2Str(N: Word): String;
var
  S: String;
begin
  Str(N, S);        { Perform the conversion }
  Word2Str := S;    { Return the result       }
end;

{ Create the file and write to it }
procedure WriteFile(var F: TAryFile);
var
  MyArray: TMyArray;
  Hour,Min,Sec,H,Year,Month,Day,Weekday: Word;
begin
  if not CreateFile(F) then Error('Could not create file.');
  GetDate(Year,Month,Day,Weekday);
  GetTime(Hour,Min,Sec,H);
  MyArray[1] := ' This file was created dynamically at run time. ';
  MyArray[2] := ' It was written to disk on ' +
                   Word2Str(Day) + '/' + Word2Str(Month) +
                   '/' + Word2Str(Year);
  MyArray[3] := ' at ' + Word2Str(Hour) + ':' +
                   Word2Str(Min) + ':' + Word2Str(Sec);
  {$I-}
  Write(F, MyArray);
  Close(F);  { Be sure to Reset the file, because you }
  Reset(F);  { want to switch from write to read mode }
  {$I+}
  If IoResult <> 0 then Error('Could not write to file.');
end;

{ Read the file from disk and write it to the screen }
procedure ShowFile(var F: TAryFile);
var
  MyArray: TMyArray;
begin
  Read(F, MyArray);
  WriteLn(MyArray[1]);
  Write(MyArray[2]);
  WriteLn(MyArray[3]);
```

```
    WriteLn;
    WriteLn('Press ENTER to end this program.');
    ReadLn;
  end;

var
  F: TAryFile;

begin
  if OpenFile(F) then { If file exists, read it, }
    ShowFile(F)
  else begin          { else create and read it }
    WriteFile(F);
    ShowFile(F);
  end;
end.
```

The program's output should look like this:

```
This file was created dynamically at run time.
It was written to disk on 29/11/1992 at 16:19:12
Press ENTER to end this program.
```

Turn now to the source code. The first thing you might notice is that it is fairly long and complicated for a program that does little more than read a 768-byte file off a disk and then write it to the screen. The program is so long because it performs extensive error checking. In other words, all programs with adequate error checking are much longer than you might at first expect. The rule of thumb to follow is that adding error checking to a program usually doubles its size. This is not a particularly pleasant fact to contemplate, but it's reality.

If you move to procedure CreateFile, you can get a good look at how to actually perform error checking when working with files:

```
function CreateFile(var F: TAryFile): Boolean;
begin
  CreateFile := True;
  {$I-}                    { Turn I/O checking off }
  Assign(F, FileName);
  Rewrite(F);
  {$I+}                    { Turn I/O checking back on }
  if IoResult <> 0 then CreateFile := False;
end;
```

Notice that this is a Boolean function, and that in the first line, the result of the function is set to TRUE. In other words, the initial assumption is that all will go well.

The next step is to insert a *compiler directive* that turns I/O checking off. Compiler directives always begin with a curly brace and a dollar sign. This syntax sends a specific instruction to the compiler. In this case, you should follow the dollar sign with the letter I and a minus sign. This tells the compiler to turn I/O checking off. These conditions prevail for only two lines, and then I/O checking is turned back on. Next the program checks the variable IOResult to see whether everything has gone smoothly. If IOResult equals 0, you can assume there was no error. Otherwise, IOResult will be set to the number of the error that occurred.

This system enables you to check the result of an I/O operation for yourself and to deal with the matter as you see fit. If you don't handle things this way and an error occurs, the program will terminate immediately, leaving only a cryptic message on-screen.

Sometimes an I/O error occurs that is so serious or so peculiar that there really is no alternative but to end the program immediately. It is nice, however, to be able to explain the error to the user before terminating the program. That is what the procedure called Error does. It pops up an error message of your choosing and then terminates the program with the Halt command. You can use the Halt command whenever you want to summarily end a Pascal program.

You might want to spend a few minutes stepping through the NoFile program so that you can better understand it, but I don't think there is a need to discuss it in any great depth. You might, however, want to take a few minutes to examine the GetTime and GetDate functions, which get a rather primitive workout in this program. I also use the Str function to convert an integer type value into a string.

Find the bug in the following program:

```
program NoFile2;

const
  FileName = 'NoFile.Dta';

type
  TMyArray = array [1..3] of String;
  TAryFile= file of TMyArray;
```

```
var
  F: TAryFile;
  MyArray: TMyArray;

begin
  {$I+}
  Assign(F, FileName);
  Reset(F);
  {$I-}
  if IOResult = 0 then begin
    WriteLn('An error has occurred.');
    Halt(1);
  end;
  Read(F, MyArray);
  WriteLn(MyArray[1], #13#10, MyArray[2], MyArray[3]);
  Close(F);
end.
```

# Summary

That's enough for this lesson. The next lesson teaches you more about typed files and shows you how to pluck parameters off the command line.

# Review Questions

1. Is it possible to read a typed file as a text file? _____

2. Is it possible to read a text file as a typed file? _____

# More About Typed Files

*To learn about seeking to a specific location in text files and passing arguments to a program.*

When reading the records from the file GEN.DTA in the last lesson, you were moving sequentially through the file. That is, you started by reading the first record and continued until you had read the last record.

While this process was taking place, Turbo Pascal was somehow "remembering" the location where it last read from the file. When it was time to get the next record from the file, the program always knew where to go to get that record. The Pascal compiler does this by cleverly keeping track of an internal *file pointer* that always points to the place where you last read or wrote to the file.

As if this weren't enough, Pascal also has the ability to move at random to any particular record in a file. Although it is not unique to our language, this generous trait is part and parcel of the genial spirit of Pascal programming. This lesson begins with an exploration of this trait.

# Moving Hither and Yon Inside a File

The real power of typed files becomes apparent when you learn how to move around inside them. To understand how this works, look at the following program, which uses the data file created in the last lesson.

```
program GetRec3;
{

  Demonstration of how to seek to a place in a
  file. This program requires that a file called
  GENS.DTA is already on disk. If the file does
  not exist, compile and run GENS.PAS, presented
  in Lesson 17, to create it.
}
uses
  Crt;

const
  CR = #10#13; { A carriage return line-feed string }

type
  TGeneration = Record
    Name: String;
    Dates: String;
    Trait: String;
  end;

var
  F: File of TGeneration;
  Gen: TGeneration;

begin
  ClrScr;

  { Open file }
  Assign(F, 'Gens.Dta');
  Reset(F);
```

```
{ Read third record using zero-based number line }
Seek(F, 2);
Read(F, Gen);

{ Handle screen I/O }
with Gen do WriteLn(Name, CR, Dates, CR, Trait);
WriteLn;
WriteLn('Press ENTER to end this program');
ReadLn;
end.
```

The program's output looks like this:

```
Boomers
1943 - 1960
Moralists - Fickle


Press ENTER to end this program
```

Notice that this program introduces the Seek procedure, which enables you to move to a particular place in a file:

```
Seek(F, 2);
```

The data file you are working with was created by GENS.PAS. This file contains four records of type TGeneration. GetRec3.Pas *seeks* to a particular place in that file so that it can read the third record.

Notice that two parameters are passed to Seek. The first is the file variable and the second is the number of the record you want to find. The first record in the file is considered to be record zero; the second record, one; and the third record, two. Therefore, the Seek command issued in this program gets record three, even though it is passed the number 2 as a parameter.

Take a moment to track down the bug in this program:

```
program GetRec4;
{

  Demonstration of how to seek to a place in a
  file. This program requires that a file called
  Gens.Dta be on disk. If the file does not
  exist, compile and run Gens.Pas to create it.
}
uses
  Crt;
```

```
const
  CR = #10#13; { A carriage return line-feed string }

type
  TGeneration = Record
    Name: String;
    Dates: String;
    Trait: String;
  end;

var
  F: File of TGeneration;
  Gen: TGeneration;

begin
  ClrScr;

  { Open file }
  Assign(F, 'Gens.Dta');
  Reset(F);

  { Read third record using zero-based number line }
  Seek(F, 4);
  Read(F, Gen);

  { Handle screen I/O }
  with Gen do WriteLn(Name, CR, Dates, CR, Trait);
  WriteLn;
  WriteLn('Press ENTER to end this program');
  ReadLn;
end.
```

Rather than moving on without comment as I usually do, I would like to take a moment to discuss the bug in this program. When you run the program, it bombs out with Run Time Error 100 on the line that reads:

```
Seek(F, 4)
```

The IDE finds the line this error occurred on and prints a description of the error. This is fairly helpful, but at the end of the programmer's guide that came with your version of Turbo Pascal is a more in-depth description of all the compiler and runtime errors. The entry for Error 100 looks like this:

```
100 Disk read error
```

```
Reported by Read on a typed file if you attempt to read past the
end of the file.
```

This information obviously is much more helpful than the information printed by the IDE. Take the time to find where in the manual these error messages are printed and refer to them as often as necessary. Remember also that short descriptions of the errors are listed in the online help (see Figure 18.1).

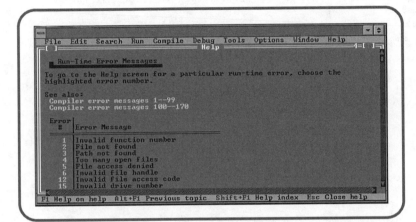

*Figure 18.1.*
*The online help has a list of error messages.*

The second point I want to make about the Find the Bug program is a seemingly picayune syntactical matter that can drive beginning programmers mad. If it makes you feel any better, it also drives writers of beginning programming books mad too! Nevertheless, we have to focus in on this issue. Notice that the type of the file variable is in the global variable section instead of in the type section. In other words, it is declared like this:

```
var
    F: File of TGeneration;
```

instead of like this:

```
type
    TGenFile: File of TGeneration;
```

GENS.PAS utilizes this second technique because that program passes the file variable to several different procedures. This meant there had to be multiple instances of the very same type of file.

It might seem possible to declare the type of the variable in the header of each procedure that used it. In other words, it would seem just as acceptable to write:

```
procedure OpenFile(var F: File of TGeneration);
```

as:

```
procedure OpenFile(var F: TGenFile);
```

But this is not the case. You must use the syntax evident in the latter example. In fact, using the first format generates a compile-time error stating that a parenthesis is missing! Unless you understand what you have just read, you might be baffled when you get this error message.

The point is that every declaration of a type is considered a new type, even if the new type is declared exactly as the first type is declared. Take the time to be sure—absolutely positive—that you understand this important point.

For instance, the following two legal declarations declare two separate and distinct types, and they cannot be used interchangeably:

```
type
    F : array[0..10] of Integer;
```

and

```
    F1: array[0..10] of Integer;
```

Don't make the mistake of thinking that F and F1 are of the same type. They aren't!

 Find the bug in the following program:

```
program TypeBug;

type
    TMyArray = Array[1..2] of Integer;

procedure WriteAry(MyArray: TMyArray);
var
    i: Integer;
begin
    for i := 1 to 2 do
        WriteLn(MyArray[i]);
end;

var
    MyArray: Array[1..2] of Integer;

begin
    MyArray[1] := 42;
```

```
    MyArray[2] := Round(Sqrt(42));
    WriteAry(MyArray);
end.
```

# Plucking Parameters Off the Command Line

So far you have run all the programs in this book from inside the IDE. When other people use your programs, however, they will run them from the DOS prompt.

The programs run from the DOS prompt usually have an extension of .EXE or .COM. The files you create when using Turbo Pascal always have an .EXE extension. These files usually are referred to as executables because they can be *executed* from the command line. When referring to these files, programmers often call them "exies."

> **NOTE:** The Pascal compilers make it extremely easy to create an executable. But it will take me a moment to explain the process, because the language now ships with such a wide array of compilers.

Perhaps it would be best to start with the simplest cases. If you are using BPW.Exe or BP.Exe, both of which ship with BP7, then executables will be created automatically every time you compile. But if you are using Turbo.Exe or TPX.Exe, then before you can create executables, you must open up the Compile menu and set the Destination option so that it reads Disk. By default, destination is set to memory.

Often when you run an executable from the DOS prompt, you can pass it a parameter. For instance, if you start up Turbo Pascal, you can pass it the name of the file you want to edit. If you have Borland Pascal 7.0, you might start up with the following command:

```
bp myfile.pas
```

to begin your Pascal session by editing program MyFile.

Or, if you have Turbo Pascal 7.0, you might begin with this command:

```
turbo myfile.pas
```

The following program shows how you can add this feature to your own executables:

```pascal
Program ReadProc;
{

  Example of how to pass a parameter to a program.
  You must run the program called MakeInfo at least once
  before you run this program. MakeInfo creates the data
  files that this program reads.

  Usage: ReadProc <FileName>
  Where FileName is either DosProc or SysProc.
  Example: ReadProc DosProc
}

uses
  Crt;

type
  TProcInfo = Record
    Name: String;
    Description: String;
    NumParams: Integer;
    IsFunction: Boolean;
  end;

  TPInfoFile = File of TProcInfo;

{ Explain how to use the program. Called only if a user
  passes the wrong parameter or if an error occurs. }
procedure Explain;
begin
  WriteLn('This program writes out a description of ');
  WriteLn('several Pascal procedures. To use it, pass' );
  WriteLn('in either the word DosProc or SysProc as');
  WriteLn('a parameter. For instance: ');
  WriteLn;
  WriteLn('ReadProc DosProc');
end;

{ Report a fatal error }
```

```pascal
procedure Error(S: String);
begin
  WriteLn('Error: ', S);
  Explain;
  Halt(1);
end;

{ Write a record to the screen }
procedure WriteInfo(ProcInfo: TProcInfo);
begin
  with ProcInfo do begin
    WriteLn('Routine name: ', Name);
    WriteLn('Description: ', Description);
    WriteLn('Takes ', NumParams, ' parameters.');
    Write('Type: ');
    if IsFunction then WriteLn('Function')
    else WriteLn('Procedure');
  end;
  WriteLn;
  WriteLn;
end;

var
  F: TPInfoFile;
  ProcInfo: TProcInfo;

begin
  ClrScr;
  if ParamCount < 1 then Explain;

  {$I-}
  Assign(F, ParamStr(1) + '.Dta');
  Reset(F);
  {$I+}

  if IoResult <> 0 then Error('Could not find file');

  while not Eof(F) do begin
    Read(F, ProcInfo);
    WriteInfo(ProcInfo);
  end;
```

```
   WriteLn;
   WriteLn('Press any key to end this program');
   ReadKey;
end.
```

Sample output from this program is visible in Figure 18.2. Note that the program won't run correctly unless you first run the program MakeInfo, included on this book's disk.

*Figure 18.2.*
*The output from*
*READPROC.PAS.*

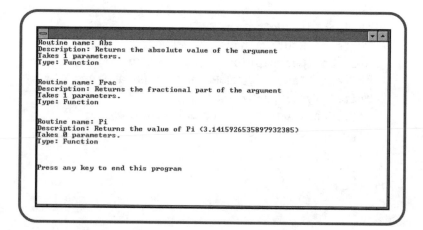

By now, most of this program should be entirely self-explanatory. Notice, however, the use of the ParamCount and ParamStr functions.

The ParamCount function tells you how many parameters are being passed to a program. For instance, if you write:

```
ReadProc DosProc
```

ParamCount will be set to 1 because you are passing one parameter to the program.

To find out what the value of this parameter is, you can examine the ParamStr function, which itself takes an integer as its sole parameter. Assuming that the variable S was declared as a string, if you wrote:

```
S := ParamStr(1);
```

S would be set to the value of the first parameter passed to the program.

I should add that the best way to run ReadProc is to first build the program, then exit the IDE to run the executable you have created. There is, however, a second method. Inside the IDE you can pull down the Run menu to get access to the Parameters option. You can use this option to pass a parameter automatically to your program without having to leave the IDE, as Figure 18.3 shows. This functionality is provided primarily to aid programmers during the testing phases of program production.

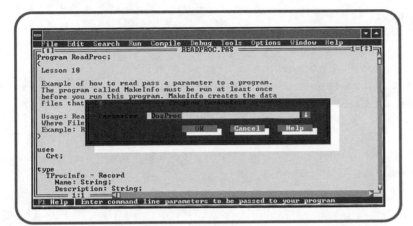

*Figure 18.3.*
*Use the Parameter option to pass arguments to your program.*

Finish the following program so that it successfully tells the user which two parameters were passed to it.

```pascal
program TwoParam;
{
 Lesson 18
 }

procedure Explain;
begin
  WriteLn(' Pass two parameters to this program and it ');
  WriteLn(' will print them both out for you!');
end;

begin
  if ParamCount <> 2 then Explain;
```

_____

_____

_____

243

Before you finish this lesson, look at one more short program.

The following program generates Error 100, described earlier in this lesson. Find the problem area and repair it.

```
program GetRec5;
{

  Demonstration of how to seek to a place in a
  file. This program requires that a file called
  Gens.Dta be on disk. If the file does not
  exist, run Gens.Pas to create it.

  Pass the number of the record you want to read in
  as a parameter.
}
uses
  Crt;

const
  CR = #10#13; { A carriage return line-feed string }

type
  TGeneration = Record
    Name: String;
    Dates: String;
    Trait: String;
  end;

procedure Explain;
begin
  WriteLn('This program will access a file which contains');
  WriteLn('four different records numbered 1 through 4.');
  WriteLn('If you pass the number of one of these records');
  WriteLn('to this program as a parameter, then it will ');
  WriteLn('access that record for you.');
  WriteLn;
  WriteLn(' Example: ');
  WriteLn;
  WriteLn('GetRec5 2 ');
  Halt(1);
end;
```

```
var
  F: File of TGeneration;
  Gen: TGeneration;

var
  Code,
  N: Integer;
  S: String;

begin
  ClrScr;

  if ParamCount <> 1 then Explain;


  { Open file }
  Assign(F, 'Gens.Dta');
  Reset(F);


  Val(ParamStr(1), N, Code);
  Dec(N);
  Seek(F, N);
  Read(F, Gen);

  { Handle screen I/O }
  with Gen do WriteLn(Name, CR, Dates, CR, Trait);
  WriteLn;
  WriteLn('Press ENTER to end this program');
  ReadLn;
end.
```

# Summary

That's enough about typed files for now. In the next lesson, I teach you how to break code into modules called units and show you a method used by professional programmers for getting input from users.

# Review Question

1. What are some differences between the following pieces of syntax:

_____

_____

```
var
   MyFile: File of TMyRecord;
```

and

```
type
   TMyFile = File of TMyRecord;
```

# Review Exercises

1. Write a program that reads five parameters and writes them back in the reverse order from which they are passed to the program.

2. Write a program that takes two numbers as parameters and then multiplies them together and shows the result to the user. (*Hint:* Use the Str procedure.)

3. Discover a way to modify the previous program so that it can do multiplication, division, or subtraction, depending on the third paramter passed to the program. For instance:

```
Mather 3 2 +
```

would produce 5, whereas

```
Mather 3 2 *
```

would produce 6.

# urbo Pascal
## CLASSROOM 6

# The Modular Structure of Large Programs

**Notes**

# Units: The Key To Creating Large Programs

*To explore a way to reuse code and to learn how to break large programs into manageable units.*

We expect modern programs to have pull-down menus, pop-up windows, mouse support, online help, and an intuitive, easy-to-use interface. All these fancy features have evolved over the years to the point where they have become necessities. As a result, even programs that perform relatively simple tasks require hefty stacks of code.

So far, all the programs in this book have been relatively short—approximately 100 lines or less. But many real-world programs, especially those with the features just mentioned, require between 10,000 and 100,000 lines

of code. Some require even more. Programs that guide rockets through space or that control a phone system frequently consist of several million lines of code.

If you picture for a moment all those reams of code stacked in a tall pile, it should be easy to understand why programmers have spent so much time finding ways to manage their bulging programs. Most of the work that has been done in this area can be boiled down to two key methods. The first is the divide-and-conquer strategy associated with structured programming, and the second is the efforts of programmers who have found ways to group related fragments of code into objects.

Unfortunately, there is not enough room in this book to discuss objects. I have, however, introduced you to procedures and functions, which are the bricks and mortar of which structured programs are built. The next most important aspect of good structured programming is called *modularization.*

# units and Include Files

In Pascal, when you want to divide programs into modules, you usually create something called a unit.

I have created a very simple program to introduce you to units. It is unlike any other program presented so far because its source is divided into two separate files. One file is the source code for the main program, and the other file is the source code of the unit that is "attached" to the main program.

First look at the main program, which won't compile correctly until the unit that belongs to it is created:

```
program UseUnit;
uses
  MyUnit;

begin
  SayGoodnightDick;
end.
```

It is hard to imagine a much simpler program than this. It consists primarily of a single line that calls a single procedure:

```
SayGoodnightDick;
```

I hope by now you can guess that a procedure with a silly name like SayGoodnightDick was created by me and not by the people who wrote Turbo Pascal.

If I wrote the procedure, then where in the world is it?

Well, I've got it hidden away in its own separate file called MyUnit. If you take a second look at the program, you can see that it does, in fact, reference MyUnit in the program's uses clause:

```
uses
  MyUnit;
```

If you are seated at your computer, press Alt-F to bring up the File menu, then press N to start a new file. Now type the following into the file:

```
unit MyUnit;

interface

procedure SayGoodnightDick;
implementation

procedure SayGoodnightDick;
begin
  WriteLn('Goodnight Dick');
end;

end.
```

When you finish typing this unit, first check that it compiles, and then save it under the name MyUnit. Be sure you type the name exactly right. It is important that the filename and the unit name be identical.

Now go back and compile and run the main program. If all goes well, you will see that it prints the words Goodnight Dick to the screen. To understand how this happened, you have to look at the unit in more depth.

Like all units, this very simple unit has two sections. The first, the interface, begins right after the keyword interface. The second section, the implementation, begins right after the keyword implementation.

It is easier for me to discuss the implementation first:

```
procedure SayGoodnightDick;
begin
  WriteLn('Goodnight Dick');
end;
```

As you can see, the `implementation` consists solely of a simple procedure called `SayGoodnightDick`. This procedure is very much like the ones you have seen many times before in this book. The only unusual thing about it is that it is being called not from some other place inside this file, but from the main body of the program, which is in a totally different file.

The big mystery is how the main body of the program knows to look for this procedure in the `implementation` of this unit. The clues, however, aren't so hard to follow. First, because you put the identifier `MyUnit` in the `uses` clause of the main program, the program knows that there is something in the file called `MyUnit` that it needs to know. Second, the compiler helps the main program scan through the `interface` of `MyUnit` to see what is there. When it looks through the `interface` of `MyUnit`, the compiler finds the following declaration:

```
procedure SayGoodnightDick;
```

The compiler "memorizes" this procedure name and skips back to the main body of the program, where it finds a call to a procedure with the same name. The final and obvious step is for the compiler to *link* the code from the unit's `implementation` into the main program so that the main program knows how to perform the actions specified in `procedure SayGoodnightDick`.

Think about this process for a moment. First the compiler checks the `uses` clause to see which files belong to this program. Then it scans through the `interface` of the files to see what is there and matches what it finds in the `interfaces` with calls made in the main body of the program. Finally, it links the code from the `units` into the main program. This is, of course, a grossly oversimplified explanation of how the separate modules of a program are linked to its main body, but for now it should be enough to give you a general feel for how the process works.

To wrap up this introductory section of the lesson, I should mention that every `unit` ends with the keyword `end` followed by a period. Notice also that it is very important that the declaration of a procedure or a function in the `interface` exactly match the actual header of the function as declared in the `implementation`.

The following `unit` is filled with mistakes I sometimes absentmindedly make when creating `units`. See whether you can find them.

```
Unit BugUnit;

procedure Rimbaud(var S: String);
interface;
```

```
procedure Rimbaud(S: String);
begin
  WriteLn('Pity the man who traveled all the way downtown');
  WriteLn('to see a movie called Rambo because he thought');
  WriteLn('it was about the life of a French poet.');
  WriteLn;
  Write('The first name of that poet was: ');
  ReadLn(S);
end;

end;
```

# Include Files

Because units are so important, I discuss them in more depth in the next lesson. Right now I will digress in order to mention a second, and now somewhat outdated, way to link code into a module. This second method involves creating something called *include files*, which are very much like units—only different!

The difference between include files and units is both syntactical and technical. That is, you use a different syntax to bring include files into your programs than you do to bring units in. I will explain the syntactical differences in a moment. First I want to mention the technical differences, which are very significant, though perhaps somewhat difficult for you to understand at this time.

When you were studying arrays, I mentioned that no single array can be larger than 64K. It so happens that this same limitation applies to the code you write.

> **NOTE:** I should take a moment to remind you that writing 64K is only a shorthand way of writing 65,536. The letter K stands for kilobyte, which in turn means 1,000 bytes. And yes, when we write 1,000 bytes, we really mean 1,024 bytes; and 64 times 1024 equals 65,536. But that's a whole other story that I don't want to go into right now!

The Pascal code you write is translated into machine code by the compiler and then stored on disk. When a program is run, this code is loaded into memory the same way an array, an integer, or a string is loaded into memory. To explain much more about this concept would be to step well outside the scope of this book. For now, all you need to know is that the instructions that run a computer, the things we call a program, also can be loaded into that 640,000-byte memory theater that I keep mentioning. When a program executes, it reads a byte or two from that code, which is loaded into memory, then it does what those two bytes ask it to do. Next it reads a few bytes more, and then it does what those bytes ask it to do. Though the actual implemen- tation is in fact very complicated, the basic concept is really that simple.

I hope some of that last paragraph makes sense to you. You don't have to understand it completely. But if some of it has sunk in, you can understand what I mean when I say that there is a 64K limitation on the size of any one location, or *segment*, in memory dedicated to code. In other words, just as no one array can be larger than 64K, no one *code segment* can be larger than 64K.

In the bad old days, this used to mean that no one Pascal program could be larger than 64K. In practice, this meant that you would write some code, and then watch as it was compiled and stored on disk. When you ran the program, that code would be loaded into memory, and you might find that it occupied 20K. Then you would go back and add a few more routines to the program. When you loaded that into memory, you might find that it occupied 33K, and so on until you reached 64K. Then you were out of room.

When Turbo Pascal 4.0 was released, units were introduced. One of the most important things about units is that *each unit has its own code segment!* This means that if one of your programs appears to be out of space because it occupies 64K of code, all you have to do to remedy the situation is put half of it into a unit, and suddenly your main program takes up only 32K!

When you fill one unit with code, you can in turn divide it into two 32K segments, and so on, until you fill the whole 640K of available memory theater. (Starting with Borland Pascal 7.0, you can write protected-mode Pascal programs that break even the 640K barrier!)

At any rate, I introduced this rather lengthy discussion of code segments in part to make it clear that units do more for you than include files; they divide your program up into different code segments so that you can write really large programs. But you will not get this benefit from using include files.

The moral of this tale is that normally you should use units rather than include files. In fact, units so thoroughly supersede the functionality of include files that I mention them only because you might run into them when studying someone else's code. In your own code, however, you probably should use units instead. At any rate, you should use units unless you have some specific reason for using include files.

Well, after that incredibly lengthy introduction, you are ready for an example that shows you how to use include files. The listings here include both the main module and the include file. Be sure to place each in a separate file, just as was done with the units example.

Here is the main program:

```
program UseInc;
{

  The purpose of this program is to demonstrate how to use
  an include file. Notice the include directive listed in
  curly braces below.
}

{$I WriteXY.Inc}

begin
  WriteXY(10, 10, 'Hello');
  WriteXY(10, 11, Int2Str(234));
  WriteXY(10, 12, Int2Str(BigNum));
end.
```

Here is the include file:

```
{

  This is an include file that goes with
  program UseInc. The purpose of this code
  is to demonstrate how to use include files.
}
uses
  Crt;
```

```
const
  BigNum = 1345645;

function Int2Str(N: LongInt): String;
var
  S: String;
begin
  Str(N, S);
  Int2Str := S;
end;

procedure WriteXY(X, Y: Integer; S: String);
begin
  GotoXY(X, Y);
  Write(S);
end;
```

This program simply writes the word Hello to the screen at a certain *x,y* coordinate and then writes 234 and BigNum to the screen right beneath it.

As you can see, include files are very easy to use. The include file itself simply contains the code or any constants you want to declare. To bring this code into the main module, use the following syntax, which takes the form of a compiler directive:

```
{$I WriteXY.Inc}
```

Here I surround the name of the include file with curly braces. Notice that immediately after the first curly brace I include a dollar sign followed by the letter I. If I left the dollar sign out, or if I placed a space between the dollar sign and the left curly brace, the compiler would treat the statement as a comment, and it would have no effect on the code.

You should also note that naming the file WRITEXY.INC instead of WRITEXY.PAS is simply a matter of convention. Traditionally, include files have had the .INC extension, but there is no rule stating that they must be written this way.

The following program uses the same include file you just created. Find four reasons why it won't compile:

```
program IncBug;
{
}
{I WriteXY}
```

```
begin
  WriteXY(1, BigNum, 'Hi');
  WriteXY(1, 9, 345);
end.
```

# Summary

This is the end of Lesson 19. The next lesson continues the exploration of units.

# Review Questions

1. In what version of Turbo Pascal were units first introduced? _____
   _____

2. Suppose you created an include file that had no extension. How would you write the compiler directive to include the file in your unit? _____

# Review Exercise

1. In the file called WRITEXY.INC, you learned how to declare a constant inside an include file. Create a unit that declares a constant, then write a program that uses your unit and its constant.

## 20

*L e s s o n*

# Storing Often-Used Routines

*To introduce the ToolBox unit, which stores useful routines that can be used repeatedly.*

units perform three important functions. The first is to divide portions of code into logical subsets of a whole. The second is to create multiple code segments so that you can have programs that contain more than 64K of code. The third is to make it easy for programmers to reuse code.

Perhaps without realizing it, you have been taking advantage of this feature since the earliest lessons of this book. Think for a moment of the ClrScr procedure you have used so often. Every time you have used this procedure you have first added the identifier Crt to the uses clause of the program.

By now it should be obvious to you that the procedure called ClrScr is in fact defined inside a unit called Crt. The same is true of the GotoXY, Delay, ReadKey, TextColor, and TextBkGround routines that you have used in one place or another in this book.

The point to remember is that the creators of Turbo Pascal made one unit called Crt that you have used over and over.

There is no substantial difference in form between the Crt unit and the units created in the last lesson. They both follow the same set of rules. Of course, the units you create and the Crt unit contain different sets of procedures and functions, but the basic principles are the same.

If you want to learn more about the procedures and functions in the Crt unit, you can look in the *Programmer's Reference Guide* and the *Language Guide* or you can pop up the index to the IDE's online help and search for references to *Crt Procedures* and *Crt Functions*. If you are at all curious, go ahead and do this; it is well worth the effort. You should take the time to become familiar with the contents of all the main Pascal units, and in particular, with the DOS and Crt units.

> **NOTE:** Four books come with Turbo Pascal 7.0. They are the *Language Guide*, the *Programmer's Reference Guide*, the *User's Guide*, and the *Turbo Vision Guide*. For now, the *Programmer's Reference* and the *User's Guide* are the documents you will use most often. As your programming skills develop, you will probably find many uses for the more advanced *Language Guide*.

When you look in the online help or in the *Library Reference Guide*, you will see that the name of each routine's unit usually is included in the procedure or function's definition. Figure 20.1 shows a portion of the maximized help screen for the GotoXY procedure.

*Figure 20.1.*
*The online help screen for* GotoXY.

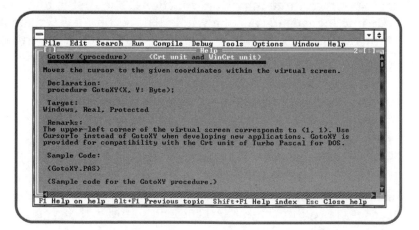

Notice the portion at the top that looks like this:

```
GotoXY (procedure)      (Crt unit and WinCrt unit)
```

Here the help screen is telling you that the GotoXY procedure is declared in the DOS Crt unit and the Windows WinCrt unit. Occasionally you will see entries that don't mention a unit name. Most of these procedures, functions, or constants are declared in the System unit, which is always linked to your program automatically.

# A Useful unit

Now that you understand something about placing reusable code inside units, you can begin constructing your own ToolBox unit, which you will continue to develop throughout this book. I could simply give you the entire unit now, but I'm afraid its size and complexity would be a bit overwhelming. So instead, you will begin with a relatively small ToolBox unit and slowly add to it as the book progresses. When you're done, you will have a unit filled with useful routines you can use repeatedly.

**NOTE:** TPW users should check the disk for alternate copies of the ToolBox unit.

Here is the beginning of your ToolBox unit:

```
unit ToolBox;

interface
{
 Copyright 1992 by Charlie Calvert

 You are welcome to use and distribute this code in any
 manner whatsoever so long as it is free. In other words,
 this code is being released as a contribution to the
 programming community. The only thing you may not do
 with it is call it your own and/or charge a fee for it.
}
uses
```

```
  Crt;

procedure Beeper(Freq, Time: Integer);
procedure CenterStr(Row: integer; S: String);
function CreateAttr(Fg, Bg: Integer): Integer;
procedure DrawBox(X, Y, W, H: Byte; DrawAttr: Integer);
procedure SetTextColor(Fg, Bg: Integer);
function Upper(S: String) : String;
procedure WriteChar(X, Y: Byte; Num: Integer;
                    C: Char; Attr: Byte);
implementation


{-------------------------------------------------
        Name: Beeper
 Declaration: CenterStr(S: String; Y: Integer);
 Result Type: None
        Type:
 Description: Makes a noise
----------------------------------------------}
procedure Beeper(Freq, Time : Integer);
begin
  Sound(Freq);
  Delay(Time);
  NoSound;
end;


{-------------------------------------------------
        Name: CenterStr
 Declaration: CenterStr(Row: Integer; S: String);
 Result Type: None
        Type:
 Description: Centers a string in the current window.
             Makes allowances for coordinate changes
             due to the Window command.
----------------------------------------------}
procedure CenterStr(Row: Integer; S: String);
var
  Width: Integer;
begin
  Width := Lo(WindMax) - Lo(WindMin);
  GotoXY(((Width div 2) + 1) - (Length(S) div 2), Row);
  Write(S);
```

```
end; { CenterStr }

{ - - - - - - - - - - - - - - - - - - - - - - - - - - - - - - - - - - - - - - - -
        Name: CreateAttr
 Declaration: CreateAttr(Fg, Bg: Integer);
 Result Type: Integer
        Type:
 Description: Centers a string in the current window.
              Makes allowances for coordinate changes
              due to the Window command.
- - - - - - - - - - - - - - - - - - - - - - - - - - - - - - - - - - - - - - - -}
function CreateAttr(Fg, Bg: Integer): Integer;
begin
  CreateAttr := Fg + Bg * 16;
end;

{ - - - - - - - - - - - - - - - - - - - - - - - - - - - - - - - - - - - - - - - -
        Name: DrawBox
 Declaration: DrawBox(X, Y, W, H, DrawAttr: integer);
 Result Type: None
        Type:
 Description: Draws a box in text mode in a certain
              attribute.
- - - - - - - - - - - - - - - - - - - - - - - - - - - - - - - - - - - - - - - -}
procedure DrawBox(X, Y, W, H: Byte; DrawAttr: integer);
const
  Num: Byte = 1;
  HorzByte: Char = #205;
  VertByte: Char = #186;
  TopLeft: Char = #201;
  TopRight: Char = #187;
  BottomLeft: Char = #200;
  BottomRight: Char = #188;

var
  i : byte;
  Attr : Integer;
begin
  WriteChar(X + 1, Y, W - X, HorzByte, DrawAttr);
  WriteChar(X + 1, H, W - X, HorzByte, DrawAttr);

  for i := (Y + 1) to (H - 1) do begin
```

263

```
      WriteChar(X, i, Num, VertByte, DrawAttr);
      WriteChar(W, i, Num, VertByte, DrawAttr);
    end;

  WriteChar(X, Y, Num, TopLeft, DrawAttr);
  WriteChar(W, Y, Num, TopRight, DrawAttr);
  WriteChar(X, H, Num, BottomLeft, DrawAttr);
  WriteChar(W, H, Num, BottomRight, DrawAttr);
end;


{-----------------------------------------------
          Name: SetTextColor
   Declaration: SetTextColor(Fg, Bg: Integer);
   Result Type: None
          Type:
   Description: Sets colors in TextMode. Passes it
                a foreground and background color.
 ----------------------------------------------}
procedure SetTextColor(Fg, Bg: Integer);
begin
  TextColor(Fg);
  TextBackGround(Bg);
end;


{-----------------------------------------------
          Name: Upper
   Declaration: Upper(S: String);
   Result Type: String
          Type:
   Description: Returns a string in uppercase.
 ----------------------------------------------}
function Upper(S : String) : String;
var
  i : integer;
begin
  for i := 1 to length(S) do
    S[i] := UpCase(S[i]);
  Upper := S;
end;


{-----------------------------------------------
          Name: WriteChar
```

```
    Declaration: WriteChar(X, Y, Num: Integer;
                           Ch: Byte; Attr: Integer);
   Result Type: None
          Type:
   Description: Writes a certain number of Bytes at a
                certain location in a certain attribute.
---------------------------------------------}
procedure WriteChar(X, Y: Byte; Num: Integer;
                    C: Char; Attr: Byte); assembler;
asm
  { GotoXY }
  mov ah, 2h
  mov bh, 0
  mov dh, y
  mov dl, x
  int 10h

  { Write the Char }
  mov ah, 9h
  mov al, C;
  mov bh, 0
  mov bl, Attr
  mov cx, Num
  int 10h
end;
end.
```

As you can see, this unit has seven routines. Each routine is preceded by a brief explanation of its purpose and calling conventions. Though some of these routines introduce new concepts, only the WriteChar procedure, listed last, introduces a radically new idea. The WriteChar procedure serves as a superficial introduction to the Pascal BASM services, which are nothing more than assembler code that can be embedded directly into your Pascal program. Unfortunately, there is not enough room in this book to discuss BASM in depth, but I will give a few examples which will give assembler programmers a feeling for how to proceed.

Before I begin talking in depth about any of the routines in this unit, take a moment to see what they can do.

```
program ShowBox1;
{
  Lesson 20
  Demonstrates how to use the first incarnation of the
```

ToolBox unit. This program clears the screen, draws a
border and writes a title, then creates a smaller window
and draws a second border around it. The program then
makes a short noise after prompting the user to press the
Enter key.

```
}
uses
  Crt,
  ToolBox;

var
  SaveAttr: Integer;
  S: String;
begin
  SaveAttr := TextAttr;
  SetTextColor(14, 1);
  ClrScr;
  DrawBox(1, 0, 78, 24, CreateAttr(14, 1));
  S := 'The First ToolBox Example Program';
  CenterStr(3, Upper(S));
  Window(10, 7, 70, 20);
  SetTextColor(14, 3);
  ClrScr;
  DrawBox(9, 5, 69, 20, CreateAttr(14, 3));
  CenterStr(7, 'Press enter to hear a noise.');
  ReadLn;
  Beeper(500,100);
  Window(1,1,80,25);
  TextAttr := SaveAttr;
  ClrScr;
end.
```

The output from this program should look something like Figure 20.2.

The first thing you should notice about this sample program is that it includes the ToolBox unit in its uses clause. Notice that the inclusion of these two short lines of code enables you to access more than 150 lines of code present in the ToolBox unit. A moment's contemplation should reveal that you reap enormous benefits in terms of clarity and ease of use by being able to divide your code into separate units.

In fact, the use of the ToolBox unit reduces the size of your main program from about 200 lines to only 40. This leads me to a very important point that I have so far neglected to emphasize.

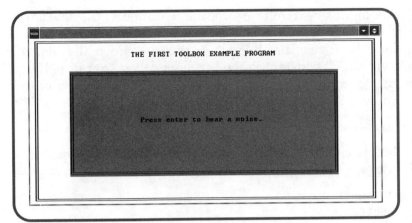

*Figure 20.2.*
*The output from*
*SHOWBOX1.PAS.*

Notice what I hope you will consider the aptness of each of the names of the routines in the `ToolBox` unit. The `WriteChar` procedure, for instance, writes a `Char` to the screen. The `SetTextColor` routine sets the colors for the output of text onto the screen. The `DrawBox` procedure draws a box on the screen. Using names that are descriptive helps make your code self-documenting.

For instance, look at these three lines of code:

```
SetTextColor(14, 1);
ClrScr;
DrawBox(1, 0, 78, 24, CreateAttr(14, 1));
```

It is evident that their purpose is to first set the text colors, then clear the screen, then draw a box using certain colors—or, as programmers tend to call them, attributes. A nonprogrammer probably would find these lines fairly cryptic, but anyone familiar with Pascal should be able to glean their approximate purpose with only a glance.

If, instead of using a descriptive naming scheme, I decided to call `SetTextColor` `Routine1`, `ClrScr` `Routine2`, `DrawBox` `Routine3`, and `CreateAttr` `Routine4`, this is what I would end up with:

```
Routine1(14, 1);
Routine2;
Routine3(1, 0, 78, 24, Routine4(14, 1));
```

Such a naming convention would make code virtually incomprehensible without the inclusion of reams of comments. So please, for everyone's sake, including your own, take the time to come up with meaningful identifiers for all the routines you create.

Now let's look at the CreateAttr procedure. Until now, the TextColor and TextBkGround procedures have always been used to set the screen's colors. It happens, however, that these two routines are really just the gateway to a "byte-sized" constant in the Crt unit called TextAttr. If you use the following formula, you can store the screen's TextColors in this attribute or in any variable declared to be of type byte:

```
TextColor := ForeGround + BackGround * 16
```

After a call to this statement, any text written to the screen will appear just as if you had written the following code:

```
TextColor(ForeGround);
TextBkGround(BackGround);
```

Although using the TextAttr constant is not quite as intuitively easy to grasp as using the TextColor and TextBkGround procedures, it does have the advantage of enabling you to store the screen's colors in a single byte. Therefore, you can store the screen's original colors in a variable called SaveAttr, then restore those same colors at the end of the program. Take the time to examine this technique, because many users believe it is the programmer's duty to leave the screen colors more or less as he or she found them.

The only thing left to say about this matter is that some people have a hard time remembering the formula used to store the foreground and background colors in a single byte. To help you, I have put together the CreateAttr procedure, which "remembers" this formula for you:

```
function CreateAttr(Fg, Bg: Integer): Integer;
begin
  CreateAttr := Fg + Bg * 16;
end;
```

Now move on to the code in the ToolBox unit. This is the WriteChar routine, which is written in BASM:

```
procedure WriteChar(X, Y: Byte; Num: Integer;
                    C: Char; Attr: Byte); assembler;
asm
  { GotoXY }
  mov ah, 2h
  mov bh, 0
  mov dh, y
  mov dl, x
```

```
    int 10h

    { Write the Char }
    mov ah, 9h
    mov al, C;
    mov bh, 0
    mov bl, Attr
    mov cx, Num
    int 10h
end;
```

Unless you know assembly language, all but the header of this procedure is incomprehensible. If this is the case, don't worry. For now there is no need for you to understand the code in the procedure's body. All you have to know is that it is written in a very low-level language called assembler, which enables you to talk directly to the operating system or to the hardware.

> **NOTE:** Assembly language mavens will notice that all I'm doing here is calling interrupt 10, functions 2 and 9.

I am including this code here in part because I needed the routine to finish the ToolBox unit. More importantly, however, I wanted you to see that you can treat a routine in a unit as a black box. You might not know any more about how the WriteChar routine works than you do about how the WriteLn procedure works. But that's not important, because all you really need to do is understand the procedure's header.

The header first asks you to pass an x,y coordinate specifying where the character will be written. Then it asks you how many times you want the character to appear. The last two parameters specify the character itself and the colors to be used on-screen. Those are the keys to the kingdom as far as this procedure is concerned.

The only thing left to explain is that I use this routine instead of the Write procedure because the Write procedure always moves the cursor one place after printing a character to the screen. As a result, the whole screen is scrolled up one line when you place a character in the lower-right corner of the screen—that is, at coordinates 80,25. When drawing a box, you want to avoid this behavior because it would scroll the top lines of the box off the screen. Therefore, I created the WriteChar procedure, which I hope you will find useful.

269

Perhaps the most important new routine from the Turbo Pascal Library introduced in this program is the Window procedure, which appears in the main module. This procedure restricts the output of any native Pascal routines to a certain area of the screen. For instance, after the following command is issued, you couldn't use the WriteLn procedure to write to the upper-left corner of the screen:

```
Window(10, 7, 70, 20);
```

In other words, the Window procedure has redefined the Pascal coordinate system so that writing

```
GotoXY(1, 1);
```

would place you 10 columns in and 7 rows down. Notice, however, that the DrawBox procedure is unaffected by the Window routine. This is because the DrawBox routine calls the WriteChar procedure, which circumvents the Pascal I/O routines.

Unfortunately, there isn't enough room in this book for me to explain all the code in these two modules in depth, but there are a few more features I should point out before you move on.

The first is the presence of the Upper and CenterStr procedures, both of which are likely to prove very useful to any Turbo Pascal program. The Upper procedure takes advantage of the relationship between strings and arrays to set all the characters of a string to uppercase. The CenterStr procedure centers a string on a particular row. It uses the WindMin and WindMax constants, declared in the Crt unit, to find the size of the current window. In other words, if you use the Window routine to change the coordinate system on-screen, the CenterStr procedure takes this fact into account and still properly centers your string.

The last procedure you should be sure to examine is the Beeper procedure, which allows your computer to make a few primitive noises. The first parameter you pass to this procedure influences the pitch of the noise, and the second changes its duration.

The following program makes several of the more classic mistakes you are likely to make while calling the current incarnation of the ToolBox unit. See whether you can straighten things out:

```
Program ToolBug1;
uses
  ToolBox;

var
```

```
  S: String;
begin
  WriteChar(1, 33, 35, #12, CreateAttr(15, 2));
  CenterStr(5, S);
  Beeper(10, 600);
  DrawBox(35, 25, 10, 10, CreateAttr(0, 2));
end.
```

# Summary

So ends this lesson. Next up is a quick look at circular unit references and some of the other fancy problems that can occur when you divide programs into units.

# Review Questions

1. What is the size of the TextAttr variable? _____

2. What is the difference between the coordinate system used by WriteChar and that used by the Write procedures? If necessary, explore this issue by using both routines to write to coordinate 1,1.

   _____

3. How does the coordinate system used by WriteChar affect the DrawBox procedure? Rewrite the DrawBox procedure so that it uses the same coordinates as the routines in the Crt unit. _____

   _____

# Review Exercises

1. When you set the TextBackGround to a particular color, the screen will be cleared to that color whenever you use ClrScr. Use this knowledge to create a program that draws three boxes, one inside another, and each one having a different background color.

2. Use the DrawBox procedure to put a border around each of the three boxes you created in the previous review exercise.

21

# Going Around in Circles

*To explore circular unit references and other potential pitfalls involving units.*

Despite the fact that units are so easy to use, problems can arise if they are not handled properly. The next two lessons look at a few of these problems and explore ways to resolve them by developing powerful debugging strategies.

Before beginning, I want to spend a moment discussing the importance of thinking ahead when you are designing units. Of course, an in-depth discussion of how to go about designing a large program is much too broad a topic for this book, but still it is possible to give a few general hints to help you organize your code.

When dividing programs up into modules, be sure that your plan is logical. For instance, small database programs often perform the following functions:

1. Read and write information from a file

2. Sort the information in various ways

3. Show the information to the user

4. Get input from the user

It might be a good idea to divide such a program into four or five modules.

The first module is the main program; the rest are units, each of which is dedicated to one of the subjects listed above. Some people might, for instance, want to divide the first topic into two units, or combine the last two topics into one unit. Regardless of how these details are resolved, it is extremely important to make a plan before beginning to write code and to stick to it.

In this lesson, I describe some of the problems that arise when programmers try to use units without first thinking about what they are doing.

# Mistake Number One Involves Scoping

Every variable, procedure, function, or constant has a certain scope, or range, over which it is valid. For instance, a global variable declared at the start of a one-module program is valid through the entire breadth of the program. To make sure you understand this idea, consider the following short program:

```
program Scope1;
{

  Sample program to demonstrate the scope of a constant.
}
Uses
  ToolBoxB;

const
  TheNumber = 42;

{ Use a global copy of TheNumber }
procedure WriteNumber;
```

```
begin
  WriteLn('WriteNumber says: ', TheNumber);
end;

{ Use a local copy of TheNumber }
procedure WriteLocal;
const
  TheNumber = 412;
begin
  WriteLn('WriteLocal says: ', TheNumber);
end;

begin
  WriteNumber;
  WriteLocal;

  { Use a global copy of TheNumber }
  WriteLn('Main says: ', TheNumber);

  PressToEnd;
end.
```

The output from this program looks like this:

```
WriteNumber says: 42
WriteLocal says: 412
Main says: 42

Press ENTER to end this program.
```

Before considering the main portions of this program, notice that it references the ToolBoxB unit. The ToolBoxB unit now contains a simple routine called PressToEnd, which holds the user screen open at the end of the program's run. This procedure encapsulates the following lines, which have ended most of the programs you have looked at so far:

```
WriteLn;
WriteLn('Press ENTER to end this program.');
Readln;
```

Take a good look at the code. You never need to write it again. From now on just reference the PressToEnd routine in the ToolBox unit.

Now to more important matters. Focus your attention on the first constant declaration in the source code:

```
const
   TheNumber = 42;
```

This identifier is considered a *global constant*. It is given this name, in part, because its scope extends globally throughout the entire program.

To demonstrate this fact, the program uses the constant in both its main body and in the procedure WriteNumber. Viewing the output, you can see that these two instances of the constant do, in fact, reference the place in memory where the number 42 is stored.

The procedure WriteLocal, on the other hand, declares its own local constant, called TheNumber, and then proceeds to write this constant to the screen:

```
procedure WriteLocal;
const
   TheNumber = 412;
begin
   WriteLn('WriteLocal says: ', TheNumber);
end;
```

This time the number 412 is printed to the screen, and not the number 42. If you want, step through the program with the debugger so that you can see exactly how this works. (See Figure 21.1.)

*Figure 21.1.*
*Use breakpoints to see how scoping affects the value of an identifier.*

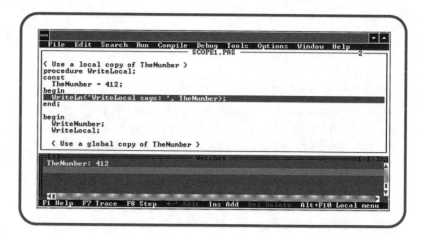

Let's discuss this situation some more, because it is absolutely essential to understand the scope of an identifier.

In two different places, this program declares a constant called TheNumber. In one place, its value is declared to be 42; in the other place, 412. The first instance of this identifier has a scope which extends throughout the entire program, and the second instance has a scope which extends only throughout the entirety of the `WriteLocal` procedure. In other words, this second declaration of the identifier takes precedence over the first declaration inside the second instance's own domain, which happens to be the `WriteLocal` procedure.

An analogy might help to clarify matters. There is the saying, "Every man's home is his castle." People pay lip service to this little cliché, but in their hearts they know that even inside the house they are supposed to obey the laws of the land. In the upside-down world of programming, however, a local variable is, indeed, king inside its limited dominion. In other words, on its own home ground, the local version of the constant in our program takes precedence over the global version of the constant, even though the global constant holds sway over a larger block of coding territory.

Consider further that these two constants have two totally different seats inside the memory theater. When this program was loaded into memory, people in one part of the theater were asked to remember the first instance of this constant, and people in another part of the theater were asked to remember the value of the second constant. This means, for all intents and purposes, that these two constants are *totally separate entities* even though they happen to share the same name.

Furthermore, the members of the audience at the memory theater remembering the value of the first constant had to keep this information in their minds throughout the entire time the program was running, but the people who remembered the local constant had to do so only while the local procedure was being executed. This will become important to you later on as you start to build large programs that push the limits of a computer's memory. The bottom line is that global variables are always taking up space in a computer's memory, whereas local variables are in memory only temporarily.

The moral here is that what happens in memory, not what is written in the source code, represents reality to a computer. In other words, the source code makes it look as though these two constants with the same name might be somehow related. But, in fact, they occupy two totally different locations inside memory, and they are treated in two totally different fashions.

In other words, even when you write programs in an elegant language like Turbo Pascal, your code is still little more than a flimsy metaphor for what is really taking place inside the computer's memory. In the long run, it is important that you learn to see through the "veil" created by the source code and into the inner workings of the computer. You can take satisfaction, too, in knowing that Pascal is probably the single most useful way that programmers have come up with for describing how to manipulate the memory inside a computer.

# Scope and Circular unit References

Most of the examples you have looked at so far involve scoping issues inside a single module. But when you bring multiple modules into the mix, scoping issues become considerably more complex.

 Consider the following program, which demonstrates a classic error:

```
program ClassErr;
uses
  UnitErr;

const
  Foo = 32;

begin
  WriteFoo;
end.
```

Here's the unit:

```
Unit UnitErr;
interface

procedure WriteFoo;
implementation

procedure WriteFoo;
begin
  WriteLn(Foo);
end;
end.
```

If you try to run the preceding program, you end up producing an `Unknown Identifier` error, as pictured in Figure 21.2.

The problem here is essentially a matter of scope. Constant `Foo` is boldly declared in the main program. You might think that it could be accessed in `UnitErr`, which is, after all, a part of program `ClassErr`. In fact, though, `UnitErr` has access to none of the variables, constants, or procedures that exist in the main module of which it eventually becomes a part. The flow of information is in the opposite direction; that is, the main module has access to any declarations made in the *interface* of its units, but the units do not have access to declarations made in the main program. Notice the emphasis on the word interface. It is important to remember that declarations made in the implementation section of a unit are not available to the main module.

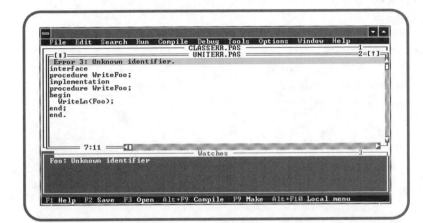

*Figure 21.2.*
*The IDE catches an error.*

By now you have had a chance to see a number of important issues involving scope, but there is still one major piece missing. A unit is permitted to include another unit in its *uses clause*. What happens, though, if a program has two units, and each one includes the other in its own uses clause?

Because the preceding sentence is not only an aesthetic monstrosity, but also a bit of a mind twister, I'll move on immediately to an example that should clarify the issue in question.

```
procedure CircBug;
uses
  CircBug1,
  CircBug2;

begin
  LetsHearFromBug1;
  LetsHearFromBug2;
end.

-------------------------------

unit CircBug1;

interface

uses
  CircBug2;
```

279

```
const
  Bug1Str = ' Hi from CircBug2 ';

procedure LetsHearFromBug1;
implementation

procedure LetsHearFromBug1;
begin
  WriteLn('Bug One says hi!');
end;
end.


- - - - - - - - - - - - - - - - - - - - - - - - - - - - - -


unit CircBug2;
interface
uses
  CircBug1;

const
  Bug2Str = ' CircBug1 says hi ';

procedure LetsHearFromBug2;
implementation

procedure LetsHearFromBug2;
begin
  WriteLn(Bug1Str);
end;
end.
```

If you try to run this program, you receive the famous `Circular unit reference` error, pictured in Figure 21.3.

This error occurs because unit `CircBug1` references unit `CircBug2` in its uses clause, and unit `CircBug2` references unit `CircBug1` in its uses clause. When the compiler tries to resolve these two references, it ends up going around and around in loop, much like a reader of the two famous sentences quoted earlier in this book:

```
The following sentence is false.
The preceding sentence is true.
```

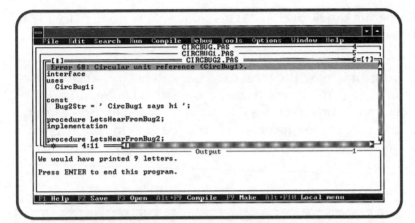

*Figure 21.3.*
*The IDE reports a*
*circular unit reference*
*error.*

As it happens, the resolution of this problem is often extremely simple. In this case, for instance, all you need do is to move the declaration of the uses clause in CircBug2 below the keyword implementation:

```
unit CircBug2;
interface

const
  Bug2Str = ' CircBug1 says hi ';

procedure LetsHearFromBug2;
implementation  { <== Implementation }
uses            { <== Uses clause    }
  CircBug1;     { <== Uses clause    }

procedure LetsHearFromBug2;
begin
  WriteLn(Bug1Str);
end;
end.
```

It is only fair to say that it isn't always so easy to resolve circular unit reference errors. There is, however, a strategy you can use that often helps you avoid this error altogether. The strategy is not entirely without drawbacks in terms of overall efficiency, but at least it is a readily accessible solution to a sticky problem, especially for beginning and intermediate programmers.

This strategy involves designating one unit as the place where all constants, types, and variables that are going to be shared by two or more

modules of a program can be declared. This unit is also a good place to put any routines likely to be used by several different modules inside your program.

In the following Finish the Program exercise, you get a chance to work with a unit containing identifiers used by several other modules. This program enables you to draw pictures like those shown in Figures 21.4 and 21.5. What these images fail to capture is that the "cursor" in our program is always in motion. In other words, the user can't stop it; rather, he or she can only change its direction.

**Figure 21.4.**
*DRAWDEF.PAS*
*sample output.*

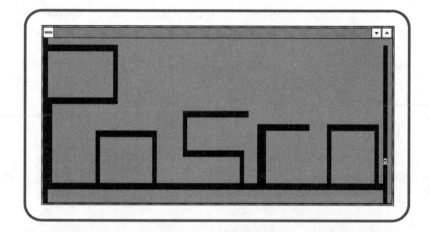

**Figure 21.5.**
*DRAWDEF.PAS*
*sample output.*

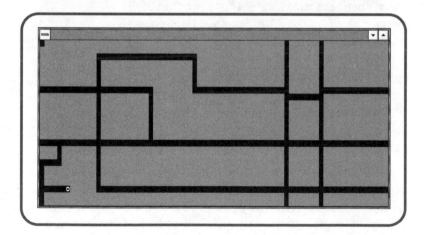

The following program contains two complete units. See if you can finish the main module which uses them:

```pascal
unit DrawDef;
{

  This unit defines the constants, etc. used
  in the Draw program
}
interface

const
  BallAttr    = 14 + 1 * 16;

  { Possible keystrokes }
  Escape      = #27;
  UpArrow     = #72;
  DownArrow   = #80;
  LeftArrow   = #75;
  RightArrow  = #77;

  { ASCII chars to draw with }
  UpChar      = #24;
  DownChar    = #25;
  RightChar   = #26;
  LeftChar    = #27;

  { Possible directions }
  Up    = 1;
  Down  = 2;
  Left  = 3;
  Right = 4;

var
  Arrow: Char;              { Holds current draw char }
  Direction : Byte;         { Holds current direction }
  Done: Boolean;            { Are we done yet?        }
  XNow, YNow: Integer;      { Current location        }
```

```
implementation
end.

. . . . . . . . . . . . . . . . . . . . . . . . . . . . . . .

unit DrawSome;
{

  This unit is part of the program Draw.
  It contains all the major routines for
  getting input and drawing to the screen.
}
interface
uses
  Crt,
  DrawDef,
  ToolBoxB;

procedure Initialize;
procedure CleanUp;
procedure Bounce;
procedure GetInput;
implementation

procedure Initialize;
begin
  CursorOff;
  TextAttr := 1 + 3 * 16;
  ClrScr;
  TextAttr := 3 + 1 * 16;
  CenterStr(1, ' Press ESCape to Exit ');
  TextAttr := 1 + 3 * 16;
  Done := False;
  XNow := 40;
  YNow := 12;
  Direction := Up;
  Arrow := UpChar;
end;
```

```
procedure CleanUp;
begin
  TextAttr := 7 + 1 * 16;
  ClrScr;
  CursorOn;
end;

{ Draw to the screen }
procedure Bounce;
begin
  WriteChar(XNow, YNow, 1, #32, BallAttr);
  Case Direction of
    Up: begin
      Dec(YNow);
      if YNow < 1 then YNow := 24;
    end;
    Down: begin
      Inc(YNow);
      if YNow > 24 then YNow := 1;
    end;
    Left: begin
      Dec(XNow);
      if XNow < 0 then XNow := 79;
    end;
    Right: begin
     Inc(XNow);
     if XNow > 79 then XNow := 0;
    end;
  end;
  WriteChar(XNow, YNow, 1, Arrow, BallAttr);
end;

{ Does the user want to go up, down, right or left? }
procedure GetInput;
var
  Ch: Char;
begin
  if KeyPressed then begin
    Ch := ReadKey;
    if Ch = Escape then Done := True;
```

```
      if Ch = #0 then begin
        Ch := ReadKey;
        case Ch of
          UpArrow: begin
            Direction := Up;
            Arrow := UpChar;
          end;
          DownArrow: begin
            Direction := Down;
            Arrow := DownChar;
          end;
          LeftArrow: begin
            Direction := Left;
            Arrow := LeftChar;
          end;
          RightArrow: begin
            Direction := Right;
            Arrow := RightChar;
          end;
        end; { case }
      end; { of Ch = 0 }
    end; { if KeyPressed }
  end;
end.


------------------------------------


program DrawFast;
{

  This study in how to use units is also
  a simple example of event-oriented programming.
  The code repeats a simple loop until the user
  sets the variable Done to TRUE. The loop continually
  checks for input from the user and then draws
  characters to the screen. After exiting the loop, the
  program calls procedure CleanUp to restore the screen
  to a normal condition.
```

```
}
uses
  Crt,
  DrawDef,
  DrawSome,
  ToolBoxB;

begin
  Initialize;        { Perform some set up }
  repeat;
```

A few things need to be said about this program.

First, you should understand that the decision to divide it up into several units is fairly arbitrary. A program this small could easily have been written in one module, or it could have been broken up in a different manner.

The system chosen does have several advantages. It divides the code up into three small, manageable modules. Each module can be grasped in a moment, and it is easy to see how the three modules fit together. All of these features make it easier to understand how the program works.

Notice the way the main block of the program is reduced to a handful of easy-to-understand commands:

```
begin
  Initialize;       { Perform some set up               }
  repeat;
    Delay(100);     { Slow things down so we can watch  }
    GetInput;       { Check for input from user         }
    Bounce;         { Draw to the screen                }
  until Done;
  CleanUp;          { Clean up the screen before exiting }
end.
```

Someone who has never seen this code before can grasp its purpose after only a few moments of study. Just imagine how this block of code would look if the contents of the GetInput procedure were inserted directly into the repeat loop. If this were the case, the program would still run the same, but the repeat loop would be so long that it would be much harder for another programmer to understand. Equally important, it would be much harder to understand if you went back to change the code a year or two down the road.

Another important point about the code in the main block of this program is that it is representative of a type of coding called *event-oriented programming*. A large portion of the code driving sophisticated programs is event oriented. This type of program gets its name because it is capable of responding to *events* that occur while it is running repeatedly through a loop. Let's examine this concept in more depth, so that you can get some feel for it.

The previous program begins by doing some initialization. Then it enters a loop, and it begins performing a particular action, which in this case happens to be drawing a line in a certain preselected direction. It continues to do this until it responds to an event, in this case, a keystroke from the user saying that it should either change directions or exit the loop.

Some people get excited about event-oriented programming because it is lively, even lifelike. In daily life, people tend to perform certain actions and respond to certain events, just as this program does. In a way, this program takes a few feeble steps toward making the computer "come alive." These are, however, only very tentative steps in a particular direction. The event-oriented paradigm does not, in and of itself, resolve any of the elusive quests for artificial, computer-simulated life.

The final things to mention here are the calls to CursorOn and CursorOff, both of which procedures have been added to the ToolBoxB unit, included here in our *uses clause*. Once again, these routines are written in BASM, so their implementation might be hard for you to understand. That isn't important right now, though, because all you need do is to call the procedures. It doesn't matter to you how, or why, they work.

The functionality offered by the easy-to-use CursorOn and CursorOff procedures is part of the whole idea of dividing code into units. The code is easy for you to access, even if you didn't write it, and even if you don't know why it works. Many professional programmers are forced to work this way at times, because the needs of their programs require them to use sophisticated routines that they buy from third-party vendors.

In all honesty, some of the world's great programmers might be inclined to object at this point and argue that you should never use any code that you do not completely understand. Admittedly, this attitude on their part has helped make them highly respected professionals. If all programmers were gifted with such brilliant minds, everyone could live by those standards. But in reality, it is necessary to make do with the familiar old rag and bone shop we call a mind. In other words, real-world programmers master the art of the possible rather than the art of the ideal.

# Summary

The plan is to continue investigating units in the next lesson. Some folks might want to take a little breather to prepare themselves to take up more or less where we left off.

# Review Questions

1. If you declare a variable inside a procedure or a function, it is a _____ variable.

2. Variables declared outside procedures and functions are _____ variables.

# Review Exercises

1. Rewrite the following unit so that the variable Time and the procedure WriteTime can be accessed by other modules that include this unit in their uses clause:

```
unit Times;
interface
uses
  Dos;

implementation

var
  Time: String;

function LeadingZero(w: Word) : String;
var
```

```
    s : String;
begin
  Str(w:0,s);
  if Length(s) = 1 then
    s := '0' + s;
  LeadingZero := s;
end;

function SetTheTime: String;
var
  h, m, s, hund : Word;
begin
  GetTime(h,m,s,hund);
  SetTheTime := 'It is now ' + LeadingZero(h) + ':' +
                LeadingZero(m) + ':' + LeadingZero(s) +
                '.' + LeadingZero(hund);
end;

procedure SetTime;
begin
  Time := SetTheTime;
end;

procedure WriteTime;
begin
  SetTime;
  WriteLn(Time);
end;
end.
```

2. Write a program that uses procedure WriteTime, as defined in the previous review exercise.

# Debugging Several Modules at One Time

*To debug modules.*

As you have seen, a price must be paid before you can enjoy the benefits of adding units to your programs. And though you may be bitter about having to pay the piper, never forget that units make it possible to break code into modules. Without that benefit, you would most likely be hopelessly mired in unresolvable debt.

To be perfectly frank, debugging a series of interrelated units can be a monumental task. Yet I believe that at heart most good programmers find

this challenge exciting. For some reason they are able to approach the whole enterprise as if it were a fantastic and pleasurable puzzle, which they feel compelled to solve.

If you feel these instincts welling up inside you at times, then perhaps you are ready to begin playing the great game. For, indeed, programming is a game. People who forget this not only make themselves miserable, but their skills usually atrophy, and their interest slowly dies away.

# Going on a Bug Hunt

Now that I've said such nice things about the process of debugging, I'm going to return to reality by plunging you into the midst of a typical hellacious debugging debacle, the kind that can be generated only by someone who has thoroughly botched the process of writing a program.

Specifically, it is time to tackle a few of the common scoping errors that occur over and over when programmers wrestle with their machines. What follows is not really so much of a Find the Bug exercise as it is an Explore the Bug exercise. The main point is to show you what a mess you can make with units if you don't organize them carefully.

As you read the next few pages of text, you are likely to become confused at times. Don't let this bother you. You are about to descend into a mire, a rat's nest, a limitless Sargasso Sea of programming frustration. In other words, I'm going to intentionally drag you into the maelstrom not only of mixed metaphors, but of the outrageous misfortune which will strike any programmer who starts to carelessly assemble modules without first thinking ahead.

To get into the right spirit for this exercise, pretend that you have progressed as a programmer far enough to get called in for advice by some friends struggling with a recalcitrant chunk of code. They want to produce a program for a group of children still learning how to count. Their goal is to write a little computerized exercise that will look like this:

```
Here's the number 5 written 5 times:
5
5
5
5
5
Add these numbers up and you can see
that five times five = 25
It is TRUE that 5 = 5
```

```
The word cat has only 3 letters.
If we wrote it out three times, like this:

Cat Cat Cat

We would have printed 9 letters.
```

Although it occurs to you that your friends may be a bit misguided, you still understand that the intent is to help children learn how to count.

After working on this project for several hours, your friends call you in for help. They have produced the following code, which is full of errors:

```
unit ScopeBug;
interface
const
  Count = 5;

function ReturnInfo: Integer;
function CheckCount: Boolean;
implementation

function ReturnInfo: Integer;
begin
  ReturnInfo := Count;
end;

function CheckCount: Boolean;
begin
  CheckCount := 5 = Count;
end;
end.


- - - - - - - - - - - - - - - - - - - - - - - - - - - - - - - - - - - - - - - -
```

And here's the main program:

```
program Scope2;
uses
  Crt,
  ScopeBug,
  ToolBoxB;
```

```pascal
const
  Count = 3;

type
  TMyArray = array[0..Count] of Byte;

var
  MyArray: TMyArray;

procedure FillArray;
var
  i: Integer;
begin
  for i := 0 to Count do
    MyArray[i] := ReturnInfo;
end;

function CheckCount: Integer;
begin
  CheckCount := Count * Count;
end;

procedure WriteInfo;
var
  i: Integer;
  Count: Integer;
begin
  Count := ReturnInfo;
  for i := 1 to Count do
    WriteLn(MyArray[i]);
end;


begin
  ClrScr;
  WriteLn('Here''s the number 5 written 5 times: ');

  FillArray;
  WriteInfo;
  WriteLn;
  WriteLn('Add these numbers up and you can see');
  WriteLn('that five times five = ', Count * Count);
```

```
      WriteLn('It is ', CheckCount,' that 5 = 5');
      WriteLn;
      WriteLn('The word cat has only ', Count, ' letters.');
      WriteLn('If we wrote it out three times like this: ');
      WriteLn;
      for i := 1 to ReturnInfo do Write('Cat  ');
      WriteLn;
      WriteLn;
      WriteLn('We would have printed ', CheckCount,' letters.');
      PressToEnd;
   end.
```

You will find both the unit ScopeBug and the program Scope2 on the disk that comes with this book. Go ahead; compile and run Scope2 once so that you can see the crazy output it produces. Then come back and read about what has gone wrong with this program.

As they now stand, these two modules produce the following absurd output:

```
Here's the number 5 written 5 times:
5
5
5
0
0

Add these numbers up and you can see
that five times five = 9
It is 9 that 5 = 5

The word cat has only 3 letters.
If we wrote it out three times like this:

Cat  Cat  Cat  Cat  Cat

We would have printed 9 letters.

Press ENTER to end this program.
```

Maybe you already spotted the errors that set this program awry, but pretend for a moment that you don't have a clue as to what has gone wrong.

When you arrive on the scene, your friends are staring morosely at this bug-ridden mess which they perhaps are beginning to suspect might be of

interest only to the most dedicated entomologists. In the midst of their frustration, though, they have done one thing right: They turned to you for help.

In situations like this, you should always nod your head sagely a few times, then quietly ask whether the compiler directives for range checking, stack checking, and strict var-strings checking are turned on. If the answer is a baffled and confused "no," then walk over to the computer and type in the following short line of code at the very top of the program:

```
{$R+,S+,V+}
```

Now, the beginning of the main module should look like this:

```
program Scope2;
{$R+,S+,V+}
uses
   Crt,
```

After stepping back for a moment to admire your handiwork, lean forward and run the program.

This time, instead of producing the same erroneous results, you see the following run-time error message:

```
Error 201: Range check error.
```

The cursor is blinking before the call to WriteLn in the WriteInfo procedure:

```
WriteLn(MyArray[i]);
```

At this point, the screen looks as it does in Figure 22.1.

*Figure 22.1.*
*The Pascal IDE as it appears immediately after a range checking error has occurred.*

```
  File  Edit  Search  Run  Compile  Debug  Tools  Options  Window  Help
[■]======================== SCOPE2.PAS ========================1=[↑]
 Error 201: Range check error.
procedure WriteInfo;
var
   i: Integer;
   Count: Integer;
begin
   Count := ReturnInfo;
   for i := 1 to Count do
      WriteLn(MyArray[i]);
end;

var
   i: Integer;
*===== 38:1 =====◄□                                                ▼
                              Watches ========================2
 Count: 3




 F1 Help  F2 Save  F3 Open  Alt+F9 Compile  F9 Make  Alt+F10 Local menu
```

In order to clarify exactly what has happened, the first thing that you should do is press F1 to pop up an online help window for this error message. Now the screen looks like it does in Figure 22.2. After studying the help window for a moment, your attention should settle on the first of the three explanations for this error:

```
The index of an array was out of range.
```

In other words, the program attempted to read beyond the end of an array.

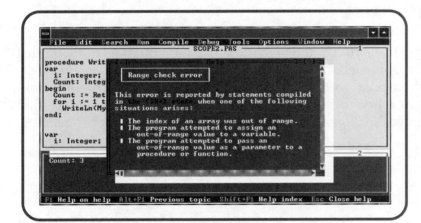

*Figure* 22.2.
*Turbo Pascal's online help detailing an error message.*

Take a moment to assess what has happened. When you first ran the program, it produced erroneous results. Then you turned on range, stack, and strict-var checking, and watched the program crash in mid-flow.

It seems as though you took a step backward. After all, before you got involved with your friends' program, it at least ran all the way to completion.

Actually, the error message you generated can help you find what is wrong with this program. Specifically, it told you that at some point during the execution of the program, the value of i in the following line of code is outside its proper range:

```
WriteLn(MyArray[i]);
```

Look at the top of the module, and you see that this array is declared to contain "Count" characters. Furthermore, you can see that "Count" is a constant with a value of 3:

```
const
  Count = 3;

type
  TMyArray = array[0..Count] of Byte;
```

297

Now take another look at the procedure where the error occurred:

```
procedure WriteInfo;
var
  i: Integer;
  Count: Integer;
begin
  Count := ReturnInfo;
  for i := 1 to Count do
    WriteLn(MyArray[i]);
end;
```

Looking at it carefully, the first thing you might notice about this procedure is that it contains another identifier called Count. At this point, warning bells should go off in your head. But before you jump to any conclusions, see whether the variable Count is set equal to the value returned by the function called ReturnInfo, which is located in the unit ScopeBug:

```
function ReturnInfo: Integer;
begin
  ReturnInfo := Count;
end;
```

Perhaps for a moment you believe that everything is fine; you can see that this function does little more than return the value of a variable `Count`. Your eyes then travel up to the beginning of the `unit` and you see the following code fragment:

```
unit ScopeBug;
interface
const
  Count = 5;
etc...
```

Wait a minute. Hadn't your friends set the value of `Count` to 3? You quickly glance back at the main module and see that they had, indeed, done so.

Suddenly a light goes on in your head. You think, "Oh my gosh, the constant `Count` has been declared twice—once in this `unit` and once in the main program. Each time it has been assigned a different value."

You point this out to your friends and they immediately blush furiously. Then all at once one of them spills the beans: "But...but that second time, here at the top of the main module, we meant for `Count` to represent the number of letters in `Cat`."

Because you are a friendly, nonjudgmental type, you nod your head and say, "Well then, you should have given that variable a different name. Maybe something like `NumLetters`."

You make this change to the source code and look through the rest of the main module, changing the identifier `Count` to `NumLetters` wherever it seems appropriate. And perhaps because you are now wise to your friends' tricks, you notice that they also declared two functions called `CheckCount`—one in the main module, and one in the `unit`.

After cleaning up the mess, you produce a main module that looks like this:

```
program Scope3;
uses
  Crt,
  ScopeBug,
  ToolBoxB;

const
  NumLetters = 3;

type
  TMyArray = array[0..Count] of Byte;

var
  MyArray: TMyArray;

procedure FillArray;
var
  i: Integer;
begin
  for i := 0 to Count do
    MyArray[i] := ReturnInfo;
end;

function ThreeCats: Integer;
begin
  ThreeCats := NumLetters * NumLetters;
end;

procedure WriteInfo;
var
  i: Integer;
```

```
    Count: Integer;
begin
  Count := ReturnInfo;
  for i := 1 to Count do
    WriteLn(MyArray[i]);
end;


var
  i: Integer;
begin
  ClrScr;
  WriteLn('Here''s the number 5 written 5 times: ');

  FillArray;
  WriteInfo;
  WriteLn;
  WriteLn('Add these numbers up and you can see');
  WriteLn('that five times five = ', Count * Count);
  WriteLn('It is ', CheckCount(Count),' that 5 = 5');
  WriteLn;
  WriteLn('The word cat has only ', NumLetters,' letters.');
  WriteLn('If we wrote it out three times like this: ');
  WriteLn;
  for i := 1 to NumLetters do Write('Cat  ');
  WriteLn;
  WriteLn;
  WriteLn('We would have printed ', ThreeCats, ' letters.');
  PressToEnd;
end.
```

You run this code and find that the program, at last, produces the correct results. Your friends all but fall over themselves thanking you for your help. Once again you nod sagely, and perhaps even smile benignly, although inside you have doubts about their futures in the programming world.

At any rate, after seeing the mess they made of their program, you know enough to be doubly careful never to fall into any of the traps that held them prisoners.

# Sailing Around the Sargasso Sea

Well, that's probably enough of my little programmer's morality tale. It is now time to assess three important lessons to learn from the previous tale.

The first lesson is to use range checking and other compiler directives to help you track down errors. These are very useful tools, which should be hauled out of your well-tended bag of tricks any time you are baffled by a seemingly inexplicable bug.

The previous tale includes an introduction to range checking errors; it is probably only fair to mention something about stack checking. As explained earlier, global variables are in memory throughout the entire run of a program, while local variables are in memory only for a limited period of time. When they are accessed, these local variables are placed in an area of memory called the stack segment. If you try to put too many local variables in memory at one time, you run out of stack space. Unfortunately, this disastrous error can occur without you being aware that anything is amiss. However, if you turn on stack checking, you are always alerted the moment this error occurs.

Of course, these compiler directives don't always help you find your errors. In fact, many times they don't do you any good at all. Even so, it takes only a moment to implement them, and on some occasions they can save you hours of work.

Many experienced programmers leave these directives turned on during the entire development cycle of their programs. They switch them off only when they are finally done working on their code. They always take this last step because stack checking and range checking tend to slow down the execution of their programs.

The second lesson to glean from my morality tale is to be careful to not give the same name to any two procedures or variables in a program. This mistake is easy to make when you are working with multiple modules, which is why so much emphasis is placed on this error. One of the best ways to avoid falling into this trap is to create very descriptive names for each of your identifiers.

This leads us to the third and last, but by no means least, lesson to learn: Don't ever use glib identifiers like Count as global constants or variables.

The word Count is much too abstract and non-specific. As a result, your poor friends ended up using the word three times—once as a global identifier in their unit; a second time as a global identifier in their main module; and a third time as a local variable in the procedure WriteInfo.

The lengthy debugging session boils down to one simple problem: Nothing worked right because the identifier Count had one value in the main module and another in the unit. If your friends had chosen a more descriptive word, this error might have been avoided.

In truth, I'm narrowing the focus a bit too much by zeroing in specifically on the identifier Count. The lesson to be learned here is really a bit broader than I have suggested so far; it applies to a slew of commonly used identifiers that, by their very nature, should always be local rather than global variables. They are identifiers like S or S1, which I often use when declaring local string variables. Other potential culprits include i, j, X, and Y, all of which are frequently used as local integer variables.

The rule here is simple: Don't ever use any of these identifiers as global variables or constants. There is simply too much chance that they might be declared multiple times, and the implications are serious, indeed. After all, the previous program contains only a few lines of code, and range checking helped uncover the error. However, if you are dealing with a program of ten thousand or more lines, and if by chance no range or stack checking errors occurred, then it could take you days, even weeks, to uncover such an error. Short debugging sessions can sometimes be fun, but nobody wants to get bogged down in a four-day-long debugging session.

 Careful, this one can hose memory bad enough to lock up your system!

```
program FromA2B;
var
  MyArray: array[1..10] of Byte;
  i: Integer;

begin
  for i := 1 to 15 do
    MyArray[i] := i;
end.
```

# Summary

This is the end of what was admittedly a somewhat experimental lesson. I hope, however, it has taught you a few useful debugging techniques and has also showed you some of things that can go wrong if you don't plan ahead when creating units.

# Review Questions

1. When you add compiler directives to your code, they always begin with a curly brace and the _____ symbol.

2. Compiler errors occur when you are trying to compile your program, but _____ errors occur while your program is executing.

3. The stack is an area in memory where _____ variables are placed when a procedure is executed.

# Review Exercises

1. The following line of code will write out the amount of available stack space in a program:

```
WriteLn(Sptr);
```

Add that line three times to the following program so that you can see how much stack space exists when the program begins, when procedure UseStack is executing, and when the program ends:

```
program BigStack;

const
  MaxSize = 10000

type
  TStackAry = array[1..MaxSize] of Byte;

procedure UseStack(StackAry: TStackAry);
var
  i : Integer;
begin
  for i := 1 to MaxSize do
    StackAry[i] := i;
end;

var
  StackAry: TStackAry;
begin
  UseStack(StackAry);
end.
```

2. Sptr is a global variable declared in the System unit. Modify the previous program so that it "remembers" the value of Sptr when the program begins and when procedure UseStack is executed. Just before it ends, have this program write out the difference between these two values.

3. Turn stack checking on for program BigStack, and then set MaxSize = 20000. Run the program.

# urbo Pascal
# CLASSROOM 7

# Sets and
# Enumerated
# Types

# Notes

# Playing a Role

 *To introduce enumerated types and typecasting.*

The main subject of this lesson is *enumerated types,* a useful and fairly straightforward topic. I should probably add that it is not a subject of earth-shaking importance, at least not when compared to most of the other topics discussed so far. This lesson also introduces typecasting, a topic important when discussing pointers and objects.

Pascal, as I have already mentioned, is a strongly typed language. This means that the compiler is very strict about ensuring that you don't confuse one type for another. Most of the time, this is a very useful feature, but you might on occasion prefer to go beyond these restrictions. In those cases, typecasting is the ticket to freedom.

## A Simple Example

Let's get started by discussing enumerated types, which you can think of as a shorthand way to avoid writing a few extra lines of code.

```
program FakeEnum;

uses
  ToolBoxB;

const
  Little = 0;
  Medium = 1;
  Big    = 2;

var
  Size: Byte;
begin
  WriteLn('In your opinion, is your home town: ');
  WriteLn('1) Little');
  WriteLn('2) Medium');
  WriteLn('3) Big');
  Write('Answer by entering a number between 1 and 3: ');
  ReadLn(Size);

  Dec(Size);
  WriteLn;

  case Size of
    Little: WriteLn('Small towns are best.');
    Medium: WriteLn('Let''s hear it for medium towns!');
    Big: WriteLn('Ah, a sophisticated big city type.');
    else
        WriteLn('Answer out of range');
  end;

  PressToEnd;
end.
```

This extremely simple program shows how to associate words with a series of numeric values. Specifically, the word Little is associated with 0, Medium with 1, and Big with 2. As a result, you can write extremely clear and easy-to-understand code like the code in the case statement in the preceding program.

A rewriting of this program shows that enumerated types are a short-hand way of associating words with a series of numeric values. Enumerated types also allow you to use Pascal's strong type-checking abilities to ensure that you are writing valid, bug-free code.

Consider this rewrite of the FakeEnum program:

```
program RealEnum;
{

 An introduction of Enumerated types.
}
uses
  ToolBoxB;

type
  TSize = (Little, Medium, Big); { Declare enumerated type }

var
  Size: TSize;

begin
  WriteLn('In your opinion, is your home town: ');
  WriteLn('1) Little');
  WriteLn('2) Medium');
  WriteLn('3) Big');
  WriteLn;
  Write('Answer by entering a number between 1 and 3: ');
  ReadLn(Byte(Size));  { Type cast enumerated type }

  Dec(Size);
  WriteLn;

  Case Size of
    Little: WriteLn('Small towns are best.');
    Medium: WriteLn('Let''s hear it for medium towns!');
    Big: WriteLn('Ah, a sophisticated big city type.');
    else
      WriteLn('Answer out of range');
  end;
  PressToEnd;
end.
```

Figure 23.1 shows sample output from this program.

*Figure 23.1.*
*Sample output from the*
*RealEnum program.*

```
In your opinion, is your home town:
1> Little
2> Medium
3> Big

Answer by entering a number between 1 and 3: 1

Small towns are best.

Press ENTER to end this program.
```

The key to understanding this program is in the declaration of the enumerated type in the data section:

```
type
  TSize = (Little, Medium, Big);
var
  Size: TSize;
```

To understand enumerated types, all you need to do is see the parallel between this data section and the data section in the FakeEnum program:

```
const
  Little = 0;
  Medium = 1;
  Big    = 2;

var
  Size: Byte;
```

For most practical purposes, these two data sections are identical, except that one is a little shorter than the other. In other words, in the declaration of TSize, the byte-sized identifier Little is associated with the number 0, Medium with 1, and Big with 2.

This same pattern is followed whenever you declare an enumerated type. In the following example, the first entry is associated with the value 0, the second with 1, the third with 2, and so forth:

```
TBooks = (BookOne, BookTwo, BookThree);
```

Of course one of the main purposes of enumerated types is to allow the use of a mnemonically useful identifier like BookOne or Little, rather than a relatively meaningless numeric value like 0 or 1. Nevertheless, don't forget that enumerated types are really only cardinal numbers ranging from 0 upward to 255, the largest size a byte can hold.

This means that, in the variable section, Size is declared to be a byte-sized variable. Remember that enumerated types are always of size Byte, which means they can never contain more than 255 elements. When you think about trying to declare an enumerated type of, say, 20,000 elements, then you can understand why this size restriction is reasonable.

Some versions of Pascal enable you to use the Write or WriteLn procedure to write to the screen the identifiers associated with the elements of an enumerated set. This same action generates a compiler error if you try to do it using Turbo Pascal.

Can you find two bugs in the following program?

```
program WriteEnum;
uses
  Crt;

type
  TColors = (Red, White, Blue);

var
  Colors: TColors;

begin
  ClrScr;
  Colors := Blue;
  WriteLn(Colors);
  Colors := Green;
  if Colors = Green then
    WriteLn('The Color is green');
end.
```

# Trying a Little Typecasting

I hope that the concepts behind enumerated types are beginning to make sense to you, and that you understand the parallels between enumerated types and variables of type byte.

However, there is one issue that I have skirted over, namely, that enumerated types cannot always be treated the same way as you treat

variables of type byte. This is why you must perform a typecast in the following line from program `RealEnum`:

```
ReadLn(Byte(Size));
```

Typecasting is not really a complicated subject once you understand the few simple principles involved. As usual, the best way to help you understand these principles is to give you a few short examples.

For instance, the compiler lets you do this:

```
var
  i: Byte;
begin
  ReadLn(i);
end.
```

but it rejects this:

```
type
  TSimple = (Round, Square);

var
  Simple:  TSimple;

begin
  ReadLn(Simple);
end.
```

Specifically, this second example produces `Error 64: Cannot Read or Write variables of this Type`, as Figure 23.2 shows.

*Figure 23.2.*
*Turbo Pascal reporting an error and providing help on that error.*

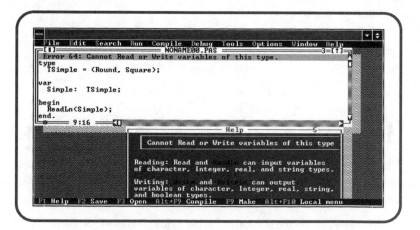

312

NOTE: It's usually simpler to remember errors by name, rather than by number. When you do reference an error by number, be sure to distinguish compiler errors from run-time errors. The former occur while you are compiling your code; the latter occur while your program is running. Their ranges, however, overlap in several cases. This means that there are, for instance, two entries for error 3. The first entry, Unknown Identifier, is a compiler error. The second entry, File Not Found, is a run-time error.

In the last example, Pascal's strict type checking ended up saddling us with error 64. You can see by reading the help screen in Figure 23.2 that the ReadLn procedure is designed to work only with characters, real numbers, integers, or strings. The ReadLn procedure can't work with an enumerated type.

To get around this limitation, you need only to typecast the enumerated type variable:

```
ReadLn(Byte(Simple));
```

This syntax tells the compiler the following story:

*Ok, I know that type Simple is an enumerated type and I know that ReadLn can only read variables that are characters, real numbers, integers, or strings. In this particular case, though, I happen to know that everything will be fine if you, the compiler, let variable Simple pretend that it is of type byte. I know that this is not the way things are usually done, but I promise everything will be fine if you just go along with this little fiction.*

The compiler, being the cooperative and friendly type that it is, allows programmers to get away with this approach. Remember, of course, that the person doing the coding is always responsibile whenever he or she typecasts a variable. Do so only if you are sure you know the implications of your action.

If you are still trying to get a handle on typecasting, perhaps it will be useful to indulge in the somewhat obvious analogy between a programmer's typecast and what takes place in film or onstage. Some actors and actresses are always, or at least often, cast to type. For instance, the perennially entertaining Peter Lorre was born to play sinister villains in spy and horror

313

films. When you watch movies from the Thirties, Forties, and Fifties, again and again you find him cast to type. Similarly, in your program, the variable Simple is, in a sense, born to play a variable of type byte, so you can typecast it in that role. (Take this analogy with a grain of salt. It is not a perfect fit, but it should serve its main purpose, which is to help you remember and understand what it means to typecast a variable.)

Return for one last look at the moment when the variable Size is typecast in the RealEnum program:

```
ReadLn(Byte(Size));
```

The issue here is that Size is an enumerated type. Therefore, you cannot read or write it. But underneath a rather shallow veneer, Size is really nothing more than a Byte in sheep's clothing, so to speak. As a result, it is safe to typecast it simply by surrounding it with parentheses and preceding it with the name of a reasonably compatible type.

Try this quick Find the Bug example so that you can see what kind of troubles arise when you are careless with typecasts.

```
program CastErr;

type
  TCountry = (America, Japan, Germany);

var
  i: Byte;
  Country: TCountry;

begin
  i := 15;
  Country := TCountry(i);
  case Country of
    America: WriteLn('America');
    Japan: WriteLn('Japan');
    Germany: WriteLn('Germany');
  end;
end.
```

# Enumerated Types in the Real World

Though I have waited until this late date to discuss enumerated types in depth, you have actually been using one since the earliest lessons. The Boolean type has, in effect, the following declaration:

```
type
  Boolean = (False, True);
```

This means that Booleans are really only a form of enumerated type. Therefore, much of the syntax associated with them can be used with any enumerated type. It also means that the Boolean expression FALSE is associated with the number 0, and TRUE is associated with the number 1.

Consider the following program:

```
program PolySci;

uses
  Crt,
  ToolBoxB;

type
  TSex = (Male, Female);

{ Write out the users sex. }
procedure ReportSex(Sex: TSex);
begin
  WriteLn;
  Write('You stated that you are ');
  if sex = Male then WriteLn('Male.');
  if sex = Female then WriteLn('Female.');
end;


{ Find out the user's sex. }
var
  Sex: TSex;
  Num: Byte;
begin
  ClrScr;
  repeat
    Write('Enter 1 if you are female, 2 if you are male: ');
```

```
    ReadLn(Num);
  until (Num = 1) or (Num = 2);
  Dec(Num);
  if Num = 1 then
    Sex := Male
  else
    Sex := Female;

  ReportSex(Sex);

  PressToEnd;
end.
```

This example is presented primarily so you can see how useful enumerated types can be when you are trying to create clear, easy-to-understand code. Statements such as:

```
if Sex = Male then WriteLn('Male');
```

are far easier to understand than some of the alternatives, such as:

```
if Sex = 1 then WriteLn('Male');
```

To make sure that you really understand the issues discussed in this lesson, try another Find the Bug exercise on typecasting.

The following program has two bugs in it.

```
program EnumBug;

type
  TComputer = (An8086, A286, A386, A486, P5);

var
  Computer: TComputer;
  Num: Byte;
begin
  Computer := A486;
  WriteLn('What type of computer do you have: ');
  WriteLn('1) An XT');
  WriteLn('2) A 286');
  WriteLn('3) A 386');
  WriteLn('4) A 486');
  WriteLn('5) A P5');
  ReadLn(Num);
  if Computer = Num then
    WriteLn('You have a fast computer.');
end.
```

# Summary

After an introduction to enumerated types, you are now ready to move on to the next lesson, where you study sets. Because the two subjects are so closely related, the next lesson picks up the discussion begun here.

# Review Questions

1. If you want to write the number associated with an enumerated type to the screen, you should typecast it as being of type_____.

2. In the following declaration, what number is associated with the word Cats?_____

   ```
   TRain = (Cats, dogs);
   ```

# Review Exercises

1. Suppose that you are writing a program for an ideal college campus that has only three buildings: a library, a dormitory, and a gym. Declare an enumerated type that would allow you to write statements like:

   ```
   if building = Gym then Result = 2;
   ```

2. Use your declaration in a short program that accepts a single parameter. If the user passes in 0, have your program write out the word library. If the user passes in 1, have your program write out dormitory. And if the user passes in 2, have your program write out gym.

# Arranging the World into Sets

*To introduce sets and set logic.*

This lesson on sets is the last of the introductory lessons. After this material, you move on to study intermediate-level issues such as longer programs, pointers, and objects.

Like enumerated types, a closely related topic, sets are not one of the most important syntactic elements in the Pascal language. Nevertheless, they are interesting, and they can prove to be extremely useful when you encounter a need for them. Most people need them only occasionally, but, of course, students of logic are likely to find this aspect of the language extremely useful.

## Learning about Sets

Every student who has taken introductory math courses has been introduced to sets. These logical entities are used to arrange groups of related

concepts under a single aegis. For instance, you might talk about the set of all American states. The set includes, among others, Alabama and New Hampshire, but it does not include Transylvania.

You might talk also about the set of all letters. From the elements of that set, you can produce the set of all the vowels and the set of all the consonants. After doing this, you can test whether the set of vowels is a subset of the set of letters, or whether vowels and consonants have any letters in common.

Pascal enables you to work with sets, provided that your sets are expressed as ordinal values with fewer than 256 members. It is also important that the base type for this set have a range between 0 and 255. The following rather long program introduces most of the major features of sets. Don't let its length intimidate you. Sets are not hard to understand, and they can be explained in one easy-to-understand program.

```pascal
program SetIntro;
{

  An exploration of the basic principles of Sets, such
  as testing for inclusion, as well as an examination of
  the union, difference and intersection of two sets.
}
uses
  Crt,
  ToolBoxB;
const
  Letters: set of Char = ['A'..'Z', 'a'..'z'];
  SmallLetters: set of Char = ['a'..'z'];
  Numbers: set of Char = ['0'..'9'];

type
  TAllChars = set of Char;
  TSomeLetters = set of 'a'..'z';

{ Show how to check whether a Char is in a set.
  The set Letters contains all 26 letters.}
procedure IntroToSets;
var
  Result: Boolean;
begin
  Result := 'a' in Letters;
  WriteLn('It is ', Result, ' that ''a'' is in Letters,');
```

```
    Result := '1' in Letters;
    WriteLn('but ', Result, ' that ''1'' is in Letters');
end;


{ Show that if we declare a set in the type section, we
  are only defining its limits, the set itself is empty }
procedure ASetType(var SomeLetters: TSomeLetters);
var
  Result: Boolean;
begin
  WriteLn;
  Result := 'a' in SomeLetters;
  WriteLn('It is ', Result,
          ' that ''a'' is in SomeLetters.');
  SomeLetters := ['a','Q','r'];
  WriteLn('Set SomeLetters equal to [''a'',''Q'',''r'']');
  Result := 'a' in SomeLetters;
  WriteLn('Now it is ', Result,
          ' that ''a'' is in SomeLetters.');
  Result := 'Q' in SomeLetters;
  WriteLn('Now it is ', Result,
          ' that ''Q'' is in SomeLetters.');
end;


{ Explore the intersection of two sets. Remember
  SomeLetters is equal to ['a','Q','r'] after
  call to ASetType }
procedure Intersection(SomeLetters: TSomeLetters);
var
  Result: Boolean;
  AllChars: TAllChars;
begin
  WriteLn;
  AllChars := SomeLetters * SmallLetters;
  WriteLn('We have set AllChars equal to the ');
  WriteLn('intersection of SomeLetters and SmallLetters.');
  Result := 'a' in AllChars;
  WriteLn('It is ', Result, ' that ''a'' is in AllChars.');
  Result := 'v' in AllChars;
  WriteLn('It is ', Result, ' that ''v'' is in AllChars.');
end;
```

```pascal
{ An empty set that can contain all chars is set equal
  to the difference between letters and SmallLetters }
procedure Difference;
var
  Result: Boolean;
  AllChars: TAllChars;
begin
  WriteLn;
  Result := 'a' in AllChars;
  WriteLn('It is ', Result, ' that ''a'' is in AllChars.');
  AllChars := Letters - SmallLetters;
  WriteLn('We have set AllChars equal to the set left ');
  WriteLn('when we subtract SmallLetters from Letters.');
  Result := 'a' in AllChars;
  WriteLn('Now it is ', Result, '
           that ''a'' is in AllChars,');
  Result := 'A' in AllChars;
  WriteLn('but ', Result ,' that ''A'' is in AllChars.');
end;


{ Show what is in the Union of SmallLetters and Numbers }
procedure Union;
var
  Result: Boolean;
begin
  WriteLn;
  Result := '1' in SmallLetters;
  WriteLn('It is ', Result, ' that ''1'' is
           in SmallLetters.');
  SmallLetters := SmallLetters + Numbers;
  WriteLn('We have set SmallLetters equal to the ');
  WriteLn('union of Numbers and SmallLetters.');
  Result := '1' in SmallLetters;
  WriteLn('Now it is ', Result, '
           that ''1'' is in SmallLetters.');
end;


var
  SomeLetters: TSomeLetters;
begin
  ClrScr;
```

```
  IntroToSets;
  ASetType(SomeLetters);
  Intersection(SomeLetters);
  Difference;
  Union;

  PressToEnd;
end.
```

This program shows the major traits associated with Pascal sets. Figure 24.1 shows the output from this program.

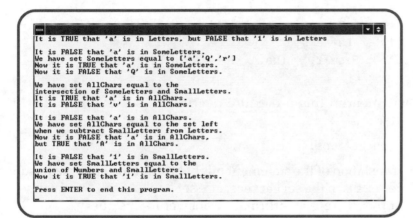

```
It is TRUE that 'a' is in Letters, but FALSE that '1' is in Letters

It is FALSE that 'a' is in SomeLetters.
We have set SomeLetters equal to ['a','Q','r']
Now it is TRUE that 'a' is in SomeLetters.
Now it is FALSE that 'Q' is in SomeLetters.

We have set AllChars equal to the
intersection of SomeLetters and SmallLetters.
It is TRUE that 'a' is in AllChars.
It is FALSE that 'v' is in AllChars.

It is FALSE that 'a' is in AllChars.
We have set AllChars equal to the set left
when we subtract SmallLetters from Letters.
Now it is FALSE that 'a' is in AllChars,
but TRUE that 'A' is in AllChars.

It is FALSE that '1' is in SmallLetters.
We have set SmallLetters equal to the
union of Numbers and SmallLetters.
Now it is TRUE that '1' is in SmallLetters.

Press ENTER to end this program.
```

*Figure 24.1.*
*The output from*
SETINTRO.PAS.

To begin an examination of this program, focus on the declarations at the top of the code:

```
const
  Letters: set of Char = ['A'..'Z', 'a'..'z'];
  SmallLetters: set of Char = ['a'..'z'];
  Numbers: set of Char = ['0'..'9'];

type
  TAllChars = set of Char;
  TSomeLetters = set of 'a'..'z';
```

First, declare Letters to be a set of Char that contains all the letters of the alphabet, both their capital and lowercase forms. Pascal provides a short-hand method to use sets of contiguous ordinal values such as chars. This shorthand frees you from having to laboriously write out each element of a set of sequential values. For instance, instead of writing:

323

```
FiveLetters: set of Char = ['A','B','C','D','E']
```

you can write this:

```
FiveLetters: set of Char = ['A'..'E']
```

To return to the study of the declarations in our example program, we can take a look at the procedure `IntroToSets`:

```
procedure IntroToSets;
var
  Result: Boolean;
begin
  Result := 'a' in Letters;
  WriteLn('It is ', Result, ' that ''a'' is in Letters,');
  Result := '1' in Letters;
  WriteLn('but ', Result, ' that ''1'' is in Letters');
end;
```

The first statement in this procedure queries the set as to whether it contains the letter a:

```
Result := 'a' in Letters;
```

A more literal translation of the statement might be: "Set the variable Result to TRUE if the letter a is in the set `Letters`, else set it to FALSE." You can see from the output that there is an affirmative answer to this query.

The next step in the program is to ask if the number 1 is in the set:

```
Result := '1' in Letters;
```

Because 1 is a number rather than a letter, you end up with a negative result.

All this is interesting, but not entirely unexpected. A more unusual result is obtained in the second procedure, when there is a query about the contents of `TSomeLetters`, which is declared as follows:

```
TSomeLetters = set of 'a'..'z';
```

After just a glance at this declaration, you might suppose that a query like the following would be answered in the affirmative:

```
Result := 'a' in SomeLetters;
```

But as the output of the program shows, it turns out that the letter a is not automatically included in the set. This is because a type declaration like the one shown above simply limits the valid entries in the set, rather than actually initializing them to any particular values. In other words, it states that this set can contain any of the small letters of the alphabet, and that it cannot, for instance, contain any numbers.

When it comes time to state which members will actually be part of the set, the following syntax is used:

```
SomeLetters := ['a','Q','r'];
```

After this assignment, the next step is to query the set again to find out whether a is a member. This time, as expected, there is an affirmative answer.

Although this code compiles cleanly and runs without error, it may surprise you to find out that Q is not a member of the set. As stated before, the reason for this is that the set is declared to contain only small letters:

```
'TSomeLetters = set of 'a'..'z';
```

As a result of this declaration, Q can never become a member of the set, even though an attempt to include it generated no errors.

The next three procedures in the program allow an exploration of the *union, difference,* and *intersection* of some of the declared sets. Table 24.1 summarizes the operators and the operations that can be performed on sets.

**Table 24.1. Operators and operations that can be performed on sets.**

| Operator | Operation |
| --- | --- |
| + | Union |
| - | Difference |
| * | Intersection |

Because you probably won't use these operators very often, you might want to remember that there are example programs in this book showing how to use them. There is also help on this subject in both the Language Guide that came with your copy of Turbo Pascal and in the online help, as shown in Figure 24.2.

The output from this program shows that the intersection of SomeLetters and SmallLetters contains the letter a but not the letter v. To make sense of this, remember that at the start of this procedure, SomeLetters contained only a and r. As a result, it is only logical that the intersection of this set and the set containing all small letters should consist of only the letters a and r.

The next procedure goes in the opposite direction when it shows you the set that is left after finding the difference between the set SmallLetters and the set Letters. Because both of these sets contain all the small letters, the difference between them is the set of capital letters. Therefore, the tests show that the resulting set contains the letter A but not the letter a.

*Figure 24.2.*
*One of several online help screens available to you if you need a quick reference on how to use sets.*

```
┌─────────────────────────────────────────────────────────────┐
│ ▼ ╪ │
│  File  Edit  Search  Run  Compile  Debug  Tools  Options  Window  Help │
│ ═[ ]════════════════════════ Help ═══════════════════?═[ ]═╗ │
│   set (reserved word)                                       ▲ │
│                                                            ▒ │
│   Syntax:                                                  ▒ │
│     set of type                                           ▒ │
│   Remarks:                                                ▒ │
│   The base type of a set must be an ordinal type with no more than 256 │
│   possible values.                                       ▒ │
│                                                          ▒ │
│   The ordinal values of the upper and lower bounds of the base type must be │
│   between 0 and 255.                                     ▒ │
│                                                         ▒ │
│   A set constructor, which denotes a set-type value, is formed by writing │
│   expressions within brackets. Each expression denotes a value of the set. │
│                                                        ▒ │
│   The notation [ ] denotes the empty set, which is compatible with all set │
│   types.                                               ▒ │
│                                                        ▒ │
│   Example:                                             ▼ │
│   { Set types }                                        ▼ │
│ ═◄════════════════════════════════════════════════════►═ │
│ F1 Help on help  Alt+F1 Previous topic  Shift+F1 Help index  Esc Close help │
└─────────────────────────────────────────────────────────────┘
```

The last example shows the union of the set SmallLetters and the set Numbers:

```
SmallLetters := SmallLetters + Numbers;
```

After this operation is performed, the tests show that the number 1 is a member of the set SmallLetters.

It is worth noting here that you can add a number to the set SmallLetters, even though no numbers were explicitly included in the original declaration:

```
SmallLetters: set of Char = ['a'..'z'];
```

In contrast, you are unable to add the letter Q to the set of type TSomeLetters:

```
TSomeLetters = set of 'a'..'z';
```

The difference is that the program explicitly says that SmallLetters can contain the set of all ASCII characters, but the range of TSomeLetters is intentionally narrow. One last point: If SmallLetters had been declared as

```
SmallLetters = ['a'..'z'];
```

then you would have received a compiler error when you tried to compile the following line of code:

```
SmallLetters := SmallLetters + Numbers;
```

# Sets Not of Type Char

So far all the sets presented in this text have been of type Char, or of some subset of that type. You can also define sets of other simple types. For instance, this program defines the set of all Intel CPU chips:

```
program SimpSet;
type
   TChips = (An8088, A286, A386, A486, AP5);
   TChipSet = set of TChips;

var
  SamsChips: TChipSet;
  JoesChips: TChipSet;
  BobsChips: TChipSet;
begin
  SamsChips := [A486];
  JoesChips := [A286, A386];
  BobsChips := [An8088, A486];

  { Check the intersection of SamsChips and JoesChips
    to see that they are not the empty set }
  if SamsChips * JoesChips <> [] then
    WriteLn('Joe and Sam have chips in common.');

  { Check the intersection of SamsChips and BobsChips
    to see that they are not the empty set }
  if SamsChips * BobsChips <> [] then
    WriteLn('Bob and Sam have chips in common.');
end.
```

**NOTE:** Notice that when I declare this enumerated type I don't write `TChips = (8088, 286, 386, 486, P5)`. The declaration can't be made this way because identifiers can never start with a number, such as the 2 in 286 or the 4 in 486. Instead, construct identifiers that start with a letter, such as A286 and A386.

The output from this program looks like this:

```
Bob and Sam have chips in common
```

The rules here are exactly the same as the rules you followed when working with sets of `Char`. This program declares a set that contains fewer than 256 ordinal members, specifically a set of `TChips`, where `TChips` is an enumerated type listing five different CPUs.

Then it declares three variables of this type of set:

```
var
   SamsChips: TChipSet;
   JoesChips: TChipSet;
   BobsChips: TChipSet;
```

When I was making up this example, I imagined that these variables might represent three friends. I then decided that it might be interesting if each of these individuals were die-hard propeller heads who were the proud owners of at least one computer. In the first few lines of this program, I assign a few computers to each of these friends.

To check which of these friends have the same type of computer, perform the actions specified in this program; that is, see whether the intersection of two sets of computers is an empty set, represented by two opposing brackets:

```
[ ]
```

If the intersection produces the null set, then you know that neither of the two friends being compared has the same computer.

I feel obliged to add that I have not found this particular capability of the Turbo Pascal compiler to be particularly useful. To be perfectly honest, I'm not sure that I've ever found a practical use for it. I do use sets of Char fairly often, however, particularly when I'm checking the exit conditions of a repeat until loop:

```
repeat
   Ch := ReadKey;
until Ch in ['Y','y','N','n'];
```

# Working with Sets and Enumerated Types

After this introduction to sets, the only thing left is to practice working with them. This Finish the Program example gives you a chance to invent a way to write the actual members of a set to the screen.

```
program SetStuff;
uses
   Crt,
   ToolBoxB;
```

```
type
  Things = (Apples, Oranges, Tables, Chairs, Cars, Peaches,
            Grapes, Hats);
  ThingSet = Set of Things;

const
  Fruit:ThingSet = [Apples, Oranges, Peaches, Grapes];
  Inanimate:ThingSet = [Tables, Chairs, Cars, Hats];
  SamsThings:ThingSet = [Tables, Peaches, Cars];


procedure WriteAnswer(Answers: ThingSet; S: String);
begin
  WriteLn;
  Write(S, ': ');
  SetTextColor(Yellow, Blue);
```

_____

_____

_____

_____

_____

_____

_____

_____

_____

_____

_____

_____

_____

_____

_____

_____

```
  WriteLn;
  SetTextColor(LightGray, Blue);
end;

procedure DrawLine;
```

```
begin
  WriteLn;
  WriteLn('------------------------------------------');
  WriteLn;
end;

var
  Answers: ThingSet;
begin
  SetTextColor(Yellow, Blue);
  ClrScr;
  CenterStr(1, 'Program Write Set');
  WriteLn; WriteLn;
  SetTextColor(LightGray, Blue);
  Write('This program works with these two sets: ');
  WriteLn;
  WriteAnswer(SamsThings, 'Sam''s Things');
  WriteAnswer(Inanimate, 'Inanimate Things');

  DrawLine;
  WriteLn('It shows three different relationships');
  WriteLn('between these two sets:');

  Answers := Inanimate - SamsThings;
  WriteAnswer(Answers, 'Difference');

  Answers := Inanimate + SamsThings;
  WriteAnswer(Answers, 'Union');

  Answers := Inanimate * SamsThings;
  WriteAnswer(Answers, 'Intersection');

  DrawLine;
  PressToEnd;
end.
```

# Summary: A Simple Deck

Congratulations! You have reached the end of the sections of this book that introduce the Pascal language. From here on, most of the issues this book deals with are on the intermediate or advanced level.

From now on, most of the code presented in this book will become increasingly complex. But please don't feel that you have outgrown the first two sections of this book. On the contrary, good programmers study the basics as often as they can, or whenever they feel the need to look something up.

The big point here is that you have now covered most of the fundamental aspects of the Pascal language. You are now ready to produce some truly useful programs.

To celebrate your accomplishment, I present you with one fairly straightforward way of using Pascal to represent a deck of cards. If you want, you can build on this foundation to create an actual card game.

```pascal
program SetCards;

uses
  Crt;

type
  TSuits = (Clubs, Spades, Diamonds, Hearts);
  TNums = (Ace, Two, Three, Four, Five, Six, Seven,
          Eight, Nine, Ten, Jack, Queen, King);


  TCard = Record
    Suit: TSuits;
    Value: TNums;
  end;


  TDeck = array[1..52] of TCard;

procedure FillDeck(var D: TDeck);
var
  i: Integer;
begin
  D[1].Suit := Clubs;
  D[1].Value := Ace;
  for i := 1 to 51 do begin
    if i < 13 then D[i + 1].Suit := Clubs
      else if (i > 12) and (i < 26) then
        D[i + 1].Suit := Spades
        else if (i > 25) and (i < 39) then
          D[i + 1].Suit := Hearts
          else D[i + 1].Suit := Diamonds;
```

```
      D[i + 1].Value := TNums(i mod 13);
    end;
end;

procedure WriteSuit(C: TCard);
begin
  case C.Suit of
    Clubs: Write('Clubs');
    Spades: Write('Spades');
    Diamonds: Write('Diamonds');
    Hearts: Write('Hearts');
  end;
end;

procedure WriteValue(C: TCard);
begin
  case C.Value of
    Ace: Write('Ace');
    Two: Write('Two');
    Three: Write('Three');
    Four: Write('Four');
    Five: Write('Five');
    Six: Write('Six');
    Seven: Write('Seven');
    Eight: Write('Eight');
    Nine: Write('Nine');
    Ten: Write('Ten');
    Jack: Write('Jack');
    Queen: Write('Queen');
    King: Write('King');
  end;
end;


procedure WriteCard(C: TCard);
begin
  WriteValue(C);
  Write(' of ');
  WriteSuit(C);
end;
```

```
procedure WriteDeck(D: TDeck);
var
  Line,
  i: Integer;
begin
  Line := 1;
  for i := 1 to 52 do begin
    Write(i, ' ==> ');
    WriteCard(D[i]);
    if i mod 3 = 1 then
      GotoXY(27, Line)
    else if i mod 3 = 2 then begin
      GotoXY(54, Line);
      inc(Line);
    end else begin
      GotoXY(1, Line - 1);
      WriteLn;
    end;
  end;
end;

var
  D: TDeck;
  i: Integer;
  Dias: Byte;
  Cl: Byte;
begin
  FillDeck(D);
  WriteDeck(D);
end.
```

# Review Questions

1. What is the upper limit on the number of items you can have in a set? _____

2. How do you represent the empty set in Pascal? _____
_____

# Review Exercise

1. Write a program using a `repeat until` loop and set notation that ensures that the users won't be able to exit the loop until they enter either the letter T for TRUE or F for FALSE.

# urbo Pascal
## CLASSROOM 8

# Is My
# Computer Alive?

# Notes

# The Game of Life

*To study a longer program that uses arrays to create cellular automata.*

This lesson at long last begins an exploration of a longer program. This program, called Life, incorporates many of the concepts you have learned so far in this book. My intent in the next few lessons is to show how to construct a large program like the one presented here, and also to demonstrate a method for coordinating the many features of Pascal, so that they form a complete whole.

It is my sincere belief that merely learning the grammar of a language is not enough. Good programmers must also know how to construct a large program, and how to harmonize the disparate elements of the language so that they work in concert. Without this knowledge, even a good programmer's best efforts are bound to fail. This means that the material I have covered so far is not enough to prepare you to write real-world programs; before I am done, I must try to present you with a larger project and give you some understanding of how it works.

Before turning to the actual source code of the program Life, it might be helpful first to learn something about its history. The program in question is by no means an ordinary conglomeration of code thrown together solely for utilitarian reasons. Instead, it is one of the most well known and controversial of the "classic" programming assignments. The controversy stems from the fact that some people feel this program enables a computer to take on a life of its own.

# Stand Back! I Think It's Alive!

Most introductory computer programming books begin by introducing the reader to a few lines of code that look something like this:

```
begin
  WriteLn('Hello world!');
end.
```

This program has been presented so often, in so many different computer languages, that many people now seem oblivious to the fact that it carries a certain philosophical baggage along with it. Specifically, these few lines of code seem to imply that in some sense we as programmers are teaching the computer how to speak. As we do so, the computer supposedly raises its head from the primordial ooze and, blinking violently against the glare of the sun, greets us with its first words, "Hello World."

I am perplexed both by people who seem oblivious to the implications of this program, and by those who gleefully embrace its "hidden" message. I happen to have grave doubts about artificial intelligence (AI) and artificial life, and about the general idea that computers can be thought of as places where realized or potential lifelike minds can be generated.

Nevertheless, I vividly remember what a fellow student in a college-level computer science AI course said to me one day after the entire class had been discussing this issue rather heatedly in a seminar. The discussion had become very abstract and intellectual, although not necessarily intelligible. Afterward, he came up to me, looked me right in the eye, and said with obvious sincerity, "Charlie, I don't care what you say, or how you say it. I believe that what computers do is called thinking! They think just the way you and I think."

For some reason, his forthright emotional sincerity has always meant more to me than most of the erudite, and sometimes brilliant, arguments concerning the question of whether computers do or do not have lifelike, or mindlike, qualities.

Nevertheless, some interesting aspects of this debate are raised by the computer-based simulation called the Game of Life, which we are about to study. It has a rather illustrious history, in that it has its roots in the thinking of the brilliant scientist John von Neumann. The credit for its actual invention goes to the eminent mathematician John Horton Conway, who gave birth to the program as we know it.

The game falls into a category called cellular automata, which might be defined as a form of sophisticated puzzle where strict mathematical rules govern the behavior of a series of single cell entities, each of which is represented by a square on a grid. If the right set of rules is followed, these single cells begin to exhibit behavior that many people consider to be life-like.

Lest you fear that I have gone completely off the deep end, let me assure you that presenting the Game of Life as part of an introductory computer book is only a few steps away from being cliché, on the order of the "Hello World" program. It is a classic exercise for beginning or intermediate programmers, primarily because it gives students a chance to design a fairly lengthy program that makes heavy use of arrays.

But I am intentionally emphasizing the philosophical implications of this program because I don't want this book to consist of nothing but a series of syntactical rules. Anyway, after all the work you have done to learn the basics of the language, you have earned the right to flex your newly found programming muscles. Your being able to discuss the implications of a relatively sophisticated piece of code shows that the subject matter of this book has now progressed beyond trivial matters of syntax and structure. There is no longer a need to struggle with the basic elements of the language. Instead, it is my hope that readers of this book should now feel as though the vast world of computer programming is opening up before them like a flower.

With that image in mind, there is perhaps no better place to turn than to the Game of Life.

# Playing the Game of Life

A working version of the Game of Life comes on your disk, in the sub-directory called Life. Before beginning the discussion of this program, why don't you play the game a few times to see how it works. To get started, pull the module called LIFE.PAS up into the Pascal editor, compile it and its

units, and then run the program. At the start you should see a menu that looks like the image in Figure 25.1.

**Figure 25.1.**
*The main menu for the Game of Life.*

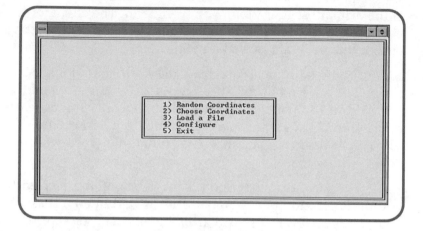

```
1> Random Coordinates
2> Choose Coordinates
3> Load a File
4> Configure
5> Exit
```

Until two or three years ago, menus that looked like this were pretty much the norm, but now they are considered a bit old-fashioned and not entirely professional. Because you are not yet ready to build the kind of sophisticated menuing system found in the IDE, this simple type of menu will do. Remember, as well, that two of the prime assets of these simple menus are that they are easy to use and relatively easy to construct. These are not trivial assets.

To prove this point, select option 1, Random Coordinates, simply by pressing the number 1 on the keypad. You are then confronted with a screen that looks like the image in Figure 25.2.

**Figure 25.2.**
*The user has just requested that the computer select 234 randomly chosen points on the playing board.*

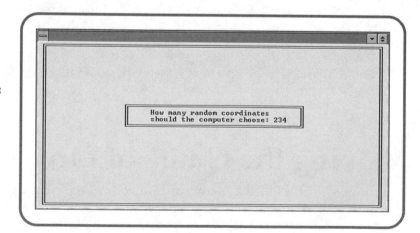

```
How many random coordinates
should the computer choose: 234
```

At this point, the user is free to type in any number under 32,000. Because I have not yet explained how the game works, you might want to trust me when I say that experience has taught me that entering numbers between 70 and 300 usually produces the best results. To see those results, press the Enter key.

You should see a series of squares appear on the screen and ripple across its surface. They either die away altogether or settle into a configuration that might look something like what you see in Figure 25.3. Should the computer, by chance, reach a stage where it oscillates back and forth between two similar patterns, you can press Escape to stop this endlessly repeating process. When the game ends, you can return to the main menu by pressing Enter one more time. From there, you may repeat the process as often as you want.

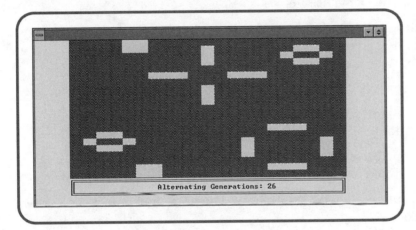

*Figure 25.3.*
*An unusually crowded board at the end of a run of the Game of Life.*

# More Syntactic Sugar

Now that you've watched at least one run of the program, you might ask, "What does this have to do with life? I mean, this may be fairly interesting to look at, but it certainly isn't anything that I would recognize as being alive!"

Such an opinion would, at least to some degree, echo my own sentiments. Nevertheless, interesting things are going on in this game that deserve some attention.

For one reason or another, programmers have always longed to create autonomous creatures that know how to act on their own. This urge has

proved so strong that it has leaked over into the public at large, which has embraced the idea with remarkable enthusiasm. Both Hal from the movie *2001* and R2D2 from *Star Wars* embody one of the primary fantasies of our age—to build a machine that comes to life!

The natural inclination is to consider building something that resembles a full grown human, or at least to build some form of mechanical robot that could be considered as sophisticated as a cat or dog. Perhaps because it so far has been impossible to achieve this goal, some scientists have considered approaching this elusive goal from the opposite end. In other words, they decided that to create lifelike creatures, they ought to start with the lowest forms of life, rather than the most sophisticated. Instead of trying to create a creature that lives on the highest end of the evolutionary scale, they decided to start with simple one-celled animals. This reasoning gave—ahem—*birth* to the Game of Life.

To play the Game of Life, imagine a sea of tiny one-celled animals, and suppose that their lives are governed by the following four rules, as put forward by the redoubtable John Horton Conway:

1. Any cell that has two or three neighbors is happy enough to survive.

2. Any cell surrounded by exactly three neighbors is happy enough to reproduce.

3. Any cell surrounded by more than three neighbors will die of overcrowding.

4. Any cell surrounded by less than two neighbors will die of loneliness.

When Conway invented this game, he wasn't thinking specifically of computers. Instead, he was thinking of ways to simulate life, ways to create self-perpetuating machines called *cellular automata*. When he came across the rules outlined above, he was amazed to see that sometimes the tiny one-celled creatures in his game came together to form multicelled creatures that survived as units, similar to the way multicelled creatures survived in the sea when life was first born.

If you want to see a picture of one of these multicelled creatures, look back at Figure 25.3. Remember how each of these little fellows was formed. First a set of random points was selected on the board located in the center of the screen; then these points were used to form the starting point from which to launch the Game of Life.

The program on your disk follows the rules of the Game of Life to the letter. The program creates new squares if a square has three neighbors, it allows squares to live if they have two or three neighbors, and it ensures that all other squares die.

When these rules are obeyed, a sea of random one-celled creatures sometimes slowly evolves into multicelled creatures like those seen in Figure 25.3. At other times, circumstances aren't right, and they simply die out, leaving the screen empty. This behavior happens to be very much like the way living creatures act in the real world.

This is the nub of the matter. Here are little one-celled creatures that act as though they are alive. They are even capable of evolving into more sophisticated creatures that seem to have an autonomous existence.

So if it looks like it's alive, and it acts like it's alive, then it must be alive. Right?

Well, possibly. Some people would argue that these little fellows aren't alive in the usual sense of the word; after all, they're just little dots on a computer screen. As such, they can't possibly have any significance. Right?

Well, maybe yes, and maybe no. There is something fascinating about these little fellows. They certainly appear to take on an autonomous existence inside the computer. And if it is possible to build these little creatures with a few lines of Pascal code, what sort of creatures might evolve out of more sophisticated games run on more sophisticated machines? Who's to say that two or more of those multicelled creatures might not come together to form an even more sophisticated entity? Who knows where this kind of thing might go?

Well, certainly not me. There are, however, factors here intriguing enough to explore in more depth.

# Summary

Congratulations. You are at the end of another lesson. Don't think lightly of these last few pages just because they don't contain any Pascal code. Becoming a good programmer isn't all a matter of learning rules and mastering syntax. Good programmers come to their machines with a sense of passion. There has to be more to it than just pure abstracted reason. Spending a few moments to think about something like the Game of Life can help you open doors that reveal a view into the realms inhabited by people with the passion required to master the art of programming.

As students of the Pascal language, you are undoubtedly anxious to move on to the next lesson. There you will look at some real code.

# Review Exercises

1. Practice using all the games features. See if you can load files from disk, and try to draw simple patterns on the board that will go on to form colonies of their own.

2. Compile the program to disk, and run it from the DOS prompt.

# 26

L e s s o n

# Saving the World from the Forces of Chaos

**OBJECTIVE**

*An examination of the Game of Life reveals how to centralize the key configurable elements of a program.*

This lesson picks up where the last lesson left off. The goal now is to get you to the point where you are ready to work on your own to add a new module to the Game of Life. Pay attention to these next few pages, for they will prepare you for the moment when you'll get a chance to write some interesting and important code.

When Conway was first exploring the Game of Life, he and his coworkers found that it generated an interesting little creature called a *Spinner*. To see Spinners at work, start the game and choose option three, Load A File. You should be greeted with a screen that looks something like the image shown in Figure 26.1.

*Figure 26.1.*
*A screen from the Game of Life that enables you to choose one of the pre-saved screens.*

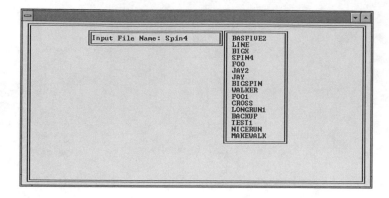

Type in either Spin4 or Spinner and press Enter. The program loads a pre-saved game and then runs it. You'll see one or more little creatures like those pictured in Figure 26.2 begin to move across the screen.

*Figure 26.2.*
*After loading the game labeled Spin4, the user has elected to terminate the game in mid-play, by pressing Escape.*

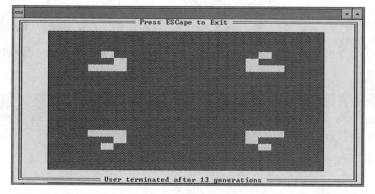

These little creatures are quite fascinating to watch. In fact, on some machines, you may feel that they are moving across the screen too quickly. In order to study them better, what is needed is a way to control the speed at which they move across the screen.

# Controlling the Game

Because of the great range in CPU speeds presented by today's computers, I have frequently discussed how to use the Delay procedure in programs. By now it should be obvious to you that you can use this procedure to set the speed at which the computer runs the Game of Life. In the examples presented so far, whenever the `Delay` procedure was needed, the call was simply inserted into the program, and a literal value was passed to it as a parameter:

```
Delay(56);
```

In the past, there was no reason not to take this approach. But Life is such a long and complex program that it is no longer recommended to be so informal.

More specifically, this new program, rather than consisting of only twenty or thirty lines, consists of over a thousand lines, and those are spread out over eight modules, as you can see here:

```
Directory of C:\PASDOS\LIFE

SETBOARD PAS       4677 12-08-92    9:52p
TOOLBOXC PAS       7405 12-07-92    6:14p
FILEIO   PAS       3189 12-08-92    9:45p
LIFE     PAS       4675 12-10-92    7:53p
GENLAWS  PAS       4791 12-08-92   10:17p
LSCREEN  PAS       2743 12-10-92    7:20p
LIFEDEF  PAS       3049 12-10-92    8:11p
CONFIG   PAS        500 12-10-92    7:13p
         8 file(s)      46402 bytes
                     17571840 bytes free
```

Now, suppose you decide to change the speed at which this program executes by inserting a `Delay` procedure in the appropriate spot. Also suppose, after considerable thought, you decide that the right place happens to be at line 63 in one of the units listed at the top of `Life.Pas`:

```
uses
  Crt,
  Config,
  Dos,
  FileIO,
  GenLaws,
  LifeDef,
  LScreen,
  SetBoard,
  ToolBoxC;
```

So you make the change, run the program, and see that it runs at just the right speed to allow for a leisurely study of the little Spinners.

347

However, now suppose that for some reason you get called away from the computer, and that furthermore, for one reason or another, it is three months before you get back to working with this particular game. By then you may have completely forgotten about the Delay procedure and may not even understand why the program is running so slowly. It might be hours, days, or even weeks before you uncover the error.

At this stage, I can imagine some readers sitting back and thinking, "Why is Charlie always making such a big point about this kind of thing? I'm never going to make a mistake that dumb. I'm just not that stupid." Well, my experience has been that everybody makes mistakes like this. In fact, some people continually get into terrible states of utter and irredeemable confusion because they don't understand that there is a way to keep these types of errors to a minimum.

To learn about one standard way of coping with this problem, take a look at procedure DefaultConfig, which appears near the bottom of the main module of this program:

```
procedure DefaultConfig(var GameInfo: TGameInfo);
begin
  CursorOff;
  TextAttr := YBAttr;
  with GameInfo do begin
    Speed := 5;
    CheckForAltGen := False;
    MaxGen := 32000;
    GameType := Classic;
  end;
  MakeRules(GameInfo);
end;
```

Notice that the sixth line of this program enables you to set a variable called Speed, which is part of a record structure called GameInfo. Right now, this variable is set to 5. As an experiment, try setting it to 50, or 200, and then load the saved game called Spinner. Now the game should move at a slower speed.

As it happens, there is a place in unit LScreen where GameInfo.Speed is passed to the Delay procedure:

```
procedure Writeboard(BoardInfo: TBoardInfo;
                     GameInfo: TGameInfo; BoardToDraw: Byte);
var
  S: String;
```

```
begin
  S := 'Generation =' + Int2Str(boardinfo.generation) + ' ';
  CenterStr(StatusLine + 1, S);
  PaintIt(BoardInfo, BoardToDraw);
  Delay(GameInfo.Speed); { Pause to check out colony.}
end;
```

If you want to change the speed in the program, however, you don't have to ever worry about unit LScreen, the WriteBoard procedure, or even the Delay procedure. All you have to do is set the speed of the game in the DefaultConfig procedure, which happens to be the first procedure the program calls.

Once you understand the principle involved in this process, it should come as no surprise to you to hear that *all* of the user configurable variables in this program can be set in the DefaultConfig procedure. That means the whole process is centralized. Therefore, it is very unlikely that you will ever have to endure the scenario outlined in the brief tale about the Delay procedure.

Furthermore, I'm sure you've noticed that all of these variables are members of one record that is of type TGameInfo. To see this record structure, open up unit LifeDef, where *all* of the program's globally used type definitions are declared:

```
TGameInfo = Record
  GameType: TGameType;
  Speed: Integer;
  MaxGen: Integer;
  Alivecount: Integer;
  Change: Boolean;
  Birth: Neighbor;
  Death: Neighbor;
  Survival: Neighbor;
  Number: Integer; { Number is number of neighbors }
  CheckForAltGen: Boolean; { Alternating generations? }
end;
```

Notice that I could have declared these variables separately rather than as members of a record, but I chose to try to create order by arranging most of the major variables used in this program into two record types. The first is shown above, and here is the other, along with the types included inside that record:

```
TBoardtype=array[1..2,1..MaxSize,1..MaxSize] of cellstate;
TSaveBoard = array[1..MaxSize, 1..MaxSize] of cellstate;
```

```
TState = (Dead, Stable, Growing, Double, UserTermination);

TBoardInfo = record
  Board : Tboardtype;
  Generation : Integer;
  New : Byte;
  Old : Byte;
  Size : 1..MaxSize;
  State :TState;
  IsDouble: Boolean;        { False if not double         }
  SaveSecond: TSaveBoard;   { Save board to check repeats }
  Finished : Boolean;       { Make menu run               }
end;
```

It's not important at this point that you understand what all of these variables do in the program. In fact, you shouldn't be worrying about that at all right now. Nor is it really important whether you think this is the best possible way of encapsulating the variables used in this program into useful and logical records.

What is important is that you understand that there has been an attempt to bring order to the different portions of this program. Furthermore, you should understand that this goal has been achieved by concentrating all of the major variables in one of two records, and that all of the user configurable variables can be changed in one single procedure.

Now that you understand a little of what is going on here, take a look at the other configurable variables in the record:

```
with GameInfo do begin
  Speed := 5;
  CheckForAltGen := False;
  MaxGen := 32000;
  GameType := Classic;
end;
```

Some of them are easy to understand. MaxGen, for example, specifies the maximum number of generations the program will run through before stopping. If you set this to 32, the program will always stop after 32 generations of one-celled creatures have come and gone.

The other two identifiers, however, are a bit harder to understand. CheckForAltGen makes it easy to check for the condition that occurs when two generations alternate back and forth indefinitely between two different states. Set this variable to TRUE, and then load the saved game called Cross; you will notice that the game will halt after eight generations, as shown in

Figure 26.3. Set it to FALSE, and you will see it alternate back and forth in a continuous, pendulum-like motion.

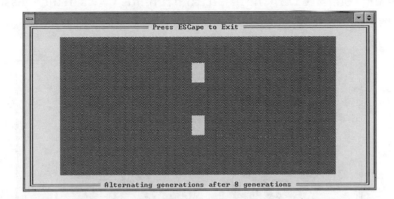

***Figure 26.3.***
*The game called* `Cross`
*will end after eight*
*generations when the*
*variable called*
`CheckForAltGen` *is set*
*to TRUE.*

Once again, it is not important right now that you understand how the program checks for alternating generations, only that you see how easy it is to control this feature. This lesson is concentrating on design issues, which are every bit as important as the actual implementation of any one of the program's features.

Last but not least, I want you to take a look at the `GameType` variable, which is an enumerated type. The declaration for this type looks like this:

```
TGameType  = (Classic, ManyBirths, MuchSurvival);
```

The three identifiers that make up the elements of this type refer back to the rules of the game, which were enumerated in the last lesson. As you recall, the classic configuration of this game states the following:

```
3 Neighbors = Birth
2, 3 Neighbors = Survival
0, 1, 4, 5, 6, 7, 8 Neighbors = Death
```

However, you might want to try a configuration where there are many births, such as

```
3, 4 Neighbors = Birth
2, 3, 4 Neighbors = Survival
0, 1, 5, 6, 7, 8 Neighbors = Death
```

or one where there is much survival, such as

```
3 Neighbors = Birth
2, 3, 4 Neighbors = Survival
0, 1, 5, 6, 7, 8 Neighbors = Death
```

To see what effect these have, you might want to set GameType to MuchSurvival, and then load the game called Cross. You can see the result in Figure 26.4, which you should compare with the result from running Cross in the Classic configuration.

*Figure 26.4.*
*The result of loading the saved game* Cross *when the variable* GameInfo.GameType *is set to* MuchSurvival.

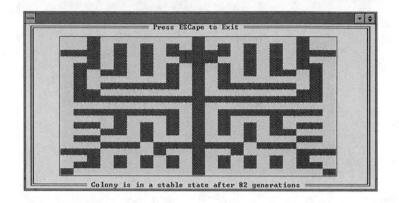

# A Hands-On Example

Before this lesson ends, let me take this situation one step further and show how this arrangement of the code enables you to find a sensible way to add a new feature to the program.

As it is now, whenever the user loads a saved game, the original shape of the board immediately begins mutating so quickly that it is almost impossible to see what the original configuration looks like. But the original seed configuration can be important to a user, especially to one who wants to use the Game of Life's menu option 2 to create and save game boards.

How is it possible for you to get the game to pause for a moment after loading the board from the disk and writing it once to the screen? Well, it happens that a good place to do that is in procedure RunGame, which is found in the main module:

```
procedure RunGame(var BoardInfo: TBoardInfo;
                  var GameInfo: TGameInfo);
begin
  DrawBorder;
  GameInfo.Change := True;
  CenterStr(1, ' Press ESCape to Exit ');
  WriteBoard(BoardInfo, GameInfo, BoardInfo.Old);
  GameLoop(BoardInfo, GameInfo);
end;
```

In the seventh line of this procedure, there is a call to `WriteBoard`, which is located in unit `LScreen`. It should be no surprise that `WriteBoard` got its name because it draws the playing board to the screen. Knowing this much, you should be able to deduce that immediately after the call to `WriteBoard`, you can place a `Delay` procedure that pauses the screen long enough for you to look at it:

```
procedure RunGame(var BoardInfo: TBoardInfo;
                  var GameInfo: TGameInfo);
begin
  DrawBorder;
  GameInfo.Change := True;
  CenterStr(1, ' Press ESCape to Exit ');
  WriteBoard(BoardInfo, GameInfo, BoardInfo.Old);
  Delay(500);
  GameLoop(BoardInfo, GameInfo);
end;
```

This is the right way to go about it, isn't it? After all, if a programmer wants to make the delay a little longer or shorter, or to remove it altogether, all that is needed is to go back and change the parameter passed to `Delay` from 500 to, say, 300. Right?

Of course not! By now it should be clear that there is a much better way to add configurable features to this program. The correct approach, of course, is to add a new field to `TGameInfo` and then to find a way to adjust this field in method `DefaultConfig`:

```
TGameInfo = Record
  FirstScreenDelay: Integer; { Delay before 1st Screen }
  GameType: TGameType;
  Speed: Integer;
  MaxGen: Integer;
  Alivecount: Integer;
  Change: Boolean;
  Birth: Neighbor;
  Death: Neighbor;
  Survival: Neighbor;
  Number: Integer; { Number is number of neighbors }
  CheckForAltGen: Boolean; { Alternating generations? }
end;

procedure DefaultConfig(var GameInfo: TGameInfo);
begin
  CursorOff;
```

353

```
    TextAttr := YBAttr;
    with GameInfo do begin
      Speed := 5;
      CheckForAltGen := False;
      MaxGen := 32000;
      GameType := Classic;
      FirstScreenDelay = 500;
    end;
    MakeRules(GameInfo);
  end;
```

# Summing It Up

Some of the major themes of this book are going to come together in the next few sentences, when I describe what will be, for this book, a kind of penultimate Finish the Program exercise.

This lesson talks a good deal about the DefaultConfig procedure and some of the key fields in TGameInfo. If you have played with option 4 in the Game of Life menu, you know that one of these fields is configurable from inside the game. In other words, the user can change the value of the GameInfo.Speed variable while the game is running.

"So," you might ask, "how come the user can't change the rest of the configurable fields from inside the game?" Well, as you may have guessed, the reason is that I've been saving that part of the program for you!

In this create-your-own Finish the Program exercise, you should go in and find a way to enable the user to change all the main configurable variables discussed in this lesson; that is, the ones that are visible in DefaultConfig procedure.

Here is the heart of the matter: you will be able to do all but one tiny portion of your work inside of the unit called Config, where the SetSpeed procedure already resides. In other words, the new routines you write should reside inside this unit. There is no need for you to examine or change the code that resides in any of the other units. It simply doesn't matter whether or not you understand how the rest of this program works.

The reason you don't need to concern yourself about this stems from the fact that the Game of Life is divided up into modules that are totally separate from each another. You can work inside of unit Config without ever having to get involved with most of the rest of this program.

This is what structured programming is all about. You divide your program up into modules and work on those modules one at a time. Any routines or types that all the modules absolutely have to share belong in a single unit, which in this case is called LifeDef. This identifier stands for *Life Define*, because it is where the types and routines that the rest of the program relies on are *defined*. Of course, you can also call on the routines in ToolBoxC, which contains code that can be linked into multiple programs.

As for the rest of the Game of Life, you need only change one line, which appears in the ChooseMethod procedure:

```
function ChooseMethod(var BoardInfo: TBoardInfo;
                      var GameInfo: TGameInfo; Ans: Char): Word;
var
  Option: Char;
begin
  case Ans of
    '1': Option := 'c'; {Computer picks random coordinates }
    '2': Option := 'u'; {user designates places            }
    '3': option := 'f'; {files option                      }
    '4': SetSpeed(GameInfo);
    '5','x','q','e': BoardInfo.Finished := True;
  end; {case}
  if Option in ['c','u','f'] then { Start colony }
    Start(BoardInfo, GameInfo, Option);
end;
```

The line in question is the one that calls the SetSpeed procedure.

# Another One Bytes the Dust

After you wrestle with rewriting this program for a while, you can move on to the next lesson, which talks a bit more about the structure of the Game of Life.

# Exploring Life's Genetic Laws

*A look at how to embody a set of rules inside the code of a Pascal program.*

One of the challenges every programmer faces is finding a way to embody facets of the real world inside a program. For example, if you are building a program that helps a company balance its books, you need to find a way to represent the company's financial structure inside a program. Or, if you are going to build an inventory system, you need to find a way to model the company's existing stocking system inside a computer.

When studying the Game of Life, programmers are presented with the same type of challenge because they need to find a way

to embody the rules governing the birth and death of individual cells. I have discussed these rules several times already, but here they are one more time so you can have a handy reference while you are reading this lesson:

```
3 Neighbors = Birth
2, 3 Neighbors = Survival
0, 1, 4, 5, 6, 7, 8 Neighbors = Death
```

These rules explain that if any one cell has three neighbors, it gives birth to another cell; if it has two or three neighbors, it survives; otherwise, it dies.

Certainly these rules are not particularly difficult to understand, yet they have a degree of complexity sufficient to pose a challenge for programmers who attempt to embody them inside computer programs. To meet a challenge like this, it is necessary to develop a coherent strategy or else face the possibility of becoming hopelessly mired in a swamp of incomprehensible code.

It is probably worth re-emphasizing that both amateur and professional programmers face this kind of challenge over and over again. The ability to effectively embody simple rules in code makes the difference between a successful and a failed project. Merely knowing the grammar of a language is never enough; you also have to know how to put a program together.

The two great strategies for performing this task are called *structured programming* and *object-oriented programming*. In this lesson we will continue our examination of structured programming.

# Designing a Module

By now you probably understand enough about this implementation of the Game of Life to understand that the choices the user makes while looking at the main menu are handled in the file called Life.Pas. Once all the possible courses that the game flow can take are sorted out, the focus of attention becomes unit LRunGame. It is here that the actual body of the game is executed, and it is from here that you can watch the evolutionary ebb and flow of a colony of one-celled creatures.

Take a look at the main loop that guides this portion of the game:

```
procedure GameLoop(var BoardInfo: TBoardInfo;
                   var GameInfo: TGameInfo);
begin
  with BoardInfo do begin
```

```
    repeat
      GeneticLaws(BoardInfo, GameInfo);
      WriteBoard(BoardInfo, GameInfo, New);
      Evaluate(BoardInfo, GameInfo);
    until GameOver(State, Generation, GameInfo.MaxGen);
  end; {with}
end;
```

Although the actual source code on the disk contains some extra comments not included here, it is still easy to understand the basic flow of a colony's life simply by taking a brief look at this one procedure.

In the beginning, a set of genetic laws are enacted that govern the birth, death, and survival of individual cells. After these laws have been executed, a new board has been created—that is, a new generation of one-celled creatures has been produced. It follows that the next step should be to draw the new board to the screen. While the user is looking at the new generation, the program evaluates the impact the laws had on the colony. For example, the code checks to see if there are no cells left, of if the game is in a stable state. Finally, in the Boolean function GameOver, the program "reads the report" produced during its evaluation of the colony in order to see if the game is over and if it is time to exit the loop.

If it is not time to exit the loop, the process is repeated. That is, the genetic laws are used to create a new board and the result is shown to the user. After evaluating the result, a decision is made whether to exit or continue the cycling through the loop.

**NOTE:** This is a good time to point out once again the elegance of Pascal. Notice that the language can capture the essence of a logical flow in only a few clearly written lines. Many other computer languages fail to produce such readily comprehensible code.

Notice that back in the main module, the loop that drives the course of the entire game follows a similar pattern:

```
var
  Ans: Char;
  BoardInfo: TBoardInfo;
  GameInfo: TGameInfo;
begin
  DefaultConfig(GameInfo);
```

```
repeat
  Initialize(BoardInfo);
  Ans := DoMenu;
  ChooseMethod(BoardInfo, GameInfo, Ans);
until (BoardInfo.Finished = true);

ClrScr;
CursorOn;
end.
```

The repeat loop in this code fragment iterates through a simple, readily comprehensible process. First, the code initializes some variables that need to be reset before each run of the game. Then the menu system processes input from the user. The final step is to sort out which options the user chose.

Just to make sure there is no unnecessary confusion, I should point out that it is just coincidence that there are three routines called inside each of the repeat loops examined in this lesson. It doesn't matter whether there are three routines, two routines, or ten routines; it only matters that the essence of a loop can be distilled into a few short commands that are readily comprehensible.

Furthermore, my point here is not that I have found the ideal way of breaking this program up into modules and routines. In fact, writing about this code has helped me see a number of improvements I will enact in my next version of this program. So it is not the actual implementation of these guidelines that you are primarily concerned with, but rather the guidelines themselves. In other words, the idea that code needs to be broken into readily comprehensible modules and procedures is much more important than the actual way the process is enacted in this particular example.

# The Genetic Laws

You should be beginning to understand the way this program is broken down into carefully encapsulated sections that act like a series of Chinese boxes. That is, the loop in the main module of the program is opened, only to reveal that it contains another loop—namely the GameLoop procedure—contained in unit LRunGame. As you no doubt suspect by now, the GameLoop procedure can in turn be opened only to reveal another loop, called procedure GeneticLaws, which is found in unit GenLaws:

```
procedure GeneticLaws (var BoardInfo : TBoardInfo;
                       var GameInfo: TGameInfo);
```

```
var
  i,j: Integer;
begin
  with BoardInfo do begin
    GameInfo.AliveCount := 0;
    GameInfo.Change := False;
    if GameInfo.CheckForAltGen then IsDouble := True;
    for i:= 1 to size do
      for j:= 1 to size do begin
        CountNeighbor(BoardInfo, i, j, GameInfo.Number);
        Board[New,i,j] := Empty;
        LawNumberOne(i, j, BoardInfo, GameInfo);
        LawNumberTwo(i, j, BoardInfo, GameInfo);
        LawNumberThree(i, j, BoardInfo, GameInfo);
        if GameInfo.CheckForAltGen then
          CheckForDouble(i, j, BoardInfo, GameInfo);
      end;
  end {with}
end; { GeneticLaws}
```

This lesson began by stating that we were going to discuss how to encapsulate a set of rules inside a Pascal program. Well, by showing you the GeneticLaws procedure, you have taken the first step toward that goal. That essential first step is to encapsulate all the rules inside one isolated portion of your program.

It is almost impossible to emphasize this point too often. *The key to making a real-world program work is to encapsulate each of the program's major functions inside a relatively isolated unit.* This means that you cannot afford to have a series of complicated cross calls between your *isolated* unit and all the other modules in your program. If you don't follow these guidelines—that is, if you have all your code mixed together in a great tangled ball of thread—you are never going to be able to maintain your code, and you are going to spend ridiculously long periods of time tracking down bugs.

Don't be fooled by people who claim that the overhead of a procedure call or of jumping to another unit is so great that it will make your code too slow. These people are a classic demonstration of what it means to be "penny wise and pound foolish." Their code may run imperceivably faster, but the project itself is never going to be finished, or if it is finished, it won't be finished on time, and it will probably never be thoroughly debugged. Heaven help the team members on this project when it comes time to update the program for a second version.

> **NOTE:** Unfortunately, the evolution of the computer business has been such that many programming team leaders do not yet understand even the elementary guidelines for producing good programs that are discussed in this book. If you find yourself laboring under such conditions, simply try to find a way to follow the principles of good structured programming while seemingly following your boss's misguided desires. For instance, if your boss insists that you combine your code into one module, or that you write longer procedures, go ahead and do so, but make sure that each of your modules and procedures are divided into clearly definable sections.

Returning to the examination of the GeneticLaws procedure, you can see that it enters a loop wherein each individual square on the 21-by-21 matrix is subjected to scrutiny by five procedures, as shown in the following code fragment:

```
for i:= 1 to size do
  for j:= 1 to size do begin
    CountNeighbor(BoardInfo, i, j, GameInfo.Number);
    Board[New,i,j] := Empty;
    LawNumberOne(i, j, BoardInfo, GameInfo);
    LawNumberTwo(i, j, BoardInfo, GameInfo);
    LawNumberThree(i, j, BoardInfo, GameInfo);
    if GameInfo.CheckForAltGen then
      CheckForDouble(i, j, BoardInfo, GameInfo);
end;
```

Here the code encapsulates all of the game's logical rules in just a few lines of code. First, the program counts the number of neighbors surrounding a position on our matrix designated by the coordinates i and j. Notice that the matrix being examined at this time is the matrix for the "old" board—that is, the one that is currently on the screen. After you have examined this matrix, you will create the next generation in the "new" board.

For clarity's sake, let me take time to point out that the two boards are defined in the following excerpt from the type definitions in unit LifeDef:

```
TBoardtype =
  array[Old..New, 1..MaxSize, 1..MaxSize] of Cellstate;
```

Yes, this is a three dimensional array, but don't let that fact intimidate you. All that occurs here is that two boards are declared, one sitting right in front of the other, as depicted in Figure 27.1. One board is called the *Old* board, the other is called the *New* board.

*Figure 27.1.*
*A visual representation of how* TBoardType *looks in memory.*

When a new generation is created, the program looks at the contents of the old board, examines them in the light of the rules, and uses that information to create the new board. This process is conducted by the three procedures called LawNumberOne, LawNumberTwo, and LawNumberThree.

Once the laws have been applied, the program looks to see if the user wants to check for alternating generations. If this is indeed what the user wants, a call is made to the CheckForDouble procedure.

The last few paragraphs can be summed up by saying that the GeneticLaws procedure first counts the number of neighbors surrounding a cell on the old board. After initializing the corresponding cell in the new board to empty, it allows the rules governing the game to mark that square as occupied, if indeed the rules designate that it should be occupied. The loop ends by checking to see if there are alternating generations.

As for the rules themselves, none of them are particularly complicated. For instance, rule one looks like this:

```
procedure LawNumberOne(i, j: Integer; var BoardInfo: TBoardInfo;
                       var GameInfo: TGameInfo);
begin
  with BoardInfo do begin
    if (Board[old,i,j] = Empty) and
       (GameInfo.Number in GameInfo.Birth) then begin
      Board[New,i,j] := Occupied;
      GameInfo.Change := True;
      Inc(GameInfo.AliveCount);
    end;
  end;
end;
```

All that's going on here is that the program checks to see if a square is empty, and if the square has the right number of neighbors to produce life. If it does, the square is marked as occupied, and then a little bookkeeping is done before exiting. If this game were following the classic rules, then steps would be taken to check if the square had three neighbors; if it did, the square would, in effect, give birth to a new cell.

LawNumberTwo is equally trivial:

```
procedure LawNumberTwo(i, j: Integer; var BoardInfo: TBoardInfo;
                          var GameInfo: TGameInfo);
begin
  if (BoardInfo.Board[Old,i,j] = Occupied) and
     (GameInfo.Number in GameInfo.Death) then
       GameInfo.Change := True
end;
```

Assuming the classic rules are still being followed, this procedure does little more than check whether a previously occupied cell has zero, one, five, six, seven, or eight neighbors. If it does, that cell has died, and the procedure notes that the board has changed. There is no need to specifically designate the cell as empty, because all the cells were initialized to that value.

And, finally, here is the last law:

```
procedure LawNumberThree(i, j: Integer;
                          var BoardInfo: TBoardInfo;
                          var GameInfo: TGameInfo);
begin
  with BoardInfo do begin
    if (Board[Old,i,j] = Occupied) and
       (GameInfo.Number in GameInfo.Survival)
      Board[New,i,j] := Occupied;
      Inc(GameInfo.AliveCount);
    end;
  end;
end;
```

This procedure checks to see if a previously occupied cell has the right number of neighbors to survive.

# An Elegant Simplicity

This lesson has taken a look at six routines:

> The main block from Life.Pas
> The GameLoop procedure for LRunGame
> The GeneticLaws procedure from GenLaws
> The LawNumberOne procedure from GenLaws
> The LawNumberTwo procedure from GenLaws
> The LawNumberThree procedure from GenLaws

All of these routines are exceedingly easy to understand. The only possible exception is GeneticLaws, which is certainly not what most programmers would call a complicated routine.

I hope that examining these routines has shown you that structured programming can help you reduce a relatively complex task to a series of pellucid exercises that flow together effortlessly. In other words, it is the very triviality of these routines that is interesting.

This leads to the last insight to be drawn from the infinitely fascinating Game of Life. Anyone who has played the game for any length of time is bound to be impressed by the complex interweaving of patterns that it creates. However, the rules that govern it are really fairly simple. Out of these few simple rules is born a kind of majesty, a kind of rococo-like complexity.

Good programs should work the same way. They should be built out of very simple, intuitively obvious routines. But the overall effect can be, at least at times, dazzling in its complexity.

# Summary

I hope you have found this examination of the Game of Life useful. These last three lessons are the only ones that I had not more or less fully envisioned before I began the process of writing this book. Instead, they emerged after I began churning out lessons. I knew from the beginning that I wanted to examine at least one longer program, but I didn't envision the process turning out quite like this. I hope that you've found the exercise instructive.

Before signing off for this lesson, you might want to try a little exercise first shown to me by a former teacher of mine named Wayne Simila-Dickinson. Just so you're sure you understand how the Game of Life is structured, you can try detecting patterns that repeat not every other generation, but every third generation. The saved game called *Jay*, named after a classmate who discovered it, is an example of this type of pattern. If you can complete this exercise, you can rest assured that you understand the Game of Life.

# Review Question

1. Why is encapsulation important? _____

_____

_____

_____

_____

# urbo Pascal
## CLASSROOM 9

## Introduction to Pointers

# Notes

28

# An Introduction to Pointers

OBJECTIVE

*To take an in-depth look at the Memory Theater to reveal the mysteries behind pointers.*

The information presented so far is sufficient to show you how to begin creating serious programs. All the key factors are already in place. Some of the early lessons in this book covered simple data types such as integers and bytes. The text then went on to cover looping and branching, as well as complex data structures such as strings, arrays and records. The next step was to introduce text and typed files and to show you enough about structured programming so that you could divide your code into procedures, function, and units.

If not for an accident of history, these basics tools would be sufficient to enable you to create all but the most complex programs. Unfortunately, there is one last major impediment between you and programming bliss. That impediment exists primarily because early PCs were 16-bit systems rather than 32-bit systems. As a result, most PCs run either DOS or a combination of DOS and Windows 3.x, which are both 16-bit operating systems.

When you are wrestling with this subject, there is no need for you to feel alone. This same impediment is the stumbling block currently holding up vast portions of the American computer profession. At times called the *sixteen-bit limit*, and other times the *64K limit*, it is currently planted firmly between programmers and many of their most ambitious programming objectives.

Fortunately, there is at least a partial solution to this problem. It consists of using something called *pointers*. If not for the 64K limit, most people could regard pointers as little more than a relatively obscure advanced technique used primarily for optimizing code. But because we have a 16-bit operating system, pointers have become an essential part of Pascal programming on the intermediate level and beyond.

The next two lessons take a look at pointers, concentrating first on a practical introduction to the subject, and then discussing two different layers of theory.

My reasoning here is that there are some very important and relatively easy ways to use pointers that you can master before you dig into the really tough material. Whatever happens, you need to have knowledge of these few relatively simple pointer techniques to write solid intermediate-level programs in Turbo Pascal. There is a big leap, however, from the moment when you learn to use pointers in these relatively simple ways to the moment when you can master the intricacies of the subject. So my goal is to start with the practical and then move to the esoteric once you know the essentials.

> **NOTE:** Even in the most technical parts of the discussion that follows, there are going to be a number of oversimplifications. If for some reason you need a detailed technical explanation of this subject, I recommend reading *Modern Operating Systems* by Andrew S. Tanenbaum, published by Prentice Hall.

# The 64K Limit

Before you can understand what pointers are, you have to understand why they are needed. The simplest possible explanation is that you need a way to get around error message 49, `Data Segment Too Large`, and error message 96, `Too Many Variables`.

The following short program demonstrates a situation where the latter error occurs:

```pascal
program BigError;

const
  MaxSize = 30000;
type
  TMyArray = array [1..MaxSize] of Integer;

var
  MyArray1,
  MyArray2: TMyArray;

var
  i: Integer;
begin
  for i := 1 to MaxSize do begin
    MyArray1[i] := i;
    MyArray2[i] := i;
  end;

  for i := 1 to 10 do begin
    WriteLn(MyArray1[i]);
    WriteLn(MyArray2[i]);
  end;
end.
```

When you try to compile the BigError program, you end up with the compiler giving you the message seen in Figure 28.1.

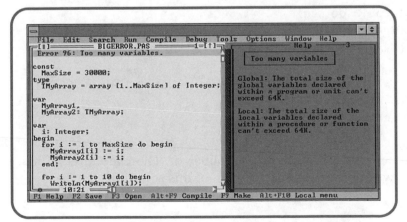

*Figure 28.1.*
*The IDE arranged so that you can see both the source of program BigError and the Help screen about the error message it generates.*

The problem here is that there are two global arrays declared that have a total size larger than 64K. Later in this lesson I will explain why we can't do this, but for now just accept the fact that it is illegal.

As I implied above, there is a solution to this kind of problem. That solution involves converting the array variables into *pointers to arrays*. Here's how it works:

```pascal
program BigFix;

const
  MaxSize = 30000;
type
  PMyArray = ^TMyArray;
  TMyArray = array [1..MaxSize] of Integer;

var
  MyArray1,
  MyArray2: PMyArray;

var
  i: Integer;
begin
  New(MyArray1);
  New(MyArray2);

  for i := 1 to MaxSize do begin
    MyArray1^[i] := i;
    MyArray2^[i] := i;
  end;

  for i := 1 to 10 do begin
    WriteLn(MyArray1^[i]);
    WriteLn(MyArray2^[i]);
  end;

  Dispose(MyArray1);
  Dispose(MyArray2);
end.
```

BigFix.Pas will compile and run without error. There are three primary differences between it and the first version of this program.

The first difference is that a type was declared that points to the array, and then variables were declared to be of that type:

```
type
  PMyArray = ^TMyArray;
  TMyArray = array [1..MaxSize] of Integer;

var
  MyArray1,
  MyArray2: PMyArray;
```

These statements say that PMyArray is a type that points to TMyArray, and that MyArray1 and MyArray2 are of type PMyArray.

Notice that in the type declaration TMyArray is referred to before it is actually declared. This type of situation, where you are declaring a pointer to a data type, is the *only* time when you are allowed to refer to a type before it is declared. The developers of Turbo Pascal allowed this exception to a rule because it helps programmers write clear, readily understandable code.

The fact that the pointer to the array is called PMyArray rather than, say, ZMyArray or MyArrayPtr, is purely a matter of convention. However, it is a convention that I strongly recommend you use. Life is simpler for programmers if they can distinguish pointer types from conventional types at a glance.

Another matter of convention is the way in which the declaration of the pointer is read out loud. My preference is to translate the line

```
PMyArray = ^TMyArray;
```

into spoken English by saying either "PMyArray is a pointer to TMyArray," or "PMyArray equals a pointer to TMyArray." Other commonly used methods are "PMyArray equals caret TMyArray" and "PMyArray equals hat TMyArray." Neither of these latter methods feature a clear explanation of the actual meaning of the syntax, so I prefer the former translations, but this is just a matter of taste.

The second big difference between BigError and BigFix is the calls to New and Dispose:

```
New(MyArray1);
New(MyArray2);

...

Dispose(MyArray1);
Dispose(MyArray2);
```

When you declare a pointer, you almost always have to allocate and deallocate memory for it. You do this by the simple expedient of calling `New` and `Dispose`. Pascal provides two alternative methods for achieving the same goal:

```
GetMem(MyArray1, SizeOf(TMyArray));

...

FreeMem(MyArray1, SizeOf(TMyArray));
```

These two methods have the exact same effect as calls to `New` and `Dispose`, but when using them you have to specify exactly how many bytes you want to allocate or dispose. You do this by calling the `SizeOf` function, which returns the number of bytes occupied by a data type or variable.

The third and final difference between these two programs is that the pointer symbol is used to *dereference* the pointers:

```
MyArray1^[i] := i;

WriteLn(MyArray1^[i]);
```

The pointer symbol, sometimes called a *caret*, is found on the numeric keyboard just above the number 6. When using pointers, this symbol must be added to tell the compiler that we are interested in the values that the pointer addresses, rather than the pointer itself.

In other words, in this case `MyArray` refers to an actual pointer in memory which is just four bytes long, whereas `MyArray^` refers to a 60,000-byte area in memory addressed by this pointer.

This last statement, though relatively concise, may confuse you a bit because it introduces a number of new concepts. But don't worry; most of the rest of this book will be dedicated to describing exactly how pointers work. Before opening the entire can of worms, I want to show you `BigFix.Pas`, which is a simple and practical example of how to use pointers to overcome compiler errors 49 and 96.

Many programmers who are in the process of making the transition between the beginning and intermediate skill levels find themselves confronted with a problem similar to the one presented in BIGERROR.PAS. Pointers offer an easy-to-use solution to this problem, and there is no real need to have a thorough understanding of the technical details involved. If you want, you can just sail on past the 64K barrier without fully understanding why or how the tricks you employ in the process work.

Here's a Finish the Program example that will give you a chance to review the material on pointers presented so far. This time you are working with an array of strings instead of integers, but all the principles discussed so far are the same.

```
program PStrAry;
{
  This program prompts the user for the first
  three elements of a pointer to an array of strings.
  It then copies these strings to a second array and
  prints them to the screen.

  In the process, it uses two procedures, one called
  GetInput and the other called WriteInput. The first
  prompts the user for input and records what he writes,
  the second writes this input to the screen.

  In this program the whole breadth of the array is not
  used. That is, we use only the first 3 elements of a
  200 element array.
}
uses
  Crt,
  ToolBoxC;

type
  PStringAry = ^TStringAry;
  TStringAry = array[1..200] of String;

var
  SAry1,
  SAry2: PStringAry;

{ Read data into each of the first three elements of the array }
procedure GetInput(SAry1: PStringAry);
begin
  Write('Enter a person''s name: ');
  ReadLn(SAry1^[1]);
  Write('Enter a second name: ')
```

```
ReadLn(SAry1^[2]);

  Write('Enter a third name: ');
  ReadLn(SAry1^[3]);
end;

{ Write the output to screen by dereferencing the pointers }
procedure WriteInput(SAry2: PStringAry);
```

_____

_____

_____

_____

_____

_____

_____

_____

_____

_____

_____

Here is how the output from your version of this program might look:

```
Enter a person's name: Sam
Enter a second name: Joe
Enter a third name: Mike

String 1: Sam
String 2: Joe
String 3: Mike

Press ENTER to end this program.
```

There are several different ways to finish this program. If you look at the sample answer provided on disk, however, you will see that one solution involves using the Move procedure to copy information from one array to another:

```
Move(SAry1^, SAry2^, SizeOf(TStringAry));
```

376

I'm making a point of showing you this code because it is an example of an extremely efficient way of accomplishing your goal. Of course, there is no reason why you couldn't write code that looks like this:

```
for i := 1 to 3 do
  SAry2^[i] := SAry1^[i];
```

In fact, this latter example is a fine, even exemplary, solution to one of the problems posed by this Finish the Program exercise. It will not execute as quickly, however, as the blazingly fast Move procedure.

The Move procedure always copies code from a source to a destination. The third parameter is used to specify how many bytes of code will be transferred. When creating this last parameter, it is usually best to use the SizeOf procedure, which automatically calculates how many bytes are involved. Finally, notice that you have to dereference the pointers when using the Move procedure. If the code example had been written like this:

```
Move(SAry1, SAry2, SizeOf(TStringAry));
```

the system most likely would have crashed down around our ears.

# A Closer Look at Pointers

Although everything discussed so far in this lesson has been useful, it still falls short of providing a complete explanation of pointers. It will take two lessons to finish that job, but you can begin to dig a bit deeper if you can come to terms with the famous DOS 64K barrier.

You have already wrestled with the 64K limit, at least to a—ahem—limited degree. The subject came up in the discussion about the maximum size of an array. I said that no single array can have more than 64K of data in it.

The primary reason for this is that 8088 and 286 computers have something called a *16-bit bus*. This bus, which you can think of as merely a series of 16 wires, is the primary means of communication between the CPU and the rest of the computer. In particular, when the computer wants to talk to RAM—what I am calling the Memory Theater—communications are conducted along a 16-bit path.

Because there are 8 bits in a byte and 16 bits in a word, the word is the standard means of addressing memory in a 16-bit operating system. The largest number a word can hold is 65,535, which is 64K.

That's pretty much the whole story right there. Because of a hardware limitation on 8088 and 80286 computers, the operating system addresses memory 64K at a time. That means we can't declare variables larger than 64K. More specifically, we can't have an array that contains more than 65,520 bytes.

That's all you really need to know for now about the 64K limit. The rest of the story involves delving into the PC's way of addressing memory through segments and offsets, but I don't want to open that can of worms quite yet.

# The Data Segment

With this somewhat oversimplified explanation of the 64K limit fixed firmly in your mind, take a look at something called the *data segment*. Whether you know it or not, you have been dealing with data segments since the very beginning of this book. In fact, every program you have written has a data segment.

The data segment is a place in RAM where all the global variables in a program are stored. For instance, in the following short program, the variable W resides in the data segment, but the variable x does not:

```
program VerySimple;

procedure Foo;
var
  x: Word;
begin
  x := 2;
end;

var
  W: Word;
begin
  W := 2;
  Foo;
end.
```

The variable x is not part of the data segment because it is a local variable, and local variables end up in what is called the *stack segment*.

378

Whenever you want to see the size of the data segment, all you need to do is press Alt-C to open the Compile menu, and then press I to select the *Information Dialog*. Figure 28.2 shows what the Information Dialog looks like after compiling the following extremely abbreviated program:

```
begin
end.
```

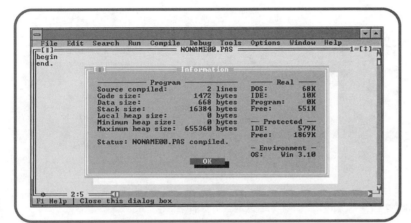

***Figure 28.2.***
*Press Alt-C, and then press I to bring up the dialog shown in this screen shot.*

Notice that in this particular example the data size is shown as occupying 668 bytes. Because you aren't declaring any variables in this program, it's only fair to ask from where these bytes are coming. The answer is that there are a number of global variables and constants declared in the System unit, which is automatically linked into every Pascal program. These identifiers can be seen in the online help, as shown in Figure 28.3.

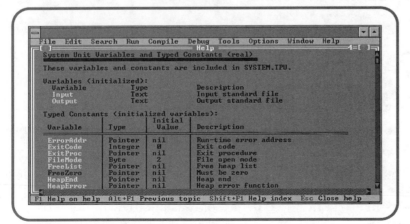

***Figure 28.3.***
*A portion of the help screen showing the constants and variables in SYSTEM.TPU.*

As an illustration of exactly how the data segment works, see Figure 28.4, which shows how the Information Dialog looks after we compile the following short program:

```
var
  W: Word;
begin
  W := 2;
end.
```

**Figure 28.4.**
*Compare the data size in this screen with the data size in Figure 28.2.*

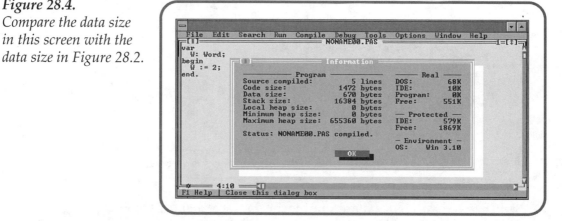

As you can see, the data segment in this example is exactly two bytes larger than the data segment in the previous example. This is because a single global variable of type word was added to the program. As I explained in the very beginning of this book, word variables are two bytes in size. That is why the data segment grew by two bytes, from 668 to 670.

# The Data Segment of the Memory Theater

Before moving on, take a moment to fit the data segment into the seats of the Memory Theater.

So far, whenever I have talked about the Memory Theater I have regarded it more or less as an undifferentiated array of seats, and I have described the data as being as likely to fit into one part of it as another. In point of fact, however, the seats in nearly every real-life theater are divided up into different sections, and people pay different prices to sit in different parts of the theater.

A vaguely analogous situation occurs in the Memory Theater, which is divided into at least four different sections. One section is called the *data segment*, another the *stack segment*, a third the *code segment*, and a fourth the *heap*. I have already discussed the data segment, and I have mentioned that local variables end up on the stack segment.

The code segment consists primarily of the procedures and functions you have written or called. After these lines of code are compiled and loaded into memory, they end up in the code segment. Nearly all the rest of the memory in the 640K Memory Theater can be allocated to the heap.

The Memory Theater analogy can be a bit misleading here, because the various sections of a real theater almost always have the same physical proportions and location. That is, the orchestra section is always in the same place, and every time you walk into your favorite movie house, the balcony has probably remained the same size.

This is not true of the sections in the Memory Theater. The data segment may end up in one part of the house during one run, and another part of the house during another run. The same is true of the code segment, stack segment, and heap. Each of these segments can also grow and shrink in size.

But some things in the theater remain constant. For instance, the data segment and stack segment can never be larger than 64K. They can, however, as we have already seen, be considerably smaller. The code segment also has a 64K limitation, but fortunately you are allowed to have multiple code segments in your programs. In fact, every time you create a new unit, you are usually creating a new code segment.

The size of the heap can vary from program to program. It is controlled by the Memory Compiler directive, which might look like either of the following two examples:

```
{$M 16384, 0, 655360}
```

```
{$M 2048, 0, 2048}
```

In the first instance, the default memory sizes for a Turbo Pascal program are simply being declared. Specifically, the first example asks for a stack segment of 16,384 bytes, a minimum heap size of zero, and a maximum heap size of 640K. The second example is declaring a very small stack and heap, but still designates the minimum heap size as zero.

Admittedly, the latter half of this lesson is discussing very abstract concepts. I hope that at least some of it is starting to make sense to you.

Just try to sit back for a moment and picture the Memory Theater spread out before you, with certain seats roped off as the data segment, other seats roped off as the code and stack segments, and most of what is left designated as the heap. This analogy is actually fairly accurate. It isn't perfect, and I am still omitting some important aspects of the lower 640K that are definitely way outside the scope of this book, but the overall picture presented here is still reasonably true to what is actually going on inside the computer.

So now you are ready for the final piece that will hopefully bring the major points of this lesson home to you. Okay, this is the big enchilada, the main point of the lesson:

> *When you declare a normal array, it ends up in the data segment. However, when you declare a pointer to an array, you move that array out of the data segment and onto the heap.*

Consider the following program:

```
program MaxAry;

type
  TMyArray = Array [1..32426] of Integer;

var
  MyArray: TMyArray;

begin
  MyArray[1] := 1;
end.
```

When this code is compiled, it creates a data segment of 65,520 bytes (see Figure 28.5), which happens to be the maximum size for a data segment.

*Figure 28.5.*
*The Information Dialog for a program that completely fills the data segment.*

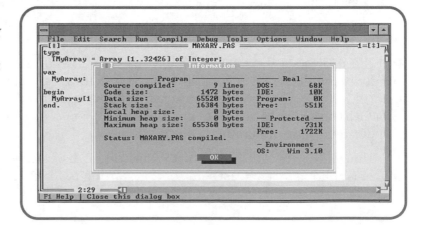

Now take a look at this program:

```
program MaxAryP;

type
  PMyArray = ^TMyArray;
  TMyArray = Array [1..32426] of Integer;

var
  MyArray: PMyArray;

begin
  New(MyArray);
  MyArray^[1] := 1;
  Dispose(MyArray);
end.
```

Program MaxAryP creates a data segment of only 674 bytes. That's a change of 64,846 bytes! And where did that information go? Well, it didn't just disappear. It has been moved from the data segment to the heap.

# Summary

This lesson is packed with very technical information. In fact, the material covered is advanced enough that many intermediate level programmers wouldn't necessarily understand everything it discusses. So take a moment to feel good about what you have been working on in these last few pages. You're in the big leagues now, discussing serious programming issues.

Nevertheless, there's nothing here so tough that you can't come to terms with it if you try. The concepts aren't really all that difficult.

If it's all starting to jell in your mind, well then, you're on your way to becoming a programming guru! At any rate, this is certainly the road that leads in the right direction. Understand memory and learn to recognize every seat in the Memory Theater. That's the foundation upon which all the best programmers build.

# Review Question

1. What is the 64K barrier, and why does it exist? _____
   _____
   _____
   _____
   _____
   _____

29

# Exploring the Heap

***To examine pointers and linked lists.***

This last lesson presents a powerful way to use pointers to break the 64K barrier. The technique is called a *linked list*. Linked lists are really only another type of data structure, such as an array or a record. By definition, however, linked lists exist only on the heap. Because the heap is usually much larger than 64K and can contain multiple segments, it can be used to store much more than 64K of data. In other words, linked lists can hold more information than any of the data structures you have seen so far.

Linked lists are not innately complicated data structures. Nevertheless, they can be devilishly hard to comprehend if you do not have a thorough understanding of pointers. So before beginning an exploration of linked lists, here's one last very close look at pointers.

# More About Pointers

In the last lesson you examined pointers to arrays. There is no reason why there can't be pointers to strings, records, integers, reals, or to virtually any data type imaginable. If something resides in memory, then you can declare a pointer to it.

Here is a short program that shows how to declare pointers to two commonly used data types:

```
program ManyPtr;

uses
  Crt,
  ToolBoxC;

var
  S: ^String;
  B: ^Byte;

begin
  ClrScr;
  New(S);
  New(B);
  S^ := 'Hello';
  B^ := 123;
  WriteLn('A String called S: ', S^);
  WriteLn('A Byte called B: ', B^);
  WriteLn;
  WriteLn(' Size of B: ', SizeOf(B));
  WriteLn(' Size of what B points to: ', SizeOf(B^));
  WriteLn(' Size of S: ', SizeOf(S));
  WriteLn(' Size of what S points to: ', SizeOf(S^));
  Dispose(S);
  Dispose(B);
  PressToEnd;
end.
```

ManyPtr's output looks like this:

```
A String called S: Hello
A Byte called B: 123

  Size of B: 4
  Size of what B points to: 1
```

386

```
Size of S: 4
Size of what S points to: 256

Press ENTER to end this program.
```

The exact same thing is going on here as in the last lesson. Most of this program is presented simply as a template you can use in the future. For instance, the following two lines remind you how to dereference pointers:

```
S^ := 'Hello';
B^ := 123;
```

There is nothing new here as compared with what you saw in the last lesson, but perhaps it is helpful to see that the same rules used with arrays also work with strings and bytes.

Of more interest is the code that writes out the size of the data types used in this program:

```
WriteLn(' Size of B: ', SizeOf(B));
WriteLn(' Size of what B points to: ', SizeOf(B^));
WriteLn(' Size of S: ', SizeOf(S));
WriteLn(' Size of what S points to: ', SizeOf(S^));
```

Notice in particular that the pointer to a byte and the pointer to a string are the exact same size, even though the things they point to are of radically different sizes.

This last sentence is absolutely crucial to your understanding of pointers, yet even if you read it over two or three times, you might not understand all the implications of the issues being discussed. To make things a bit more comprehensible, take a look at the IDE's watch window midway through a run of this program (see Figure 29.1).

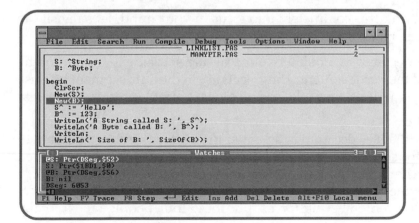

**Figure 29.1.**

*The watch window in the IDE can explain a lot about pointers.*

Start this examination by taking a look at the two different views you get of the pointers:

```
@S: Ptr(DSeg,$52)
 S: Ptr($1BD1,$0)
```

The first view of S tells where the pointer itself resides. You get this information by preceding the variable with the @ symbol, which is sometimes called the "at" symbol. This syntax makes the debugger cough up the actual address where S lives.

To understand exactly what this means, pause for a moment to think about the "true inner nature" of S, about the Zen of S. This variable is declared as a pointer to a string, but its true inner nature is not really what it is pointing to, but what it happens to be. It so happens that what ties it to all other pointers is that it *occupies a four-byte space in memory where addresses can be stored*.

That S occupies a four-byte space in memory is obvious from the program. There the SizeOf function was used to obtain the size of the variable, and a glance at the screen reveals that the pointer does occupy exactly four bytes in memory. Furthermore, a second glance at the program's output reveals that B also occupies exactly four bytes.

When we declared a four-byte variable in the past, it was because we wanted to keep data in it. For instance, LongInts take up four bytes, and you have seen that these four bytes belonging to LongInt can be used as a place to store numbers within a certain range.

The four bytes allocated to pointers, however, are not used to store traditional data, at least so far as data has been defined in this program. Rather than a number or a string, those bytes are used to store the address of some other data.

To try to bring this completely into focus in your mind, let's revisit the Memory Theater.

When S is declared as a pointer, four seats are set aside in the part of the theater called the data segment. These seats are in the data segment because S is declared as a global variable, and all global variables reside in the data segment.

You know that S is declared as a pointer to a string. So when you want to know about the string, you go to the four seats assigned to the pointer. When you get there, however, something very unusual happens. Normally, people in the data segment of the Memory Theater cheerfully cough up the numbers they have been remembering for us, but these four people take a totally different approach. When asked about their data, they all stand up on their chairs, point dramatically toward the heap, and say, "It's out there, in section 1BD0, seat 0!"

These last numbers are the ones that they have been remembering for us. In other words, the knowledge they have is not a traditional piece of data like a number or a string; instead, they know where in the Memory Theater our string is being kept. That is to say, they know an *address* in memory.

To accomplish the task of remembering an address, they divide into two groups. The members of the audience in the first two seats remember the section number, and those in the second two seats remember the seat numbers.

If you're having trouble grasping what I'm talking about, don't worry. This is a difficult subject. However, there is almost no way to exaggerate its importance. If you ever want to become a really good programmer, you have to understand pointers.

So take another look at the output you saw in the watch window:

```
@S: Ptr(DSeg,$52)
S: Ptr($1BD1,$0)
```

The first address is where the pointer S resides. The second address is where the people in these seats are pointing.

To fully understand this, you have to know that the Pascal Ptr function converts a segment and an offset into a pointer. You already know what segments are, because you have looked at the data segment, the code segment, and the stack segment. The offset part of the formula is nothing more than an index into a particular segment. So in the case of S, the watch window tells you that the variable resides in DSeg, which for now you can think of as shorthand for the data segment. Furthermore, you can see that S is at an offset 52 hex bytes into the data segment.

If you have had advanced math, you probably know about hexadecimal numbers. Hexadecimal numbers are numbers that use a base of 16 rather than a base of 10.

If you don't know anything about hexadecimal numbers, maybe this will be the moment when you throw your hands up in the air and say, "Forget it, this is just too complicated. I'm never going to absorb all this information." At any rate, that was more or less how I felt when writers first tried to explain pointers to me. The whole subject just seemed impossibly remote. But I stuck with it, and now pointers are old hat (or at least they are most of the time).

At any rate, the good news here is that you don't really need to understand hexadecimal numbers. When you see $52 on the screen, you can turn to your hex calculator (if you have one handy) and convert this to the number 82 in the base ten system. Therefore, you know that the variable S resides 82 bytes from the beginning of the data segment.

When you look there, you see that S is pointing out into the heap, toward the string. In fact, it can tell you the very seat in the Memory Theater where the string begins.

With this whole image hopefully clear in your mind, take a look at two pieces of syntax:

```
S^ := 'Hello';
S := 'Hello';
```

The first line tells us that the string S is pointing to should be set to the word Hello. The second is simply a nonsense statement saying that S itself should contain the address Hello.

In other words, the first example says "Go to the people in the data segment who are associated with variable S. Ask them where the data is to which they are pointing, and then tell the people that S is pointing to that they should remember the word Hello." This process is called *dereferencing* a pointer. The second example tells you to set the address that the people at S are remembering to the word Hello. Because Hello isn't any kind of proper address, the compiler rejects this latter statement.

You now have enough information to understand a very common and very frustrating bug called *memory corruption*. Memory corruption occurs when an area in the data segment is accidentally filled with a string like Hello, or with some other bogus information masquerading as an address. When this happens, your machine will most likely crash. The reason this crash takes place is that when the computer tries to reference the variable that has been corrupted, it ends up jumping to some nonsense address spelled out, for instance, by the ASCII value of the letters in the word *Hello*. When it gets to this address, it finds only random data. Confused by yet more bogus data, it doesn't know what to do next, and ends up crashing.

At first, this will probably happen to you a lot when you are working with pointers. Welcome to the grand tradition. Finding pointer bugs is a task that truly separates the women from the girls and the men from the boys in the programming world.

```
program PtrBug;

type
  PString = ^String;

var
  S: String;
  S1: PString;

begin
  New(S);
  S1 := 'Mother';
  S := ' Nature';
  Write(S1);
  WriteLn(S);
  Dispose(S1);
end;
```

# A Quick Look at nil Pointers

If you look at the watch window in Figure 28.1, you will see the following information:

```
@B: Ptr(DSeg,$56)
 B: nil
```

At the time this screen shot was taken, I had stepped through the part of ManyPtr.Pas where memory was allocated for S with the New procedure, but I had not yet reached the line where memory was allocated for B.

As a result, the address of B in the data segment is readily available, but the people sitting in that part of the Memory Theater don't remember a real address in the heap. In fact, what they remember is nothing at all, absolutely "nil."

Regardless of what it means in common English, in Pascal nil is a keyword that pointers can be set equal to when they are not holding any valid address. This is so pointers can be clearly marked as uninitialized. That is, you can test whether a pointer is equal to nil, and then take a certain action depending on the result of the test.

Before New is called, the variable B has no memory allocated for it, so it can either be pointing at some random, meaningless address or it can be set equal

391

to nil. In version 7.0, the Turbo Pascal compiler frequently sets uninitialized pointers to nil, but if you want to be sure of this result, you should explicitly set a pointer as being equal to nil:

```
B := nil;
```

After I took the screen shot shown in Figure 28.1, I continued to step through my program, executing the line where New was called with B as a parameter. As a result, the variable B in the watch window took on a different look:

```
@B: Ptr(DSeg,$56)
B: Ptr($1BE1,$0)
```

Here you can see that B is no longer pointing to nil. Instead, it references a valid byte of memory residing on the heap.

# A Linked List

You are finally ready to take a look at linked lists. As I said before, linked lists reside entirely on the heap, or, rather, all but at least one four-byte pointer in a linked list resides on the heap. You can think of that one pointer as being the start of a long swirling trail of data that floats in the heap above the data or stack segment like a huge long-tailed kite.

To get a better feeling for this situation, suppose for a moment that a single pointer resides in the data segment. Furthermore, suppose that it points to a data structure on the heap, and that the data structure on the heap also contains a pointer that points to another data structure on the heap. Also suppose that data structure points to yet another data structure, which in turn points to yet another, and so on (see Figure 29.2). If you can picture this long chain of linked items, then you can begin to visualize the way linked lists are put together in memory.

*Figure 29.2.*
*The first pointer in a linked list points to a data structure on the heap. That in turn points to another, and so on.*

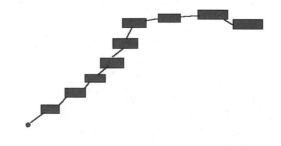

The amazing thing about this long trail of data structures is that it does not reside in either the stack segment, code segment, or data segment. Instead, each node in the long list of nodes can reside in its own segment, if indeed things happened to work out that way. As a result, there is no 64K limitation on this data structure.

It is now time to take a look at an example linked list. It begins with a pointer called First, which points toward a structure on the heap. That structure looks like this:

```
PMyRecord = ^TMyRecord;
TMyRecord = Record
  Name: String;
  Next: PMyRecord;
end;
```

As you can see, this record contains a pointer that points to a structure of type PMyRecord. This, of course, is the link to the next node on the list. Because that node will in turn contain another pointer of type PMyRecord, it also will be able to point to another data structure of the same type.

This chaining process can go on until there is no more heap space. Because you need a way to mark the end of the chain, always be careful to set the last pointer in the linked list to nil. That way you can always check to see if you are at the end of the list.

Well, that's about it for linked lists. As I said above, they aren't really very complicated data structures, but they can be nasty little fellows to pin down, especially if you don't understand the exact nature of those wily little creatures called pointers.

```
program LinkList;
{
  A simple linked list
}
uses
  Crt;

type
  PMyRecord = ^TMyRecord;
  TMyRecord = Record
    Name: String;
    Next: PMyRecord;
  end;
```

```pascal
var
  Total: Integer;

procedure CreateNew(var Item: PMyRecord);
begin
  New(Item);
  Item^.Next := nil;
  Item^.Name := '';
end;

function Int2Str(l:LongInt): string;
var
  S:string;
begin
  str(l,s);
  Int2Str := s;
end;

procedure GetData(var Item: PMyRecord);
begin
  Item^.Name := 'Sam' + Int2Str(Total);
end;

procedure DoFirst(var First, Current: PMyRecord);
begin
  CreateNew(Current);
  GetData(Current);
  First := Current;
end;

procedure Add(var Prev, Current: PMyRecord);
begin
  Prev := Current;
  CreateNew(Current);
  GetData(Current);
  Prev^.Next := Current;
end;

procedure Show(Head: PMyRecord);
begin
  while Head^.Next <> nil do begin
    WriteLn(Head^.Name);
```

```
    Head := Head^.Next;
  end;
  WriteLn(Head^.Name);
end;

procedure FreeAll(var Head: PMyRecord);
var
  Temp: PMyRecord;
begin
  while Head^.Next <> nil do begin
    Temp := Head^.Next;
    Dispose(Head);
    Head := Temp;
  end;
  Dispose(Head);
end;

var
  i: Integer;
  First,
  Prev,
  Current: PMyRecord;
  Start: LongInt;
  Size: LongInt;
begin
  ClrScr;
  Total := 1;
  DoFirst(First, Current);
  repeat
    Inc(Total);
    Add(Prev, Current);
  until Total > 20;
  Show(First);
  FreeAll(First);
  ReadLn;
end.
```

Linked lists are a subject that have probably generated nearly as many different approaches as there are programmers. The particular example I present you with here is therefore meant as little more than a place from which you can start your exploration of these fascinating, albeit at times frustrating, data structures.

Also, I should mention that there are a number of very effective substitutes for linked lists available on the market. One of them, called *Collections*, even ships with Turbo and Borland Pascal. Other alternatives involve special double-linked lists or trees that contain at least two pointers in each record—one pointing to the data item that is next in the list, and the other pointing to the previous item in the list.

The possibilities here are too many to mention at this time. I leave you with a final exercise that involves extending the example above so that it includes a procedure for finding a particular item in the list.

In this Finish the Program example, you should create a procedure that can be called like this:

```
FindItem(First, 'Sam16');
```

where `First` is a pointer to the first node in the list, and `'Sam16'` is the string for which to search. Here's the header for your function:

```
procedure FindItem(Head: PMyRecord; S: String);
begin
```

_____

_____

_____

_____

_____

_____

_____

_____

_____

_____

# Heap Overflow: We're Out of Bytes

Well, I'm afraid that's about it. Like Andrew Marvell, we have neither world enough nor time to explore any further.

As for where you go from here, I can only recommend that you code as much as possible and that you read everything you can find on the subject of Pascal, computers, and especially anything you can find on what I have called the Memory Theater. Subscribe to magazines, read books, and if possible, join programmer's user groups and even bulletin board systems (BBSs) such as CompuServe.

My final words of advice are to never write a line of code unless you enjoy what you're doing. Even if you are paid for your work, coding should always be an avocation rather than a vocation. Let management tend to the work; we're here to tend to the aesthetics of our art, which happens to be called programming. They spend the money, we make it.

I'm not really very good at good-byes, so I'll just bid you adieu by wishing you good luck with your programming.

Appendix

# Installing Turbo Pascal

The aim of this appendix is to give you a brief overview of the Pascal family of products and to help you get your copy of Borland Pascal up and running. If you are an experienced computer user, there is probably little in this section that will prove new to you. But if you are new to computers, or if you are having trouble with the installation process, this portion of the book should help get you over the initial hurdles. When you are done, you will be free to work on the real business at hand, programming.

The main difficulty that I, as a writer, face working on this appendix is that you could own any one of three products: Borland Pascal, Turbo Pascal, or Turbo Pascal for Windows. Each of these tools has its unique set of system requirements. For instance, there are only a few things I can say about installing Turbo Pascal for Windows that also apply to the installation of Borland Pascal.

As a result, portions of this appendix will be broken up into three sections, one for each of the members of the Pascal family.

# About the Pascal Family

As I write, there are three Pascal products on the market. One is called Turbo Pascal 7.0, another Borland Pascal 7.0, and the third Turbo Pascal for Windows 1.5.

Turbo Pascal 7.0 is a DOS-based product that takes up about 5 megs of disk space on your hard drive. It is an excellent product to buy if you are new to Pascal programming. It is priced to sell to almost any computer owner, yet it comes equipped with the tools necessary to build blazingly fast, bullet-proof applications that can wow users with their power and flexibility.

Turbo Pascal for Windows 1.5 is a Windows-hosted environment that takes up about 11 megs on your hard drive. It allows you to build applications that utilize the full scope of the exciting new Windows environment. Unlike many Windows tools, TPW allows you access to the entire Windows command set, while at the same time providing you with an easy-to-use set of programming tools and a powerful, intuitive programming environment.

Borland Pascal for Objects 7.0 is a superset of TP7.0 and TPW1.5. In other words, everything that is included in the first two products is also included in BP7.0. In addition, you will also find a number of handy tools, utilities, and pieces of source code that help make this the premier professional programming environment in the world today. Borland Pascal is a big, professional programming tool that, when fully installed, takes up 28 megs on your hard drive.

If you own any of these three products, you will be able to use this book to help you learn how to program in Pascal. Having said this, I must add that this is not a Windows programming book. In fact, there is no question but that the Pascal Windows programming environment at this time is not the ideal place for anyone to learn how to program. So, if you are a beginner, you are definitely better off if you own either Turbo Pascal or Borland Pascal. However, I am very much aware that many beginning programming students do own copies of TPW. As a result, I have added Appendix B, "Using Pascal with Windows," which should make it possible for you to use this book as your guide while you learn about Turbo Pascal.

All right. With these preliminaries out of the way, the next step is to discuss the installation process.

# Install Preliminaries

The installation process is effortless 99.9 percent of the time. Borland has made every attempt to make an install program that is entirely self-explanatory. As a result, by far the easiest way to use the install program is simply to proceed without reading these long and rather detailed instructions. But if you are confused by some aspect of the install process, or if you are one of the very rare users who have found what appears to be a bug in the install programs, you should continue reading this section.

Let me begin the general section of the install guide with a single piece of advice: Accept the defaults. If you are having trouble with the installation process, don't try to fine-tune it beyond what is necessary to specify your target drive. The goal is to get you up and running, and the simplest way to do that is to take the path of least resistance.

A second piece of general advice is not to install Pascal on a compressed drive. If you have Stacker, or some other general data compression product, my advice is to set aside some noncompressed space on your drive for any development tools you want to install on your system.

There are two reasons for this. The first is that most installation problems with Pascal occur on systems with compressed drives. This does not mean that I have any reason to believe that you can't install Pascal on a compressed drive; the process will go smoothly the vast majority of the time. But in my experience, there is a slightly higher incidence of trouble with installing Pascal on compressed drives than on noncompressed drives.

The second reason for not installing on a compressed drive is that programming can be a very subtle endeavor. You will have enough to worry about without having to consider whether some error in your program is the result of a bug you have introduced, or the result of a failure on the part of your data compression system.

Please don't interpret this as a criticism of any data compression product. In fact, I use one of these fine tools on my own system at home. Nor am I trying to deny the inevitable: A data compression system is slated to ship with MS-DOS 6.0. All I'm trying to do is get you up and running with the least amount of fuss possible. To help you achieve this goal, I suggest you do what I do at home, which is to install Pascal on a noncompressed portion of the hard drive.

A final piece of preliminary advice: Don't choose Pascal to be the first product you run on a computer. Pascal is a very powerful and easy-to-use programming language. It is an excellent choice for anyone who wants to

401

find a first programming language. It is also a very fine professional tool used to write some of the best applications on the market today. It is not, however, an ideal introduction to computers.

For instance, if you don't know drive A from drive C, or if you don't know what a subdirectory is, you probably are not yet ready to learn how to program.

This is by no means a hard and fast rule. Nor am I implying that you need to be an experienced computer user before you learn how to program. All I'm saying is that you will probably live a longer, happier, more fulfilled life if you know a little something about DOS before you begin programming. Even a couple weeks or a month of experience should be sufficient to get you over the first hurdles you need to master before you begin to write code.

# Install Basics

I want to take a few moments now to step you through the basics of the installation process. This section of the appendix includes three subsections: one for Turbo Pascal, one for Borland Pascal, and one for Turbo Pascal for Windows.

## Turbo Pascal Users

The instructions for Turbo Pascal depend on whether you are using a hard drive or a dual-floppy system.

### Turbo Pascal Users with Hard Drives:

1. Exit any programs you are in and return to DOS.

2. Place the install disk in either drive A or drive B.

3. Make the drive you choose the default drive. For instance. If you placed the install disk in drive A, type:

   ```
   a:
   ```

   and then press the Enter key.

4. Type the word Install and press Enter. You should now be looking at the screen in Figure A.1.

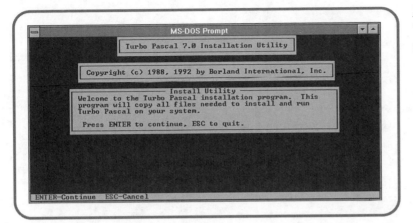

***Figure A.1.***
*The Turbo Pascal*
*installation screen.*

5. Press Enter three more times to accept the default choices.

6. If you are installing your system onto drive C, press the up-arrow key once, to highlight the words `Start Installation`. If you are going to install onto another drive, press Enter while the words `Turbo Pascal Base Directory` are still highlighted. Now change the drive letter to the appropriate setting as shown in Figure A.2. Now highlight the words `Start Installation`, as shown in Figure A.3.

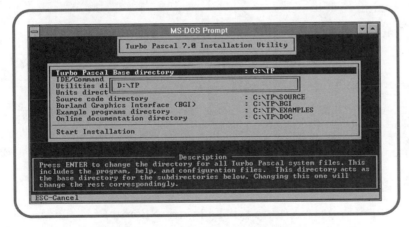

***Figure A.2.***
*Designating a*
*different drive.*

7. Press Enter one more time to start the installation process. The install program prompts you when it is time to enter another disk in your floppy drive.

8. Once the installation process has finished, be sure to modify your path, as explained later in this appendix.

403

*Figure A.3.*
*Starting the installation process.*

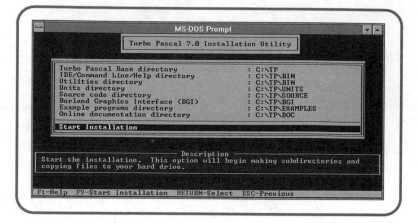

## Turbo Pascal Users with Floppy Drives:

You must have a dual-floppy system to use this option.

1. Format two floppy disks. Make sure they are completely clean, with no other files on them whatsoever, including hidden files or copies of 4DOS, COMMAND.COM, or any other system files.

2. Exit any programs you are in and return to DOS.

3. Place the install disk in drive A.

4. Be sure that drive A is your default drive. To do this, type:

   a:

   and then press Enter.

5. Type the word Install and press Enter. You should now be looking at the screen visible in Figure A.1.

6. Press Enter two more times to accept the default choices. Now use the arrow keys to highlight the words Install Turbo Pascal on a Floppy Drive.

7. Place the first of your two floppy disks in drive B and Press Enter. When the install system prompts you to change disks, do so.

8. Once the installation process has finished, be sure to modify your path, as explained later in this appendix.

I said that you must have two floppy drives to choose this option. If you have a single high-density drive, it is still possible for you to continue, so long as you are an experienced computer user. To run Turbo Pascal, you need only the files TURBO.EXE and TURBO.TPL together in a single directory. If you have already installed Pascal on a system, or if you know how to use the unzip utility, you can copy TURBO.EXE and TURBO.TPL onto a high-density floppy and run Pascal from there.

## Borland Pascal Users:

1. Exit any programs you are in and return to DOS.

2. Place the install disk in either drive A or drive B.

3. Make the drive you choose the default drive. For instance, if you placed the install disk in drive A, type:

    a:

    and then press Enter.

4. Type the word Install and press Enter. You should now be looking at a screen similar to the one visible in Figure A.1.

5. Press Enter two more times to accept the default choices.

6. If you are installing your system onto drive C, skip immediately to Step 7. If you are going to install onto another drive, press Enter while the words Borland Pascal Directory are still highlighted. Now change the drive letter to the appropriate setting as shown in Figure A.4.

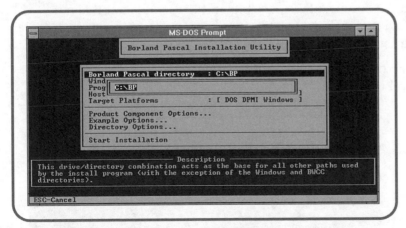

*Figure A.4.*
*Setting up for an install on drive C.*

7. If you are going to install all 28 megabytes included in the Borland Pascal package, you should skip immediately to Step 8. If you want to install only part of Borland Pascal, I can give you an example of

what you might want to do by showing you how to install only the DOS-related tools. To do this, use the arrow keys to highlight the words `Host Platforms`. Press Enter once, and then use the arrow keys to highlight the word `BPW.EXE`. Press Enter once more. The screen should now look as it does in Figure A.5.

*Figure A.5.*
*Performing a partial install of Borland Pascal.*

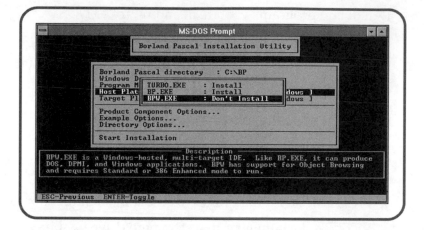

Press Escape once. Now you need to go through this same process again by first highlighting the words `Target Platforms` and pressing Enter, and then by highlighting `Windows Support` and pressing Enter. When you are done, press Escape and go on to Step 8.

There are, of course, other possible partial installs, but it is not practical to cover all the possibilities here. Just use this one example as a template you can modify to achieve your own ends.

8. Use the arrow keys to highlight the words `Start Installation`, as shown in Figure A.6.

*Figure A.6.*
*Starting the installation process.*

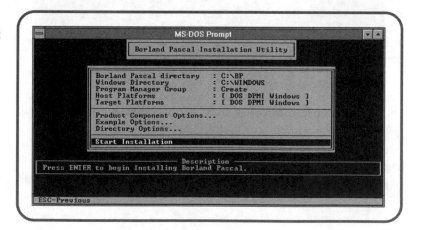

9. Press enter one more time to start the installation process. The install program will prompt you when it is time to enter another disk in your floppy drive.

10. Once the installation process has finished, be sure to modify your path, as explained later in this appendix.

## Turbo Pascal for Windows Users:

1. Place your install disk in either drive A or drive B.

2. Go to the Program Manager and click once on the word File and then again on the word Run.

3. Type the drive letter where you installed Turbo Pascal and add a backslash and the word install, as shown in Figure A.7.

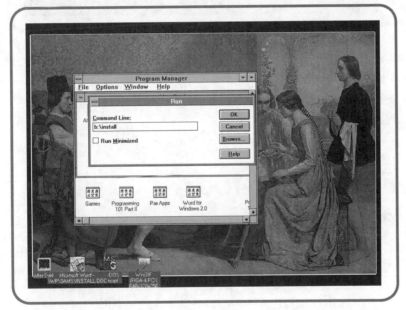

*Figure A.7.*
*Beginning the TPW install process.*

4. Press Enter to bring up the TPW install screen.

5. If you want to install to drive C, just click on the Install button. If you want to install to another drive, then go to the Install To edit box and enter the correct path (see Figure A.8). Now click on the Install button.

*Figure A.8.*
*Preparing for a TPW install on drive D.*

6. The installation program will automatically prompt you when it is time for you to enter another disk.

7. Once the installation process has finished, be sure to modify your path, as explained in the next section.

# Don't Forget to Modify Your Path

Borland's Pascal products will not automatically update your AUTOEXEC.BAT file. The install programs work this way because they aim to be polite. Most Pascal users are experienced programmers who have set up their machine to run in a particular way. It would be rude for Pascal to modify their system files automatically.

As a result, it is up to you to change the path on your system. To do this, start an editor such as Turbo Pascal, DOS's EDIT.COM, or Windows' Notepad. Then bring up your AUTOEXEC.BAT file and add the main Pascal subdirectories to your path.

Suppose that you are installing to drive C and have an initial path that looks like this:

```
c:\windows;c:\dos;c:\wp;c:\pdox40
```

If this is the case, your path should look like one of the following examples when you are done.

Turbo Pascal:
```
c:\windows;c:\dos;c:\wp;c:\pdox40;c:\bp
```

Borland Pascal:
```
c:\windows;c:\dos;c:\wp;c:\pdox40;c:\bp
```

Turbo Pascal for Windows:
```
c:\windows;c:\dos;c:\wp;c:\pdox40;c:\tpw;c:\tpw\utils
```

Of course, you may need to make modifications to these examples depending on the actual details of your particular setup. The basic idea, though, is to add c:\bp to your path for Turbo and Borland Pascal, and to add c:\tpw;c:\tpw\utils to your path for Turbo Pascal for Windows 1.5 or 1.0.

# A Broken Install

This section is for people who have followed the directions outlined above, but who find that for some reason the install process doesn't function correctly. Two problems fitting into this category are the termination of the install process with an error message or a seemingly illogical complaint from the install process regarding the amount of disk space you have available. At the very end of this section, I add a few general tips useful to people who are having trouble with the install process or to those who want to customize their setup heavily.

The easiest install problems to resolve involve confusion over the amount of disk space necessary to complete an installation. The figures I have presented above, for example, refer to the amount of space these programs take up *after* they are installed. During the installation process, however, they can take up considerably more room, especially if you are working on a compressed drive.

BP7, for example, requires 65 megs of free space on your hard drive before it will install onto a compressed drive. TPW is also greedy; it wants some 21 megs of free space before it will install without complaint onto a compressed drive.

With megabyte requirements like these, you might have to *delete* something else before you can install Pascal. Once you are done with the installation process, you may find that you now have enough room to reinstall the product you just finished deleting. That may not be what you want to hear, and it may not even make much sense, but that's the way the system works!

I want to emphasize that the figures I just mentioned pertain to compressed drives. On a normal hard drive, you may be forced to clear out more space than the installed product will use, but the situation is not nearly so dire as it is on a compressed drive.

So what happens if you have *lots* of free space on your hard drive, and yet you are *still* getting an install error regarding the amount of free disk space available? Well, you need to understand that you have slipped through the cracks in the partition dividing normal installation problems from serious ones. In other words, you are now down there with the folks who've had their install process terminate with some ugly, incomprehensible error.

If you find yourself in this category, the first thing to do is relax. Sit down. Maybe get yourself a cup of tea, orange juice, coffee, whatever. The situation is not so dire as it might seem. Borland is a big company with an excellent reputation. It is not going to stick you with a broken product. Just calm yourself first, and then take a look through the next few paragraphs to see whether there isn't something that can be done right away.

If you are getting error messages that don't make any sense at all, or if the install process terminated abnormally, the first thing you should do is boot clean, as described in the next paragraph. Of course, if you are trying to install TPW, or if you are working on a compressed drive, you won't be able to boot completely clean, but you can come close.

To boot clean, you need to eliminate your AUTOEXEC.BAT completely and then reduce your CONFIG.SYS file to the following two lines:

```
Files=20
Buffers=20
```

The simplest way to do this is to have a boot disk handy that is empty except for a command processor, your hidden system files, and a copy of your CONFIG.SYS. Once you insert this disk in drive A, you can reboot your system by pressing Ctrl-Alt-Del.

Another way to boot clean is to go to the DOS prompt, move up to the root directory, and rename your AUTOEXEC.BAT file to AUTOEXEC.TMP with the following two commands:

```
cd\
ren autoexec.bat autoexec.tmp
```

Then rename your CONFIG.SYS file to CONFIG.TMP:

```
ren config.sys config.tmp
```

Now use an editor to create a new CONFIG.SYS file like the one described above, or else type in the following lines exactly as shown at the DOS prompt:

```
C:\>copy con config.sys
files=20
buffers=20^Z
```

The part that looks like ^z is created by pressing the F6 key. When you are done, press Enter. This latter process created a new CONFIG.SYS file on your hard drive. To see its contents, execute the following command at the DOS prompt:

```
type config.sys
```

If, after you've typed the file, you see that you made an error entering it, you should delete the file and try again to create it:

```
C:\>del config.sys


C:\>copy con config.sys
files=20
buffers=20^Z
```

When you are done, press Ctrl-Alt-Del.

Now you should be able to boot clean, unless you are using TPW or running on a compressed drive. If you are running Windows, the issue is fairly simple. You can afford to eliminate every line from your CONFIG.SYS except for your files and buffers statements and the line that loads HIMEM.SYS. One way to do this is to take your CONFIG.SYS file into an editor and put the word rem in front of every line you don't need. For instance, here is my current CONFIG.SYS stripped down to a bare bones Windows boot:

```
FILES=40
BUFFERS=40
DEVICE=C:\WINDOWS\HIMEM.SYS
rem DEVICE=C:\DOS\EMM386.EXE ram
rem DEVICEHIGH=C:\DOS\SETVER.EXE
rem DOS=HIGH,UMB
rem SHELL=C:\DOS\COMMAND.COM C:\DOS\  /p
rem STACKS=9,256
```

If you are working on a compressed drive, you cannot afford to eliminate every line in either your CONFIG.SYS file or your AUTOEXEC.BAT file. However, you must type rem before every line that is not absolutely essential.

411

Specifically, this means that you should have no path and no prompt statement in your AUTOEXEC.BAT file. Once you have achieved this state of relative purity, reboot your computer by pressing Ctrl-Alt-Del.

When you have finally managed to boot clean, or as near to clean as possible, resume the install process exactly as before. This time everything should go well, unless you are a Windows user. In that case, you need to remember to change into the Windows subdirectory before you can type `Win` and start up Windows. This step is necessary because you no longer have a path. Here's how to start Windows when there is no path and no prompt:

```
cd\windows
win
```

Remember that any time you become hopelessly confused by the lack of a prompt, you can always type the following to restore it:

```
prompt $p$g
```

But don't restore the prompt until *after* you have completed the install process.

Okay. So what happens if you have *lots* of disk space, you have booted clean, and yet you *still* can't complete the install process? You have one last hope if you find yourself in this dire situation.

This last cure will also resolve problems for people who are running into problems because they copied 5.25-inch install disks onto 3.5-inch install disks, or vice versa. Don't ask me how or why, just accept the fact that problems can happen.

If you find yourself in this situation, or if you are one of the very few people who have serious install problems, try creating a temporary subdirectory on your hard drive called INSTALL. Now switch into that subdirectory. Here are the DOS commands for performing these two tasks:

```
md Install
cd Install
```

Place your first disk in either drive A or drive B, and type one of the following lines at the DOS prompt:

```
copy a:\*.*
copy b:\*.*
```

Now try running the installation process from inside this new subdirectory. When you are done, you can delete the files from the subdirectory and remove the directory itself from your system.

These remedies should take care of all but the most dire installation problems. If you have tried them all, and yet still find that you can't install, the problem might not be with the Pascal software but with your system.

I've used up my bag of tricks regarding the install process, except for one last piece of information I want to pass on to you. On your install disk, you will find two files that can help you with your install problems. One is called FILELIST.DOC, and the other is called either UNZIP.EXE or UNPAK.EXE.

FILELIST.DOC includes a complete listing of all the files that come with your copy of Turbo Pascal. This listing includes information about which install diskette the file was placed on at the factory. Most of these files reside on the disks in a compressed format.

Suppose that you have looked at FILELIST.DOC and found that the file you want to get at, TDW.EXE, is inside a zip file called TDW.ZIP located on disk 4 of the install set. The first thing you should do is copy UNZIP.EXE into your current subdirectory. Then place disk 4 in drive A or drive B, and type something like the following:

```
unzip a:\tdw tdw.exe
```

The result is that TDW.EXE is unzipped and copied into the current subdirectory. If you want to unzip the entire contents of TDW.ZIP, then you could type the following:

```
unzip a:\tdw
```

If you are using TPW 1.5, you will want to use the UnPak program rather than the UnZip program. First, copy UNPAK.EXE into the current subdirectory. Here's what you would type if you wanted to unpack a file called TDW.EXE from a packed file called TDW.PAK residing on drive A:

```
unpak x a:\tdw tdw.exe
```

If you want to unpack the whole file, you could type:

```
unpak x a:\tdw
```

Before wrapping this appendix up, I want to point out that this whole long section on installing Turbo Pascal has nothing to do with programming. It's fun to write code and to learn new facts about programming. All the Borland Pascal compilers are very clean and powerful. So, if you had a hard time installing your version of Borland Pascal, put it behind you. Just forget what happened, and, instead, prepare yourself to have some fun.

# Using Pascal with Windows

This appendix explains how to use this book if you own Turbo Pascal for Windows, or if you own BP7 and want to try to work out of the Borland Pascal for Windows IDE.

Turbo Pascal has become a much more complex product than it was when it was first released about ten years ago. Since then many new features have been added, and one of the biggest has been the introduction of Windows programming tools.

From one point of view, Windows can sometimes seem like little more than an extension to DOS. When seen from a slightly different perspective, however, Windows is revealed as an entirely new operating system that gives the user an entirely different access to the machine lurking beneath the layers of code which encase it.

Given this latter set of circumstances, it might seem as though users of Turbo Pascal for Windows would have no use for a book like this one, which is aimed primarily at DOS programmers. In fact, this is not the case. It is possible for you to use Turbo Pascal for Windows while working through this book. It's just going to require a bit of effort.

# Preliminaries

Before I begin in earnest, let me get a few important matters out of the way. First and foremost, understand that given the current state of the available tools, there is no question that the DOS IDEs such as TURBO.EXE and BP.EXE are by far the best ways for anyone to learn how to use Pascal. Of course, owners of Turbo Pascal for Windows will have no choice but to work out of the Windows IDE and to produce Windows executables.

Take a moment to be sure you know what this means. Owners of Turbo Pascal for Windows 1.0 or 1.5 are never going to be able to use that product to produce DOS applications; it can produce only Windows applications. The same thing holds true for Turbo Pascal 7.0 owners; these individuals will be able to produce only DOS applications. The two groups who have flexibility in this matter are people who own both products or those who own Borland Pascal for Objects 7.0. These individuals will be able to pick and choose which environment they want to use and what kind of applications they want to produce.

Finally, let me make clear that there is a big distinction between Borland Pascal for Windows (BPW), which ships with Borland Pascal 7.0, and Turbo Pascal for Windows (TPW). From the outside they look very much alike, but BPW has the ability to produce DOS applications, which is something TPW cannot do. This means it would be possible for someone using BPW to run all of the code presented in this book exactly as it is written. The only thing these people will not be able to do is debug these programs inside the IDE.

These latter two subjects, namely, how to produce DOS apps from inside BPW and how to debug those applications, will be broached briefly at the end of this appendix. My main goal in these next few pages is to focus on Turbo Pascal for Windows owners. Once these people are straightened out, I can turn to the BPW users, who are not in such dire need of assistance because they can always fire up TURBO.EXE if they want.

# Using DOS Apps in TPW

If you are going to use TPW to work through the programs in this book, the first thing you must understand is that what you will be doing is not standard Windows programming. Instead, you will be able to use a very limited subset of the standard DOS Pascal programming commands that have been ported to Windows by Borland specifically to form a sort of artificial bridge between DOS and Windows.

I think this is a very important point, so I want to be as specific as possible. What I'm going to do now is show you two pieces of code, labeled WinSimp1 and WinSimp2. WinSimp1 is an example of the kind of code you, as a TPW owner, will be writing in this book:

```
program WinSimp1:

program Hello;
uses
  WinCrt;

begin
  WriteLn('Hello');
end.


{==============================}
{==============================}
```

The preceding program is one of the simplest meaningful applications that can be written using the techniques discussed in this appendix. The following program is one of the simplest programs that can be written using standard Windows programming techniques.

```
program WinSimp2;

uses
  WinTypes, WinProcs;

const
  AppName = 'WinSimp';


function WindowProc(Window: HWnd; Message, WParam: Word; LParam:
                    Longint): Longint; export;
var
  PaintInfo: TPaintStruct;
  PaintDC: HDC;

begin
  WindowProc := 0;
  case Message of

    wm_Paint: begin
      PaintDC := BeginPaint(Window, PaintInfo);
```

417

```
      TextOut(PaintDC, 10, 10, 'Hello', 5);
      EndPaint(Window, PaintInfo);
    end;

    wm_Destroy: begin
      PostQuitMessage(0);
      Exit;
    end;
  end;
  WindowProc := DefWindowProc(Window, Message, WParam, LParam);
end;

procedure WinMain;
var
  Window: HWnd;
  Message: TMsg;
const
  WindowClass: TWndClass = (
    style: 0;
    lpfnWndProc: @WindowProc;
    cbClsExtra: 0;
    cbWndExtra: 0;
    hInstance: 0;
    hIcon: 0;
    hCursor: 0;
    hbrBackground: 0;
    lpszMenuName: AppName;
    lpszClassName: AppName);
begin
  if HPrevInst = 0 then
  begin
    WindowClass.hInstance := HInstance;
    WindowClass.hIcon := LoadIcon(0, idi_Application);
    WindowClass.hCursor := LoadCursor(0, idc_Arrow);
    WindowClass.hbrBackground := GetStockObject(white_Brush);
    if not RegisterClass(WindowClass) then Halt(255);
  end;
  Window := CreateWindow(
    AppName,
    'Turbo Pascal Simple',
    ws_OverlappedWindow,
```

```
      cw_UseDefault,
      cw_UseDefault,
      cw_UseDefault,
      cw_UseDefault,
      0,
      0,
      HInstance,
      nil);
    ShowWindow(Window, CmdShow);
    UpdateWindow(Window);
    while GetMessage(Message, 0, 0, 0) do
    begin
      TranslateMessage(Message);
      DispatchMessage(Message);
    end;
    Halt(Message.wParam);
  end;


begin
  WinMain;
end.
```

WinSimp2, as you notice, is considerably longer than WinSimp1, but they both produce essentially the same output, which is visible in Figure B.1.

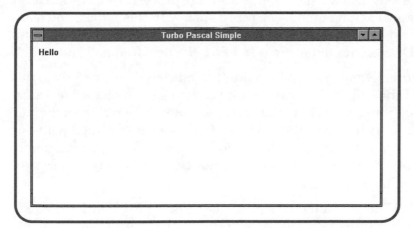

***Figure B.1.***
*The output from*
*WinSimp2.*

Obviously, these are two very different methods of producing essentially the same output. It happens that the second technique is both more complex and more powerful than the first technique. So let there be no mistake about what is going on here. I'm going to show you a way to write Windows applications, but I am not going to introduce you to "true" Windows programming.

419

A second important point I want to make is that this appendix is not going to tell you everything you need to know to begin programming. To glean that much information you will have to jump back and forth between this appendix and the main text of the book several different times. My personal suggestion is that you read this appendix all the way through once, and then begin reading the main text of the book. If there are times when you feel uncertain about how you, as a TPW owner should proceed while reading this book, you can refer to this section to help clarify matters.

You must understand that there are going to be many places in the main text where I will discuss matters that do not apply directly to Windows programs. For instance, in Lesson 1, I spend a good deal of time talking about how DOS users can view the watch window or watch screen. Windows users will simply have to ignore those passages, as they have no relevance to the IDE of TPW.

In other words, it is going to be an uphill battle for TPW users. I know that a good number of people who bought TPW need a basic introduction to Pascal, so I am providing this appendix in an attempt to reach out to those people and to show them that they can, indeed, use their product to learn the fundamentals of the Pascal language.

If you do have TPW, you should take consolation from knowing that in the long run you will probably be better off than those who do all their work in DOS. Right now every reasonable sign points to Windows as the platform of the future. Taken as a whole, Windows is more powerful, more fun, easier to use, and more exciting than DOS. If you stick with this project and learn to program using TPW, you will have a big jump on your peers who are still stuck in the DOS environment. So take heart; the news isn't all bad.

Furthermore, let me say that I wouldn't be adding this appendix to this book unless I thought it was feasible for you to learn the basics of Pascal programming from inside TPW. The goal is definitely achievable for the vast majority of readers who pick up this book. Once you are finished with this book, you will be ready to learn more about real Windows programming, which is a goal you could never achieve without first mastering the basics of the Pascal language.

Also, all TPW users should be sure to glance at the README file which comes on the disk provided at the back of this book. This file contains hints and possible last-minute additions which could be of use to Windows programmers.

With these issues cleared up, I want to begin teaching you how to write simple Windows applications that will very nearly mirror the type of code that produces DOS applications. The key to this whole process is something called the WinCrt unit.

# Borland's **WinCrt** Unit

Every application that TPW users write while studying this book will have to begin with these two lines:

```
uses
  WinCrt;
```

There can be no exceptions to this rule. If you are going to write a program that will not die with a nasty error message, you must add these two words to your code.

For instance, early on in the main text of this book I present the reader with the following short program:

```
begin
  Write('A');
end.
```

This code will compile and run fine from DOS IDEs such as TURBO.EXE, BP.EXE, and TPX.EXE, but if it is run as is from TPW, it will produce something resembling the following error message:

```
Error
```

```
Runtime error 105 at 0001:002E
```

(If you want to see this actually happen, type the program into TPW. Then press Alt-R to bring up the Run menu, and press R to run the program.) Whenever you see a message that looks like this, remember that it has occurred probably because you forgot to put the WinCrt bit at the top of your program.

It should be obvious what you will need to do to get this program up and running inside TPW:

```
uses
  WinCrt;
```

```
begin
  Write('A');
end.
```

This tiny program will run fine from the Windows IDE.

In fact, most of the programs in this book will run fine with only this one addition to their source code. However, there are some other issues that we need to clear up.

For instance, in the first lesson you will find the following program:

```
program StrangeLoop;
uses
  Crt;

begin
  ClrScr;
  WriteLn('The following sentence is false.');
  WriteLn('The preceding sentence is true.');
  WriteLn;
  WriteLn('Press the ENTER key to end this program.');
  ReadLn;
end.
```

You can see that this program already includes a *uses clause;* that is, it has the word uses followed by the word Crt. In DOS, we have to add these two words to the program because of the use of the ClrScr command, visible right below the word begin. In other words, if we took out the ClrScr command, the program would run fine from any DOS IDE even without the uses clause:

```
program StrangeLoop;

begin
  WriteLn('The following sentence is false.');
  WriteLn('The preceding sentence is true.');
  WriteLn;
  WriteLn('Press the ENTER key to end this program.');
  ReadLn;
end.
```

Of course, we know enough to realize that as is, however, this program will not run properly inside TPW. To remedy this situation, we must link in the WinCrt unit to the program:

```
program StrangeLoop;
uses
  WinCrt;

begin
  WriteLn('The following sentence is false.');
  WriteLn('The preceding sentence is true.');
  WriteLn;
  WriteLn('Press the ENTER key to end this program.');
  ReadLn;
end.
```

This program will now run fine from inside the Windows IDE.

As you can see, in this last version of the program I have not bothered to restore the ClrScr command to its place beneath the word begin. I do things this way not because ClrScr would cause an error in the Windows IDE, but because the command would serve no purpose in this Windows program. The reason for this is that every WinCrt program you create will automatically start with a clean screen. And since the ClrScr command is meant to "clear the screen," there can never be a reason to include it at the beginning of a WinCrt program. The same is not true of DOS programs, which are likely to start with the screen full of miscellaneous data.

By making these comments on the ClrScr command, I am not implying that there is no use for the command in a WinCrt program. For instance, the program will run entirely differently if we modify the code so that it looks like this:

```
program StrangeLoop;
uses
  WinCrt;

begin
  WriteLn('The following sentence is false.');
  WriteLn('The preceding sentence is true.');
  WriteLn;
  WriteLn('Press the ENTER to clear the screen.');
  ReadLn;
  ClrScr;
  WriteLn('Press the ENTER key to end this program.');
  ReadLn;
end.
```

423

If you run this program, it presents you with two screens. The first looks like the image shown in Figure B.2, and the second looks like the image in Figure B.3.

**Figure B.2.**
*The first half of the*
StrangeLoop *program.*

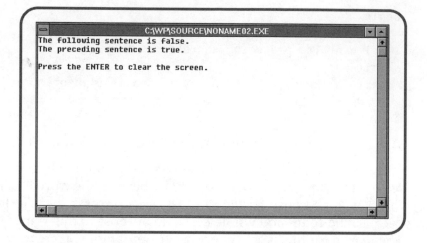

**Figure B.3.**
*The second half of the*
StrangeLoop *program.*

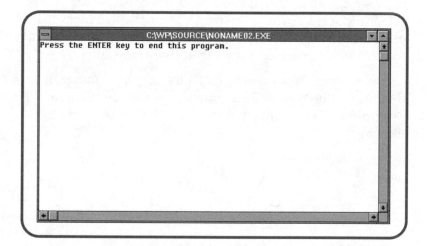

As you can see, the ClrScr command erased the first two lines printed by this program.

In this particular case, there is no good reason for inserting the ClrScr command into this program other than to show you how the command works. I hope that this example gives you a feeling for what the ClrScr command does, and for when it is useful in a Windows program. As I said above, it is unlikely to ever do you much harm, but I want to be sure that you have some feeling for what it actually does in your program.

Before we finish with program StrangeLoop, take a moment to glance at the title bar, or caption, visible at the top of Figure B.3. It looks like this:

```
( C:\WP\SOURCE\NONAME02.EXE )
```

If you follow the program's suggestion and press Enter, the screen will then look as it does in Figure B.4.

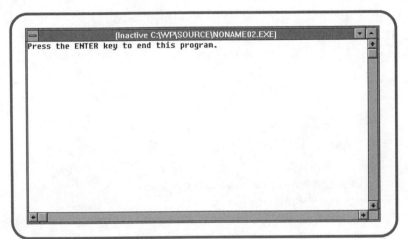

*Figure B.4.*
*An inactive WinCrt program.*

As you can see, pressing Enter changed the caption at the top of the screen so that it looks like this:

```
( Inactive C:\WP\SOURCE\NONAME02.EXE )
```

Whenever you see the word Inactive at the top of a WinCrt program, that means it has finished its run. It's over. Of course, to close the window, you still have to press Alt-Space-C, or else double-click on the icon in the upper-left corner of the screen.

This raises an interesting question: Why is the line Press ENTER to end this program appended to nearly every piece of code in this book? The reason for this is that the people who use the DOS IDE need this code to pause their programs so that they can view the results of their work. As often happens, the Windows IDE is a bit easier to use in this regard, so there is no need to include this extra line.

Therefore, the ideal way to run program StrangeLoop inside Windows is to work with code that looks like this:

```
program StrangeLoop;
uses
  WinCrt;
```

425

```
begin
  WriteLn('The following sentence is false.');
  WriteLn('The preceding sentence is true.');
end.
```

As you can see, this is a considerably simpler program than the one used by the folks who are programming for the DOS IDE.

I should add that there is a way to make program StrangeLoop act as it would in the DOS IDE, at least in regard to the manner in which the program terminates. The following code shows how this can be done:

```
program StrangeLoop;
uses
  Crt;

begin
  ClrScr;
  WriteLn('The following sentence is false.');
  WriteLn('The preceding sentence is true.');
  WriteLn;
  WriteLn('Press the ENTER key to end this program.');
  ReadLn;
  DoneWinCrt;
end.
```

If you run this program, you will never see a screen that has a caption with the word Inactive in it. Instead, the whole program will close automatically when it is through with its run, just as programs do inside the DOS IDE. The key to this process is the inclusion of the DoneWinCrt command at the end of the program. Of course, I'm not suggesting that this is the best way to run a Windows programs. I'm simply adding this information about the DoneWinCrt command so that you will have it available in case you need it.

# Code You Can't Use in TPW

As you make your way through this book you are going to find that there are things you can't do in TPW that you can do from a DOS IDE. This doesn't mean that DOS is a more powerful environment than Windows; obviously, saying something like that would be turning the world on its head. TPW is a much more powerful tool than anything that ships with Turbo Pascal 7.0. Nevertheless, there are some things you can do with DOS programs or inside the DOS IDE that you can't do when using TPW.

One simple example of this will be evident when this book introduces the Delay command. There is no equivalent of the Delay command in Windows. The reasons for this are not really germane to this book, but they all have to do with the event-oriented, nonpreemptive nature of the Windows operating system.

Whenever you see a program that uses the Delay procedure, simply delete that line from your code. If you don't, the message Error 3: Unknown identifier will appear in the status line on the bottom of the IDE window when you try to compile your code.

Consider the following program repeated verbatim from the text of this book:

```
uses
  Crt;

begin
  ClrScr;
  repeat
    WriteLn(Random(5));
    Delay(250);
  until KeyPressed;
end.
```

To translate this program into code that will run in Windows, you have to make the following changes:

```
uses
  WinCrt;                  { Change from Crt to WinCrt }

begin
  ClrScr;
  repeat
    WriteLn(Random(5));    { Omit the Delay statement }
  until KeyPressed;
end.
```

Additional changes, which are optional, might look like this:

```
uses
  WinCrt;
```

```
begin
  repeat                        { Omit the ClrScr procedure    }
    WriteLn(Random(5));
  until KeyPressed;
  DoneWinCrt;                   { Add the DoneWinCrt procedure }
end.
```

Of course it doesn't matter one way or the other whether you use the DoneWinCrt procedure. In fact, you may find it useful for the program to remain on-screen until you deliberately close its window. You're free, at any rate, to take whatever course you want in this regard.

Under normal circumstances, however, you must delete the reference to the Delay procedure. You will find that doing so will not have a negative effect on your copy of this program, because Windows code that prints to the screen usually runs much more slowly than the same code would in a DOS program.

You should also note that there is a WinDos unit included with TPW. You can use this unit in lieu of the Dos unit included in some of the example programs that come with this book. For instance, the following program will compile and run in Windows:

```
program WinSize;
uses
  WinCrt,
  WinDos;

begin
  WriteLn(DiskSize(0));
end.
```

This program reports on the size of the default disk drive. The DOS version of this program might look like this:

```
program DosSize;
uses
  Dos;

begin
  WriteLn(DiskSize(0));
end.
```

# Debugging in Windows

Given what I have said so far, some readers might be thinking that Windows programming is actually easier than DOS programming. After all, nearly every time there's been a conflict between the DOS and the Windows programming styles, the solution has been simply to delete the DOS code because it isn't needed in Windows. This seems to imply that WinCrt programs are usually shorter and, therefore, easier to write than the equivalent DOS programs.

This would indeed be the case were it not for one subject—debugging. At this stage in the evolution of the Pascal family, Windows debugging is not quite so user friendly as debugging inside a DOS IDE, but most of the basic principles that apply inside the DOS IDE also apply inside the Windows Debugger.

During the following discussion, assume that you have that old friend, the StrangeLoop program, in the TPW IDE:

```
program StrangeLoop;

begin
  WriteLn('The following sentence is false.');
  WriteLn('The preceding sentence is true.');
end.
```

In order to view this program in the debugger, you select Alt-R to bring down the Run menu and then press D to start the debugger. If all goes well, you should be able to see your code in the debugger.

If by chance you don't see your code and, instead, see a light blue screen filled with machine code, you should press Alt-X to exit the debugger. Back in the TPW IDE, press Alt-O to bring down the Options menu. Choose Linker, and then make sure the Debug Info Box has an X in front of it. When you're done, you can recompile your code and start up the debugger again.

If at any time during this process you can't proceed because you get an error message or because your screen gets so badly scrambled that you must reboot to clean it, you should see the portion of this appendix, "If You Have Trouble Loading the Debugger."

For now I'll assume that you have been able to get the debugger up and running. From here on, everything works exactly as in the DOS Debugger except for the process of creating breakpoints and for the process of actually ending your debugging session.

In DOS, you set a breakpoint by pressing Ctrl-F8; in the Windows Debugger you do this by pressing F2. In DOS, there is no need to exit the debugger formally, because the debugger and the editor are integrated into one tool. In Windows, however, you must press Alt-X to exit the debugger and return to the Pascal IDE.

Besides these two differences, all the other debugging features mentioned in this book should work the same way in DOS as in Windows. For instance, you can step through your code with the F7 or F8 key; you can open up the watch window with Ctrl-F7; and you can restart a program by hitting Ctrl-F2.

I hope that this basic introduction to the Turbo Debugger for Windows (TDW) gives you enough information to follow along with the portions of this book that refer to the built-in DOS Debugger. Whatever happens, don't let this opportunity to learn about the debugger pass you by. In this book, I say many times that it is absolutely essential for you to know your debugger inside and out. That rule doesn't just apply to DOS programmers; All programmers need to know everything they can about their debuggers.

Maybe I should qualify that last statement slightly. When you are using TDW, it probably won't take you long to figure out that it has many features that aren't included in the integrated DOS debugger. While you read this book, there is no need for you to understand the exact functioning of all those marvelous bells and whistles. You do, however, need to have a thorough understanding of the basics; that is, you need to know how to step through your code, how to put a variable in the watch window, and how to set breakpoints. If you pick up some other things along the way, that's great. But whatever you do, don't ignore the essentials.

That's about all I want to say on the issue of using TPW (and TDW) while you read this book. The point I want to emphasize is that you should be able to learn Pascal even if all you have is a copy of TPW, but that you must realize it will be a bit more difficult for you than for those who have the DOS IDE. Don't get discouraged; it can be done.

Oh, one last point. Several of the final lessons in this book are on a program called LIFE.PAS. This program must have a few modest changes before it will run under TPW. Just to avoid confusion, I have included a special Windows version of the source for LIFE.PAS. You can find this version on your disk.

Also, don't forget to check the README file included on the disk accompanying this book. That file may have important, last-minute information of interest to TPW users.

# If You Have Trouble Loading the Debugger

The Turbo Debugger for Windows (TDW) is an extremely sophisticated tool working under rather difficult circumstances. For instance, you may have noticed that it runs in text mode, while everything else in Windows runs in graphics mode. The exact reasons why the debugger runs in text mode aren't important to this book, but the fact that the debugger works this way affects many users. The unusual TDW interface is the reason why some people are unable to bring up the debugger correctly the first time they try.

There are two problems which might arise when you try to start the debugger. The first occurs when you try to bring it up and see the following error message:

```
"Can't load WinDebug.Dll"
```

This legend will be presented to every user who is trying to run TPW 1.0 under Windows 3.1. (To find out which version of TPW you have, press Alt-H for Help, and then "A" for About. If the screen you see at that time says nothing about a version, then you have 1.0, otherwise you will have version 1.5, which is clearly marked as such.)

To fix the `"Can't load WinDebug.Dll"` message, Borland recommends that you upgrade to either TPW 1.5 or BP7. To do so, dial 1-800-331-0877, and talk to the nice folks at sales. I agree with the official Borland policy that this is the best course for you to follow. If you prefer not to exercise this option, you can use your modem to download a file called TPWN31.ZIP from Borland's Download BBS. The number there is (408) 439-9096.

Let me emphasize once again that I think you will be better off upgrading. If you do download the file, however, you will be able to get up and running again by using the new copy of WINDEBUG.DLL included in TPWN31.ZIP.

To unzip this file, you should go to the DOS prompt and type one of the following commands:

```
unzip tpwn31
pkunzip tpwn31
```

If you don't have a copy of either UNZIP.EXE or PKUNZIP.EXE, you can get the former file off the download BBS.

431

Well, of the two things that can go wrong, trouble with the debugger is the one that's easiest to fix. The other problem, however, manifests itself when the screen becomes fragmented or cluttered either during the process of loading or after exiting the debugger. If this happens, you are experiencing a conflict between your video card and the drivers loaded to provide the TDW display.

There is a file called README.TDW in the DOC subdirectory on your hard drive which explains this situation and what can be done about it. The essence of it is that you need either to go to the control panel and load a standard windows video driver, or else modify your TDW.INI file, located in your Windows subdirectory.

You can change your TDW.INI file by loading it into either TPW or Notepad. When you do, you will see something that looks at least remotely like this:

```
[TurboDebugger]
VideoDLL=C:\TPW\svga.dll
DebuggerDLL=C:\TPW\tdwin.dll
[VideoOptions]
BitBlt=Y
ForceRepaint=N
Rows=25
XGA=N
DebugFile=C:\TPW\svga.dbg
SaveWholeScreen=no
Int2FAssist=no
IgnoreMode=no
```

The line which is important to you is the line that reads:

```
VideoDLL=C:\TPW\svga.dll
```

In this particular case, you are loading a file called SVGA.DLL every time you start TDW. But you may need to load a different file depending on which kind of video card you have.

You can find out about the relationship between the different cards and the different video drivers by reading README.TDW, but you might find that none of the solutions currently available does the trick. If this is the case, you should dial the Borland Download BBS and get the file labeled TDSVGA.ZIP. This file contains a wide range of up-to-date video DLLs, one of which should get you up and running regardless of what kind of card you have and what video mode you want to use.

# For BPW Users

I said I would include a few words for BP7 owners who want to use BPW rather than BP.EXE or TURBO.EXE. Let me begin by saying I don't think this is the best way to go, but you have the option if you insist.

The first step you should take is to pop open the Compile menu and choose Target. Select the Real Mode Application option. Now you will be able to produce DOS applications and run them by merely pressing Alt-R to pull down the Run menu and then selecting "R" for Run.

When you want to debug your programs you should be sure they are compiled with debug information turned on. To do this, pull down the Options menu, select Linker, and then be sure there is an X in front of the Debug Info in Exe option.

Now you must go back to the Program Manager and start the DOS Turbo Debugger program. To do this, first pull down the File menu and choose the Run option. When you start Turbo Debugger, you should designate the path to the debugger itself, and also the name of the program you want to debug. For example, you might type something like this in the Run menu:

```
c:\bp\bin\td.exe c:\wp\source\rando.exe
```

Now you can begin to debug your program, following all the same rules which are laid out above for TDW users. In other words, TD.EXE works very much the same way TDW does.

I think it's easiest to start the debugger from the Run menu. But if you want, you can follow a second plan outlined below.

Usually, the Turbo Debugger for DOS is not one of the icons automatically loaded when you install BP7. Therefore, if you want to add the icon to the Program Manager, you have to use the New option on the Program Manager's file menu to add the new icon. Once you have done this and have loaded the debugger, you can use the debugger's File menu to load your program and begin debugging.

Before closing, I want to add that I used the Program Manager explicitly in this example just because I know it is a widely-used tool. I do not mean to imply, however, that it is in any sense superior to the many fine and much more powerful Program Manager substitutes now available on the market.

# ASCII Table

| Dec $X_{10}$ | Hex $X_{16}$ | Binary $X_2$ | ASCII Character |
|---|---|---|---|
| 000 | 00 | 0000 0000 | null |
| 001 | 01 | 0000 0001 | ☺ |
| 002 | 02 | 0000 0010 | ☻ |
| 003 | 03 | 0000 0011 | ♥ |
| 004 | 04 | 0000 0100 | ♦ |
| 005 | 05 | 0000 0101 | ♣ |
| 006 | 06 | 0000 0110 | ♠ |
| 007 | 07 | 0000 0111 | ● |
| 008 | 08 | 0000 1000 | ■ |
| 009 | 09 | 0000 1001 | ○ |
| 010 | 0A | 0000 1010 | ■ |
| 011 | 0B | 0000 1011 | ♂ |
| 012 | 0C | 0000 1100 | ♀ |
| 013 | 0D | 0000 1101 | ♪ |
| 014 | 0E | 0000 1110 | ♪♪ |
| 015 | 0F | 0000 1111 | ☼ |
| 016 | 10 | 0001 0000 | ► |

| Dec $X_{10}$ | Hex $X_{16}$ | Binary $X_2$ | ASCII Character |
|---|---|---|---|
| 017 | 11 | 0001 0001 | ◄ |
| 018 | 12 | 0001 0010 | ↕ |
| 019 | 13 | 0001 0011 | !! |
| 020 | 14 | 0001 0100 | ¶ |
| 021 | 15 | 0001 0101 | § |
| 022 | 16 | 0001 0110 | – |
| 023 | 17 | 0001 0111 | ↨ |
| 024 | 18 | 0001 1000 | ↑ |
| 025 | 19 | 0001 1001 | ↓ |
| 026 | 1A | 0001 1010 | → |
| 027 | 1B | 0001 1011 | ← |
| 028 | 1C | 0001 1100 | FS |
| 029 | 1D | 0001 1101 | GS |
| 030 | 1E | 0001 1110 | RS |
| 031 | 1F | 0001 1111 | US |
| 032 | 20 | 0010 0000 | SP |
| 033 | 21 | 0010 0001 | ! |
| 034 | 22 | 0010 0010 | " |
| 035 | 23 | 0010 0011 | # |
| 036 | 24 | 0010 0100 | $ |
| 037 | 25 | 0010 0101 | % |
| 038 | 26 | 0010 0110 | & |
| 039 | 27 | 0010 0111 | ' |
| 040 | 28 | 0010 1000 | ( |
| 041 | 29 | 0010 1001 | ) |
| 042 | 2A | 0010 1010 | * |
| 043 | 2B | 0010 1011 | + |
| 044 | 2C | 0010 1100 | ' |
| 045 | 2D | 0010 1101 | - |
| 046 | 2E | 0010 1110 | . |
| 047 | 2F | 0010 1111 | / |

| Dec $X_{10}$ | Hex $X_{16}$ | Binary $X_2$ | ASCII Character |
|---|---|---|---|
| 048 | 30 | 0011 0000 | 0 |
| 049 | 31 | 0011 0001 | 1 |
| 050 | 32 | 0011 0010 | 2 |
| 051 | 33 | 0011 0011 | 3 |
| 052 | 34 | 0011 0100 | 4 |
| 053 | 35 | 0011 0101 | 5 |
| 054 | 36 | 0011 0110 | 6 |
| 055 | 37 | 0011 0111 | 7 |
| 056 | 38 | 0011 1000 | 8 |
| 057 | 39 | 0011 1001 | 9 |
| 058 | 3A | 0011 1010 | : |
| 059 | 3B | 0011 1011 | ; |
| 060 | 3C | 0011 1100 | < |
| 061 | 3D | 0011 1101 | = |
| 062 | 3E | 0011 1110 | > |
| 063 | 3F | 0011 1111 | ? |
| 064 | 40 | 0100 0000 | @ |
| 065 | 41 | 0100 0001 | A |
| 066 | 42 | 0100 0010 | B |
| 067 | 43 | 0100 0011 | C |
| 068 | 44 | 0100 0100 | D |
| 069 | 45 | 0100 0101 | E |
| 070 | 46 | 0100 0110 | F |
| 071 | 47 | 0100 0111 | G |
| 072 | 48 | 0100 1000 | H |
| 073 | 49 | 0100 1001 | I |
| 074 | 4A | 0100 1010 | J |
| 075 | 4B | 0100 1011 | K |
| 076 | 4C | 0100 1100 | L |
| 077 | 4D | 0100 1101 | M |
| 078 | 4E | 0100 1110 | N |

| Dec $X_{10}$ | Hex $X_{16}$ | Binary $X_2$ | ASCII Character |
|---|---|---|---|
| 079 | 4F | 0100 1111 | O |
| 080 | 50 | 0101 0000 | P |
| 081 | 51 | 0101 0001 | Q |
| 082 | 52 | 0101 0010 | R |
| 083 | 53 | 0101 0011 | S |
| 084 | 54 | 0101 0100 | T |
| 085 | 55 | 0101 0101 | U |
| 086 | 56 | 0101 0110 | V |
| 087 | 57 | 0101 0111 | W |
| 088 | 58 | 0101 1000 | X |
| 089 | 59 | 0101 1001 | Y |
| 090 | 5A | 0101 1010 | Z |
| 091 | 5B | 0101 1011 | [ |
| 092 | 5C | 0101 1100 | \ |
| 093 | 5D | 0101 1101 | ] |
| 094 | 5E | 0101 1110 | ^ |
| 095 | 5F | 0101 1111 | – |
| 096 | 60 | 0110 0000 | ` |
| 097 | 61 | 0110 0001 | a |
| 098 | 62 | 0110 0010 | b |
| 099 | 63 | 0110 0011 | c |
| 100 | 64 | 0110 0100 | d |
| 101 | 65 | 0110 0101 | e |
| 102 | 66 | 0110 0110 | f |
| 103 | 67 | 0110 0111 | g |
| 104 | 68 | 0110 1000 | h |
| 105 | 69 | 0110 1001 | i |
| 106 | 6A | 0110 1010 | j |
| 107 | 6B | 0110 1011 | k |
| 108 | 6C | 0110 1100 | l |
| 109 | 6D | 0110 1101 | m |

| Dec $X_{10}$ | Hex $X_{16}$ | Binary $X_2$ | ASCII Character |
|---|---|---|---|
| 110 | 6E | 0110 1110 | n |
| 111 | 6F | 0110 1111 | o |
| 112 | 70 | 0111 0000 | p |
| 113 | 71 | 0111 0001 | q |
| 114 | 72 | 0111 0010 | r |
| 115 | 73 | 0111 0011 | s |
| 116 | 74 | 0111 0100 | t |
| 117 | 75 | 0111 0101 | u |
| 118 | 76 | 0111 0110 | v |
| 119 | 77 | 0111 0111 | w |
| 120 | 78 | 0111 1000 | x |
| 121 | 79 | 0111 1001 | y |
| 122 | 7A | 0111 1010 | z |
| 123 | 7B | 0111 1011 | { |
| 124 | 7C | 0111 1100 | ¦ |
| 125 | 7D | 0111 1101 | } |
| 126 | 7E | 0111 1110 | ~ |
| 127 | 7F | 0111 1111 | DEL |
| 128 | 80 | 1000 0000 | Ç |
| 129 | 81 | 1000 0001 | ü |
| 130 | 82 | 1000 0010 | é |
| 131 | 83 | 1000 0011 | â |
| 132 | 84 | 1000 0100 | ä |
| 133 | 85 | 1000 0101 | à |
| 134 | 86 | 1000 0110 | å |
| 135 | 87 | 1000 0111 | ç |
| 136 | 88 | 1000 1000 | ê |
| 137 | 89 | 1000 1001 | ë |
| 138 | 8A | 1000 1010 | è |
| 139 | 8B | 1000 1011 | ï |
| 140 | 8C | 1000 1100 | î |

| Dec $X_{10}$ | Hex $X_{16}$ | Binary $X_2$ | ASCII Character |
|---|---|---|---|
| 141 | 8D | 1000 1101 | ì |
| 142 | 8E | 1000 1110 | Ä |
| 143 | 8F | 1000 1111 | Å |
| 144 | 90 | 1001 0000 | É |
| 145 | 91 | 1001 0001 | æ |
| 146 | 92 | 1001 0010 | Æ |
| 147 | 93 | 1001 0011 | ô |
| 148 | 94 | 1001 0100 | ö |
| 149 | 95 | 1001 0101 | ò |
| 150 | 96 | 1001 0110 | û |
| 151 | 97 | 1001 0111 | ù |
| 152 | 98 | 1001 1000 | ÿ |
| 153 | 99 | 1001 1001 | Ö |
| 154 | 9A | 1001 1010 | Ü |
| 155 | 9B | 1001 1011 | ¢ |
| 156 | 9C | 1001 1100 | £ |
| 157 | 9D | 1001 1101 | ¥ |
| 158 | 9E | 1001 1110 | $P_t$ |
| 159 | 9F | 1001 1111 | ƒ |
| 160 | A0 | 1010 0000 | á |
| 161 | A1 | 1010 0001 | í |
| 162 | A2 | 1010 0010 | ó |
| 163 | A3 | 1010 0011 | ú |
| 164 | A4 | 1010 0100 | ñ |
| 165 | A5 | 1010 0101 | Ñ |
| 166 | A6 | 1010 0110 | a |
| 167 | A7 | 1010 0111 | o |
| 168 | A8 | 1010 1000 | ¿ |
| 169 | A9 | 1010 1001 | ⌐ |
| 170 | AA | 1010 1010 | ¬ |
| 171 | AB | 1010 1011 | ½ |

| Dec $X_{10}$ | Hex $X_{16}$ | Binary $X_2$ | ASCII Character |
|---|---|---|---|
| 172 | AC | 1010 1100 | ¼ |
| 173 | AD | 1010 1101 | ¡ |
| 174 | AE | 1010 1110 | « |
| 175 | AF | 1010 1111 | » |
| 176 | B0 | 1011 0000 | ░ |
| 177 | B1 | 1011 0001 | ▒ |
| 178 | B2 | 1011 0010 | ▓ |
| 179 | B3 | 1011 0011 | │ |
| 180 | B4 | 1011 0100 | ┤ |
| 181 | B5 | 1011 0101 | ╡ |
| 182 | B6 | 1011 0110 | ╢ |
| 183 | B7 | 1011 0111 | ╖ |
| 184 | B8 | 1011 1000 | ╕ |
| 185 | B9 | 1011 1001 | ╣ |
| 186 | BA | 1011 1010 | ║ |
| 187 | BB | 1011 1011 | ╗ |
| 188 | BC | 1011 1100 | ╝ |
| 189 | BD | 1011 1101 | ╜ |
| 190 | BE | 1011 1110 | ╛ |
| 191 | BF | 1011 1111 | ┐ |
| 192 | C0 | 1100 0000 | └ |
| 193 | C1 | 1100 0001 | ┴ |
| 194 | C2 | 1100 0010 | ┬ |
| 195 | C3 | 1100 0011 | ├ |
| 196 | C4 | 1100 0100 | ─ |
| 197 | C5 | 1100 0101 | ┼ |
| 198 | C6 | 1100 0110 | ╞ |
| 199 | C7 | 1100 0111 | ╟ |
| 200 | C8 | 1100 1000 | ╚ |
| 201 | C9 | 1100 1001 | ╔ |
| 202 | CA | 1100 1010 | ╩ |

| Dec $X_{10}$ | Hex $X_{16}$ | Binary $X_2$ | ASCII Character |
|---|---|---|---|
| 203 | CB | 1100 1011 | ⊤ |
| 204 | CC | 1100 1100 | ⊩ |
| 205 | CD | 1100 1101 | = |
| 206 | CE | 1100 1110 | ⊪ |
| 207 | CF | 1100 1111 | ⊥ |
| 208 | D0 | 1101 0000 | ⊥ |
| 209 | D1 | 1101 0001 | ⊤ |
| 210 | D2 | 1101 0010 | ⊓ |
| 211 | D3 | 1101 0011 | ⊔ |
| 212 | D4 | 1101 0100 | ⊢ |
| 213 | D5 | 1101 0101 | ⊢ |
| 214 | D6 | 1101 0110 | ⊓ |
| 215 | D7 | 1101 0111 | ⊬ |
| 216 | D8 | 1101 1000 | ⊧ |
| 217 | D9 | 1101 1001 | ⌟ |
| 218 | DA | 1101 1010 | ⌈ |
| 219 | DB | 1101 1011 | ■ |
| 220 | DC | 1101 1100 | ▬ |
| 221 | DD | 1101 1101 | ▌ |
| 222 | DE | 1101 1110 | ▐ |
| 223 | DF | 1101 1111 | ▀ |
| 224 | E0 | 1110 0000 | α |
| 225 | E1 | 1110 0001 | β |
| 226 | E2 | 1110 0010 | Γ |
| 227 | E3 | 1110 0011 | π |
| 228 | E4 | 1110 0100 | Σ |
| 229 | E5 | 1110 0101 | σ |
| 230 | E6 | 1110 0110 | μ |
| 231 | E7 | 1110 0111 | τ |
| 232 | E8 | 1110 1000 | Φ |
| 233 | E9 | 1110 1001 | θ |

| Dec $X_{10}$ | Hex $X_{16}$ | Binary $X_2$ | ASCII Character |
|---|---|---|---|
| 234 | EA | 1110 1010 | Ω |
| 235 | EB | 1110 1011 | δ |
| 236 | EC | 1110 1100 | ∞ |
| 237 | ED | 1110 1101 | ø |
| 238 | EE | 1110 1110 | ∈ |
| 239 | EF | 1110 1111 | ∩ |
| 240 | F0 | 1111 0000 | ≡ |
| 241 | F1 | 1111 0001 | ± |
| 242 | F2 | 1111 0010 | ≥ |
| 243 | F3 | 1111 0011 | ≤ |
| 244 | F4 | 1111 0100 | ⌠ |
| 245 | F5 | 1111 0101 | ⌡ |
| 246 | F6 | 1111 0110 | ÷ |
| 247 | F7 | 1111 0111 | ≈ |
| 248 | F8 | 1111 1000 | ° |
| 249 | F9 | 1111 1001 | • |
| 250 | FA | 1111 1010 | · |
| 251 | FB | 1111 1011 | √ |
| 252 | FC | 1111 1100 | η |
| 253 | FD | 1111 1101 | ² |
| 254 | FE | 1111 1110 | ■ |
| 255 | FF | 1111 1111 | |

**NOTE:** The last 128 ASCII codes listed in this table, numbers 128 through 255, are specific to IBM PCs and IBM compatibles.

# Index

## G

## H

# M

# What's On the Disk

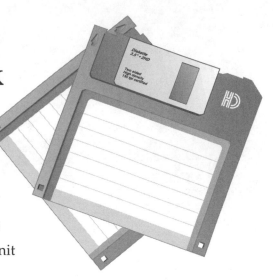

The disk contains the following:

- Programs shown in the book
- Answers to selected *Find the Bug* and *Finish the Program* exercises
- The Game of Life program
- Special Windows version of programs
- An extended version of the ToolBox unit introduced in Lesson 20
- Additional programs from the author

# Installing the Floppy Disk

The software included with this book is stored in a compressed form. You cannot use the software without first installing it onto your hard drive.

To install the files, you'll need at least 1.5M of free space on your hard drive.

1. From a DOS prompt, set your default drive to the drive that contains the installation disk. For example, if the disk in drive A:, type **A:** and press Enter.

2. Type **INSTALL** *drive* (where *drive* is the drive letter of your hard drive), and press Enter. For example, if your hard drive is drive C:, type **INSTALL C:** and press Enter.

This will install all the files to a directory called \TPP101 on your hard drive.

It's important that you read the README.DOC file, located in the \TPP101 directory on your hard drive

## License Agreement

By removing this disk, you are agreeing to be bound by the following agreement: